DATE DUE

BRODART, CO.   Cat. No. 23-221

DEC 0 8 2010

The Cultural Rights Movement

The Cultural Rights Movement

Fulfilling the Promise of Civil Rights for African Americans

Eric J. Bailey

 PRAEGER

AN IMPRINT OF ABC-CLIO, LLC
Santa Barbara, California • Denver, Colorado • Oxford, England

Library of Congress Cataloging-in-Publication Data
Bailey, Eric J., 1958–
    The cultural rights movement : fulfilling the promise of civil rights for Afri-
can Americans / by Eric J. Bailey.
        p.   cm.
    Includes bibliographical references and index.
    ISBN 978-0-313-36009-1 (hard copy : alk. paper)—ISBN 978-0-313-36010-7
(ebook)
    1. African Americans—Civil rights. 2. African Americans—Intellectual life.
3. African Americans—Social conditions. 4. Civil rights movements—United
States—History—20th century. 5. United States—Race relations—History.
I. Title.
    E185.615.B26   2010
    323.1196′073—dc22   2009042839

ISBN: 978-0-313-36009-1
EISBN: 978-0-313-36010-7

14   13   12   11   10   1   2   3   4   5

This book is also available on the World Wide Web as an eBook.
Visit www.abc-clio.com for details.

Praeger
An Imprint of ABC-CLIO, LLC

ABC-CLIO, LLC
130 Cremona Drive, P.O. Box 1911
Santa Barbara, California 93116-1911

This book is printed on acid-free paper ∞

Manufactured in the United States of America

To Gloria

Contents

Preface

The Cultural Rights Movement: Fulfilling the Promise of Civil Rights for African Americans challenges the establishment to recognize, respect, and reward African Americans not only for their cultural historical contributions to the country but also for starting a new movement that appreciates their cultural values, beliefs, and traditions. Despite having an African American in the White House, African Americans' major cultural rights still are being neglected along with experiencing significant disparities in health, income, education, and justice.

When I begin to conceive a book topic, the process usually begins with the completion of a previous book. That is exactly what happened with this book. When I was writing my previous book, *Black America, Body Beautiful: How the African American Image Is Changing Fashion, Fitness, and Other Industries*, my chapter on African American image and politics lead me to issues and individuals who I had to further investigate. After gathering additional information on the key topics and individuals, two central topics emerged—civil rights and Barack Obama.

The term *civil rights* often causes individuals to react a certain way, to think about a certain time in history, and to think about a certain group of people. On one hand, civil rights helped all of us on so many levels to achieve a better quality of life, and yet on the other hand, the images of civil rights tend to get stereotyped as being associated with one major ethnic group in the United States—African Americans. The fact that all the people, events, organizations, and issues surrounding the 1950s and 1960s civil rights movement are mainstreamed into one or two major media productions every year greatly concerns me. These one or two major media productions usually select the same individuals and same events to categorize this significant American movement. Not only does this do a disservice to the individuals and events that are selected to represent the civil rights movement, it does a major disservice for all the other thousands of significant individuals and events who were apart of this great movement.

Another major concern of mine when we talk about civil rights today is that so many other groups are using the civil rights movement of the 1950s and 1960s—the images, themes, words, and people—to lead their own new movement, cause, or even product marketing campaign. Not surprisingly, 21st-century politicians and special interest groups regularly quote passages from Dr. Martin Luther King, Jr. or other civil rights iconic speeches to make their case about a particular issue. Because these events are occurring more regularly, particularly around election time, it tells me that our society and our politicians are not only losing their creativity but also are "repackaging" the same old messages from the civil rights era into the new media outlets (Internet, blogs, podcasts, webcams, Twitter sites) for younger audiences. Thus, what seems new and fresh in the early 21st century is actually a repackaged message from the civil rights movement. This repackaging concerns me.

The other major topic from my previous book chapter on African American image and politics that sparked my interest was the then—Democratic presidential candidate Barack Obama. As I said in my previous book, Barack Obama created a new image for black politics and strategically decided to move away from those traditional images and actions. Although initially criticized for being different from the stereotypical black politician, Barack Obama's new black politician's image and strategy obviously worked. He was and is a black politician who successfully crossed over his image to mainstream society, thereby winning the pivotal votes to become the forty-fourth president of the United States.

In accomplishing this historic endeavor to become our first African American president, what price will President Barack Obama pay, and most important, what price will African Americans and all those who desire to assert their cultural and human rights pay? Time will tell whether the outcomes of his administration's initiatives during the next four to eight years will have a positive or negative impact in African American communities across this country. This impact is the central theme of this book.

Finally, as an African American professor, this is one of the most challenging and culturally sensitive book topics that I have investigated and presented. I not only will be questioned by my peers, but also by family members and friends as to why I dare to write a book like this. I understand that this will happen, and I respond to them as I have to my students in college courses for the past twenty years. I dare to speculate!

Chapter 1 opens the dialogue and debate about whether our new president Barack Obama will take the lead in overturning the litany of civil rights cases against blacks in America. As the civil rights cultural historical context is presented, a number of current issues that affect African Americans are highlighted. Issues such as discriminatory lending practices; disparities in physician care; disparity of black faculty at mainstream universities; the low number of black students in postsecondary schools; the phenomenal high rate of blacks being arrested, convicted, and incarcerated; the continual growth of black underemployment and poverty; and the near-total neglect of the reparations issue will be of increased importance to African Americans in the years to come. If these issues are not addressed seriously, then a new cultural rights movement is needed for all African Americans.

Chapter 2 relates my personal experiences during the 1950s and 1960s civil rights era. A chronology of national political and social events is presented along with key national African American civil rights leaders.

Chapter 3 examines African Americans' current poverty issues and compares them to the poverty issues of the 1960s. By revisiting the 1960s War on Poverty initiatives, we can better understand how to address and solve 21st-century poverty issues. Comparing the Obama administration's federal initiatives focusing on poverty with programs from specific states and cities suggest that the country needs to reexamine current federal poverty initiatives.

Chapter 4 recounts my personal experiences related to public education in the primary, secondary, and postsecondary school years during the 1960s and 1970s. A cultural historical review of the Chicago public school system illustrates how African Americans during the 1960s addressed the issue of inequality in the school system. A comparison of the Obama administration's federal initiatives focusing on education versus new culturally competent school systems across the country suggests that the country needs to reform its current public education system.

Chapter 5 discusses my personal experiences related to medical care during the 1960s and the type of belief systems that my family had associated with certain types of illnesses. Current African American and ethnic health disparities data illustrate how the U.S. medical and public health systems are still not connected to the cultural health component of health, wellness, and healing associated with all people. The Obama administration's federal initiatives focusing on health care reform are presented to show how severely they lack and avoid addressing the cultural component of ethnic health disparity across the country. A new ground-breaking online higher education training initiative is presented to change the perspective and approach of current and future medical and public health professionals.

Chapter 6 describes my personal experiences with the local police in the 1960s. A cultural historical review of the U.S. criminal justice system and how African Americans have been wrongly persecuted and incarcerated is presented. Contemporary crime, incarceration data, homicide rates associated with blacks, and specific examples of wrongful imprisonment of African Americans over the recent years are highlighted. The Obama administration's federal initiatives focusing on the criminal and judicial systems are presented to show that they will not significantly help reduce the massive racial disparity in the criminal justice system, particularly as it relates to African Americans.

Chapter 7 relates my personal experiences with black pride during the 1960s and 1970s and how it connects to 21st-century issues of reparations. A brief cultural history of the reparations issues is presented and key individuals involved in the movement legislatively and publicly are recognized. President Barack Obama's stance on the issue of reparations is presented before and after he became president. The Obama administration's stance has softened and he has symbolically and ceremonially apologized to the descendants of enslaved African Americans for slavery. Rep. John Conyers's bill to initiate a commission to study reparations is presented.

Chapter 8 shares my personal experiences with black and white race relations during the 1960s and 1970s. Contemporary race relations data and issues are presented. President Barack Obama's views on race relations are presented before and after he became president. Although the Obama administration is one of the most diverse cabinets in our history, the federal initiatives focusing on race relations issues are severely lacking. Former President Bill Clinton's Race Initiative is highlighted to show how a new administration can be a leader in moving our country forward in race relations issues.

Chapter 9 acknowledges how proud I am that our country elected its first African American president. This moment in history is particularly remarkable when viewed from an African American perspective. This chapter dares to ask some of the most critical questions concerning President Obama's current policies. The potential answers to these key questions lead us to my proposed cultural rights movement initiative and the key decision makers who can lead this movement nationally and locally.

Acknowledgments

This is my fifth book with Greenwood Publishing, and it has been another remarkable journey in working with my new publisher—ABC-CLIO. Throughout all the changes, I sincerely thank my incredible, caring, and insightful editor, Debora Carvalko, for working with me on yet another book project. I also want to thank Kerri Bright Flinchbaugh for reviewing earlier drafts and the soulful, inspirational songs of Sade for motivating my daily writing of this book.

I have achieved full professor status in academia—that's the culmination of more than twenty years of scholarly and professional activity, including several other universities and federal institutions, such as University of Houston, Indiana University (IUPUI, Indianapolis), Emory University, University of Arkansas Medical Sciences (UAMS), Charles Drew University of Medical Sciences, the Centers for Disease Control and Prevention, and the National Institutes of Health. I thank both of the academic departments in which I am jointly appointed at East Carolina University—the Anthropology Department and the Department of Public Health. The support I have received from these departments as well as the Thomas Harriot College of Arts and Sciences and the Brody School of Medicine has enabled me to expand my perspectives and expertise in research, teaching, and service for the university and the community at large.

In addition, I thank the two outstanding libraries at East Carolina University—The J. Y. Joyner Library and The William E. Laupus Health Sciences Library—for their excellent research journals, e-online services, and book collections as well as their outstanding administrative staff.

I also thank the incredible students I have had in all my classes during the twenty years in which I have been teaching college courses. I still remember the very first class that I taught as a doctoral anthropology instructor at Wayne State University in Detroit, Michigan. From that first class in which my students challenged me to explain concepts further to my current undergraduate and graduate courses (both face-to-face and online), I have had the thrill of sharing my knowledge, and I learn from each of my students every semester. Although teaching college courses over the years gets tedious at times, the ultimate reward is to see and hear students of all walks of life and ethnicities challenge themselves and dare to ask the questions that most people would not. That daring is what I love about teaching.

The personal stories that I included in this book are the result of being raised by two incredible, inspiring, disciplined, and loving parents—Jean Ethel and Roger William Bailey, Jr. Their tenacity, focus, downright "never giving up attitude" on improving their lives along with my brothers and I greatly influenced my early years of life. I feel blessed to have parents like my mom and dad.

I also feel blessed to have brothers like Dwight, Ronnie, Billie, and Michael Bailey. All of my brothers have played a significant role in my upbringing and I am most grateful. They may not have known how much I admired them, but I did each and every day. In addition, I thank my extended family members, past and present (aunts, uncles, and cousins).

Finally, I thank my supportive, growing, and engaging family for not only allowing me to spend the extra late nights and early mornings in writing this book but also for debating with me these serious cultural issues that needed to be investigated—my very dynamic, intelligent, artistic, beautiful wife Gloria; my high-achieving daughter Ebony; and my high-achieving sons, Darrien and Marcus. I am blessed to have a family like this.

This book is dedicated to my wife, Gloria Jean Harden Bailey. Recently, my wife and I celebrated our twentieth anniversary, and it still feels remarkable that these years have gone by so fast, but they have. In fact, I do not think that the majority of my family and friends realize that we have been together for twenty years. In sharing my early childhood personal experiences throughout this book, I quite naturally thought about my first years when Gloria and I met.

We first met when we were attending the same university—Wayne State University in Detroit, Michigan, during the 1980s. I was a doctoral student, and she was an undergraduate student. On the surface, it did not appear that we had much in common. I was seeking a degree in anthropology and she was seeking a degree in fine arts. I was originally from the Buckeye state of Ohio and she was a native of Highland Park, Michigan. I was born and raised in the small rural towns of Springfield and Wilberforce, Ohio, and she was born and raised around the big Midwestern city of Detroit. So what was it that brought us together?

Quite naturally, I was first captivated by her physical beauty, but more important as I got to know her, I was even more captivated by her internal beauty. There was something about Gloria that made her shine like a beacon of light even in the doldrums of an inner city like Detroit. She had her own voice, she had her own attitude, she had a spirit that would not be broken, and she wanted to see and experience the world.

From that very moment in which we talked on the street corner in Detroit for at least an hour and half, I knew that Gloria was the woman for me. Although it took me a long time to find her through my own trials and tribulations in life, I fell in love with her at that moment and have never looked back. Two years later, we got married in the city of Detroit.

Now that it has been twenty years, Gloria and I along with our kids have traveled, lived, and experienced all types of urban, suburban, and rural settings across America within a relatively short time period. From the Midwest, to the south central, to the southwest, mid-central, and now to the southern portion of the United States, Gloria and I adapted and made a way in each place. It has been hard on all of us, particularly for her. That's the reason I dedicate this book to Gloria: because she has continued to be the same person that I met twenty-two years ago. She still has a unique voice, her own attitude, a spirit that will not be broken, and wants to see and experience the world. I feel blessed to have Gloria Jean Harden Bailey in my life.

Chapter 1

Yes, We Can!

INTRODUCTION

In the midst of crisis, there was unbridled joy. Even though the nightly news was consistently dominated by stories of the disarray of the U.S. and global financial economy, of the foreclosure of thousands of houses across the nation each week, of layoffs of blue- and white-collar employees across America, and of the continual rise of African American men incarcerated and sent to death row, black America in 2008 also saw a positive cultural phenomenon emerge and grow. One person rekindled, stoked, and restored a new set of beliefs among African Americans about their future in America and their own African American heritage. And that person, that catalyst, was Barack Obama.

The fact that President Barack Obama virtually emerged out of nowhere as a first-term senator from Illinois to compete for the Democratic presidential candidacy among a slew of candidates, which included Vice President Joe Biden and Sen. Hillary Clinton, to win the nomination, then to beat the Republican presidential nominee, John McCain, along with his vice presidential nominee, Sarah Palin, to become the president of the United States not only shows how far race relations have changed in America but also shows how much so-called black politics has changed its political strategy on a national level in the United States.

According to author Ricky Hill (1994), who was one of the first present-day scholars to study contemporary black politics, black politics always has been burdened with the problem of duality, a duality in the sense that African Americans are constantly negotiating whether to become more a part of mainstream American politics or to be centered solely on African American political structures, institutions, leaders, and issues.[1] Historically, this problem of duality has been manifested as a conflict between inclusion and communal obligations; between integration, desegregation, and separatism; and between the yearning for universality and for black particularity. Just some of the African American leaders who struggled with this dual agenda in our American political system included Harriet Tubman, Frederick Douglass, Marcus Garvey, Booker T. Washington, W. E. B. Du Bois, Medgar Evers, Shirley Chisholm, Angela Davis, Malcolm X, Dr. Martin Luther King, Jr., and Jessie Jackson.

Some political experts would say that this issue of duality continues to exist in black politics on a local level, and its effects are as follows:

- It has hampered political development in the African American community.
- It has forced bad political decisions in the African American community.
- It has forced black politics into a dependent, reactive posture.[2]

Yet with today's prominent black politicians, such as President Barack Obama, African American politicians strive to assert more of their commonality with the mainstream populous and less with their African American base. For example, Barack Obama, the son of a Kenyan father and a white American mother and best-selling author of two books—*Dreams from My Father: A Story of Race and Inheritance*[3] and *The Audacity of Hope: Thoughts on Reclaiming the American Dream*[4]—differs markedly from the typical African American politician. When Obama delivered his inspirational keynote speech at the 2004 Democratic Convention, Americans witnessed a new image for an African American politician.

According to political reporter Benjamin Wallace-Wells, Americans encountered a new type of political character. He was black, but not quite. He spoke white, with the hand-gestures of a management consultant, but also with the oratorical flourishes of a black preacher.[5] Supporters and critics have speculated Obama's popular image and his biracial background might have been a strong factor creating the bridge between races that resulted in a persona on which each race could project its history and aspirations, as well as its support, and vote. Obama's own stories about his family's origins reinforce his "everyman" persona. In addition, Eugene Robinson, a *Washington Post* opinion columnist, characterized Obama's political image as "the personification of both-and, a messenger who rejects 'either-or' political choices, and [one who] could move the nation beyond the cultural wars of the 1960s."[6]

Thus, this is the task at hand for President Barack Obama. Being the first black person to become president of the United States is beyond historic, it is revolutionizing not only for the millions of Africans who

3

have lost their lives when they were forcibly brought to America during the 1600s and 1700s, but also revolutionizing for the native-born African Americans who adapted to this American system and fought to become an American citizen when the system denied their very existence for equal rights in all areas of life. So it is understandable that African Americans, along with all other Americans, feel a renewed sense of hope, achievement, and possibility that anyone, regardless of background, can become president of the United States to not only represent the United States on the world's stage but also live in the most powerful house in the nation—The White House.

It is also understandable that many of the civil rights cases and issues connected with African Americans and all those who have been denied equal rights for years can now be reevaluated and reassessed in an Obama administration. That is one of the major tasks at hand for President Barack Obama: Will President Obama take the lead in overturning the litany of civil rights cases against blacks in America?

Of course, only time will tell. Yet if there is any president who can and should take on this major challenge,—it is the first African American president of the United States: Barack Obama.

Nonetheless, when we speak of civil rights today, we have to consider how the term is *perceived*, because not everyone has the same view or understanding of what *civil rights* really means. Whether you are a politician, a lawyer, a professor, a high school teacher, a maintenance worker, or a plumber your interpretation of *civil rights* differs. Additionally, whether you are Caucasian, Latino, Asian American, Native American, or African American the term *civil rights* means something different to each group. Even within each racial and ethnic group, individuals have different perceptions of civil rights. So how exactly do we define *civil rights* in our United States? According to conservative scholar and author Thomas Sowell, who wrote his controversial classic book, "Civil Rights: Rhetoric or Reality?" (1984),

> Civil rights are rights guaranteed to an individual by virtue of citizenship and that all individuals should be treated the same under the law, regardless of their race, religion, sex or other social categories.[7]

Even if we embrace this definition of civil rights in America, its interpretation and enactment of the laws connected to civil rights issues varies with each ethnic and racial group because of our varied historical experiences. In other words, if an individual or individuals of a group historically experienced a denial of basic rights as a citizen of this country, then civil rights will be of major importance to those individuals and groups. Conversely, if an individual or a particular group has had limited experiences with the denial of basic rights as a citizen of this country, civil rights issues will not be as significant to that individual or group.

Yet how can these varying experiences with civil rights be so different in America given that civil rights issues and movements have been the basic cause for the nation's foundation? In fact, the early European settlers who arrived in the newly discovered continent of America came here because they were fighting for their own civil rights from their native European countries. Thus, the civil rights movement in America began a long time ago.

As early as the 17th century, blacks and whites, slaves in Virginia, and Quakers in Pennsylvania protested the barbarity of slavery. Nat Turner, Sojourner Truth, Frederick Douglass, William Lloyd Garrison, John Brown, and Harriet Tubman are but a few of those who lead the resistance to slavery before the Civil War. After the Civil War, another protracted battle began against slavery's legacy—racism and segregation. But for most Americans, the civil rights movement began on May 17, 1954, when the Supreme Court handed down the *Brown v. Board of Education of Topeka* decision outlawing segregation in public schools. The Court unlocked the door, but the pressure applied by thousands of men and women in the movement pushed that door open wide enough to allow blacks to walk through it toward this country's essential prize: freedom.

Now that blacks have this so-called freedom in America, do we still need to examine *civil rights* differently for blacks than we do for other racial and ethnic groups in America? According to Sowell, blacks in America should be examined as a special case because we can readily document their disparity statistically, behaviorally, and politically.

For example, one of the most central and controversial premises of the civil rights vision is that statistical disparities in incomes, occupations, education, and so on represent moral inequities that are caused by society. Historically, for instance, it was easy to show that segregated white schools had had several times as much money spent per pupil as in segregated black schools and that this translated into large disparities in physical plant, teacher qualifications, and other indexes of education input. Large differences in education output, such as test scores, seemed readily attributable to these input differences.[8]

Another central premise of the civil rights vision for blacks is that belief in innate inferiority explains policies and behavioral practices of differential treatment, whether expressed in overt hostility in institutional policies or in individual decisions that result in statistical disparities. Moral defenses or causal explanations of these statistical differences in any other terms tend to fall under suspicion or denunciation as racism, sexism, and so on.[9]

A third major premise for the special case for blacks is that political activity is the key to improving the lot of those on the short end of differences in income, "representation" in desirable occupations or institutions, or otherwise disadvantaged.[10] Once more, it is possible to cite such things as dramatic increases in the number of black elected officials, including President Barack Obama, after the passage of civil rights legislation of the 1960s.

Thus for blacks during the civil rights movement and even in the present, we can document this disparity statistically in a number of sociodemographic areas, such as education achievement, loans and mortgage practices, housing, income, occupations, and health status. The inequality and discrimination practices that blacks experience in all of these areas easily can be tried as civil rights cases in the courts.

Let's examine a few current civil rights issues that appear to have substantial evidence that African Americans are still subjected to discrimination.

LOAN AND MORTGAGE PRACTICES

A 2008 report entitled "Foreclosed: State of the Dream 2008" from the organization United for a Fair Economy found that major mortgage companies in the United States established more predatory loans for blacks than whites from 2000 to 2008. Key findings from their report were as follows:

- From subprime loans, African American borrowers will lose between $71 billion and $92 billion, while Latino borrowers will lose between $75 billion and $98 billion for the same period.
- Estimated total loss of wealth for people of color was between $164 billion to $213 billion for subprime loans taken during the past eight years.
- People of color are more than three times more likely to have subprime loans: high-cost loans account for 55 percent of loans to blacks but only 17 percent of loans to whites.
- Based on improvements in median household net worth before the crisis (from 1982 to 2004), it would take 594 more years for African Americans to achieve parity with whites. The current crisis is likely to make it take much longer.
- Home ownership rates for African Americans compared with whites are already starting to take back recent gains. At the current rate of improvement (from 1970 to 2006), parity will not be achieved for another 5,423 years.
- If subprime loans had been distributed equitably, losses for white people would be 44 percent higher and losses for people of color would be 24 percent lower. This is evidence of systemic prejudice and institutional racism.

- Broad racial and economic inequalities need to be addressed for the success of any policy solutions in the subprime crisis.[11]

HOUSING PROBLEMS

Another example that illustrates why blacks continue to have civil rights problems in the United States involves the well-documented discriminatory housing practices. The first phase of a national housing discrimination study sponsored in 2008 by the Department of Housing and Urban Development (HUD) and conducted by the Urban Institute found that housing discrimination against minorities still exist at unacceptable levels.[12] The greatest share of discrimination for African Americans and Hispanics/Latinos rent-seekers can be attributed to two causes: (1) being told that units are unavailable, when in fact they are available to non-Hispanic whites; and (2) being shown and told about less expensive units.

As for homebuyers, African Americans continue to face discrimination in metropolitan housing markets nationwide. White homebuyers were consistently favored over blacks in 17 percent of tests. Overall, although this special HUD study found that discrimination significantly declined between 1989 and 2000 for African Americans renters and homebuyers and Hispanic homebuyers, it also found strong evidence that discrimination against African Americans persists in all major metropolitan housing markets in the United States.[13]

DISPARITIES IN PHYSICIAN CARE

Health disparities are defined as situations in which one demographic or racial group has a higher or lower disproportionate number of deaths or disease outbreak as compared with another group. The fact that, as of 2008, African American's life expectancy for men (sixty-eight years) and women (seventy-two years) continues to be lower than white men (seventy years) and women (seventy-four years) indicates that the health and medical care systems still are not distributed and accessed equally. Unfortunately, blacks have been the recipient of poor health and medical care programs and policies for decades in our United States.

Numerous studies continue to document this health disparity between blacks and whites. Recently, one of the most profound and thorough studies that highlighted a number of health disparity issues came from the Harvard School of Public Health and the Robert Wood Johnson Foundation. This 2007 survey of 4,334 randomly selected U.S. adults compared perceptions of the quality of physician care among fourteen racial and ethnic groups with those of whites. This multiethnic focus is important because, when discussing perceptions of health care quality, prior research has tended to look at the major ethnic groups (African Americans, Hispanic and Latino Americans, and Asian Americans) as homogenous groups, although group members are from different countries and have different cultures and language backgrounds. Additionally, most prior studies have not examined the experiences of Native Americans or Alaskan Natives. Members of these subgroups may have different health care experiences than other members of their larger ethnic group.

This study's major findings, as they relate to the three subgroups of African Americans, were as follows:

- Quality of Physician Care
- Ease of Getting an Appointment
- Time with the Physician
- Listening to the Patient
- Explaining Medical Matters to the Patient
- Patient-Physician Communication
- Discomfort Asking Physician Questions

Overall, this study has implications for future research and public policy. It is clear from the results that programs and policies that focus on ameliorating the problems confronting these racial groups need to reflect some of the unequal experiences and needs that these individual minority groups confront.[14]

DISPARITY OF BLACK FACULTY AT MAINSTREAM UNIVERSITIES

Although real faculty salaries rose during much of the 1990s, according to data reported each year by the American Association of University Professors, overall increases mask persistent disparities among faculty.[15] For example, among the most persistent differences in faculty salaries are those between men and women as well as faculty at private institutions versus public institutions. Salary differences among racial and ethnic groups, although sometimes more difficult to assess because of small sample sizes, are evident as well. These gender, racial, and ethnic equity issues are particularly important to individuals currently working within the professoriate and to those who hope to attract a diverse pool of talent to the profession in the future.

In particular, the American Association of University Professors (1999) expressed specific concern about the persistent wage gap between male and female faculty members over the past two decades, noting that pay disparities have lingered despite increasing proportions

of women entering the profession. Of course, many factors contribute
to faculty salaries, and many of those factors vary by gender, race, and
ethnicity as well. To fully understand the nature of gender, racial,
and ethnic differences in faculty outcomes like salary, tenure status,
and academic rank, differences in other background characteristics also
must be fully explored and considered. Regardless of the other background characteristics, a 2002 National Center for Education Statistics
(NCES) report states that gender differences in faculty characteristics
vary across racial and ethnic groups and that racial and ethnic disparities differ for men and women.[16]

In particular, the 2002 NCES report highlighted the following data
in the overall differences between black and white faculty:

- White faculty were more likely than black faculty to teach at public doctoral universities (35 versus 23 percent), but no difference
  was found in the proportion of white and black faculty teaching
  at public two-year institutions.

- Blacks were less likely than whites to teach in the natural sciences
  and engineering but were more likely to teach in the social
  sciences.

- Black faculty, like Asian faculty, were less likely than white
  faculty to be full professors but were more likely to be assistant
  professors.

- Black faculty were less likely than white faculty to hold tenure (44
  versus 54 percent), and white faculty were more likely to hold a
  tenure-track position (26 versus 17 percent).[17]

In summary, gender, racial, and ethnic differences were observed in
faculty salaries and in many characteristics that affect salary for full-
time faculty with for-credit instructional duties. Black faculty often are
placed at a disadvantage relative to white faculty primarily because
they have less experience and lower salaries.[18]

YOUNG ADULTS AND POSTSECONDARY EDUCATION

The tradition of young adults in the United States attaining higher
levels of education than previous generations appears to have stalled,
and for far too many people of color, the percentage of young adults
with some type of postsecondary degree compared with older adults
actually has fallen.[19] According to the *Minorities in Higher Education
2008 Twenty-Third Status Report*, the percentage of young adults ages
twenty-five to twenty-nine and older adults age thirty and above with
at least an associate degree in 2006 was about the same, approximately
35 percent. For Hispanics and Native American, young adults have

received even less education than previous generations. As for African Americans, the postsecondary education attainment rates remained relatively the same for both age-groups at approximately 24 percent. Molly Corbett Broad, president of the American Council on Education (ACE), specifically stated that "It appears we are at a tipping point in our nation's history."[20]

INCARCERATION RATES

Since the early 1970s, the prison and jail population in the United States has increased at an unprecedented rate. The more than 500 percent rise in the number of people incarcerated in the nation's prisons and jails has resulted in a total of 2.2 million people behind bars.[21]

As for the African American population, it constitutes approximately 900,000 of the total 2.2 million incarcerated. Data from the Bureau of Justice Statistics document that one in six black men had been incarcerated as of 2001. If current trends continue, one in three black males born in the early 21st century can expect to spend time in prison during his lifetime. The prevalence of imprisonment for women is considerably lower than for men, but many of the same racial disparities persist, with black women being more likely to be incarcerated than white women.[22]

Although these national figures are disturbing, they mask not only the extreme state-level variations in the impact of incarceration on communities of color but also a serious underlying relationship between the criminal justice system and communities of color, particularly among blacks. The fact that so many Americans and particularly African Americans have become accustomed to seeing blacks regularly convicted, sent to jail, and even placed on death row highlights the vast racial disparity that exists within the criminal justice system.

Racial disparity in the criminal justice system exists when the proportion of a racial or ethnic group within the control of the system is greater than the proportion of such groups in the general population. The cause of such disparity may be varied and may include differing levels of criminal activity, law enforcement emphasis on particular communities, legislative policies, and decision making by criminal justice practitioners who exercise broad discretion in the justice process.[23]

In a 2008 report entitled *Reducing Racial Disparity in the Criminal Justice System*, illegitimate or unwarranted racial disparity results from dissimilar treatment by the criminal justice system of similarly situated people based on race. In some instances, this may involve overt racial bias, whereas in others, it may reflect the influence of factors that are associated only indirectly with race.

There are four key aspects to addressing racial disparity in the criminal justice system:

1. The problem of racial disparity is one that builds at each stage of the criminal justice continuum of arrest through parole, rather than the result of the actions of any single agency.

2. To combat unwarranted disparity, strategies are required to tackle the problem at each stage of the criminal justice system and to do so in a coordinated way. Without a systemic approach to the problem, gains in one area may be offset by reversals in another.

3. Each decision point and component of the system requires unique strategies depending on the degree of disparity and the specific populations affected by the actions of that component.

4. Systemwide change is impossible without informed criminal justice leaders who are willing and able to commit their personal and agency resources to measuring and addressing racial disparity at every stage of the criminal justice system, and as a result, for the system as a whole.[24]

Addressing racial disparity in the criminal justice system is entirely consistent with a commitment to public safety, to civil rights, and to a fair system of justice. If unwarranted racial disparities can be reduced, the justice system will gain credibility and serve a more effective role in preventing and responding to crime.

GENERATIONS OF POVERTY

One of the most remarkable and saddest aspects of our wealthy U.S. system is the fact that Americans have accepted that a substantial portion of citizens will live below the poverty line. Most Americans, particularly mainstream Americans, perceive those who live below the poverty line as being of the lowest caliber. Those who are impoverished, however, have little opportunity to advance out of their current economic and social situation. Furthermore, most Americans, perceive those who are impoverished as primarily associated with certain racial and ethnic backgrounds.

Without doubt, poverty affects certain racial and ethnic groups more often than others, which inhibits their ability to improve their economic and social status; however, it does not necessarily mean that we *accept* that these groups will remain impoverished for generations. Unfortunately, in America even in the 21st century, we have done exactly that.

So how do we define poverty in America? There are two basic versions of the federal poverty measure: the poverty thresholds (which are the primary version) and the poverty guidelines. The Census Bureau issues the poverty thresholds, which generally are used for statistical purposes—for example, to estimate the number of people in poverty nationwide each year and classify them by type of residence, race, and other social, economic, and demographic characteristics. The Department of Health and Human Services issues the poverty guidelines for administrative purposes—for instance, to determine whether a person or family is eligible for assistance through various federal programs.[25]

Since the 1960s, the U.S. government has defined poverty in absolute terms. When the Johnson administration declared the War on Poverty in 1964, it chose an absolute measure. The "absolute poverty line" is the threshold below which families or individuals are considered to be "lacking the resources to meet the basic needs for healthy living, [and] having insufficient income to provide the food, shelter and clothing needed to preserve health."

Today, the U.S. government and the Office of Management and Budget use an adoption of the Orshansky Poverty Threshold as the basis for measuring poverty in the United States. The Orshansky Poverty Threshold is named after an economist who worked for the Social Security Administration in the 1960s. This measure gives a range of income cutoffs, or thresholds, adjusted for factors such as family size, sex of the family head, number of children under eighteen years old, and farm or nonfarm residence.[26] Thus, when we hear and review the annual poverty rate in the United States, we are talking about families of all racial and ethnic backgrounds, heads of households and children who lack the resources to meet the basic needs of healthy living, and families with insufficient income to provide the food, shelter, and clothing needed to preserve health.

On August 28, 2007, the U.S. Census Bureau released new statistics on income and poverty for 2006. For the nation as a whole, the numbers showed the first substantial decline in the poverty rate since 2000, declining from 12.6 percent to 12.3 percent. The rate for both all blacks and black children (those under eighteen) declined as well, but it still was higher than the rate for other groups. The median household income increased for the nation by 0.7 percent to $48,201 and for blacks it increased by 0.3 percent to $31,969 (both figures are below the inflation-adjusted figures for 2000). The median income of blacks remains at 61 percent of that of non-Hispanic whites and is the lowest of any group.[27]

Although the overall poverty rate declined to 12.3 percent in 2006, that rate is still higher than in 2000 when it was 11.3 percent. The poverty rate declined for all racial and ethnic groups in 2006, but Latinos had the biggest drop (−1.2 percent), followed by Asians (−0.8 percent), and then blacks (−0.6 percent). Blacks continue to have the highest rate of people living in severe poverty (less than half the current poverty threshold): 10.9 percent of blacks were in severe poverty, compared with 7.7 percent of Latinos, 5.1 percent of Asians, and 3.5 percent of non-Hispanic whites.[28]

The poverty rate for children (under eighteen) also dropped in 2006, from 17.6 percent to 17.4 percent. At more than three times the non-Hispanic white rate of 10 percent, blacks continue to have the highest percentage of children living in poverty of any group (33.4 percent). This figure represents a 1.1 percentage point improvement from 2005, the second-biggest improvement of any group after Latinos. The elderly (sixty-five years and older) continue to have the lowest overall poverty rate at 9.4 percent, yet this rate is also higher for blacks (22.7 percent) than for any other group.[29]

Median household income increased for all groups except non-Hispanic whites in 2006, but for all groups, the inflation-adjusted median income was still less than it was in 2000. For blacks, this year's median household income was 8 percent lower than 2000. In 2006, Asians had the biggest annual increase in median income (+1.8 percent), followed by Latinos (+1.7 percent), blacks (+0.3 percent), and non-Hispanic whites (−0.05 percent). When you look specifically at different income groups, blacks continue to have far higher percentage of people at the lowest incomes (less than $15,000 a year) than non-Hispanic whites or the nation as a whole, and far fewer in the top range (more than $100,000).[30]

As for 2007, the official poverty rate was 12.5 percent just slightly up from the 2006 poverty rate (12.3 percent). In terms of actual numbers, this means that 37.3 million people in the United States were in poverty, up from 36.5 million in 2006.

Poverty rates for racial and ethnic groups remained high in 2007. The poverty rate increased for Hispanics (21.5 percent in 2007, up from 20.6 percent in 2006), whereas for Asians (10.6 percent), non-Hispanic whites (8.2 percent), and blacks (24.5 percent) the rate remained relatively the same.[31] Regardless of the year-to-year changes in the poverty rates, there is one consistent pattern—the black poverty rate is usually three times higher than the white poverty rate.

REPARATIONS

Over the past couple of decades, the word "reparations" has stirred up much controversy between blacks and whites, particularly as it relates to African Americans and slavery. The word "reparations" and discussions about reparations for African Americans as they relate to the institution of U.S. slavery invoke immediate feelings, responses, and reactions from the responsible individuals and groups. Under the Civil Liberties Act of 1988, signed into law by President Ronald Reagan, the U.S. government apologized for Japanese American internment during World War II and provided reparations of $20,000 to each survivor, to compensate for loss of property and liberty during that period. In addition, the government paid reparations to Native American tribes for compensation of their lands taken away from them through unscrupulous treaties over the years. Despite these actions, a vast majority of Americans feel ambivalent about reparations for African Americans as it relates to the centuries of institutional slavery in the United States.

So what does this word really mean? *Reparations* for slavery represents a proposal made by some people in the United States that compensation should be provided to the descendants of enslaved people, in consideration of the labor provided for free over several centuries, which has been a powerful and influential factor in the development of the country.[32] From the late 1600s when America was being first discovered by European countries to the mid-1800s when America was formulated and declarized into "these United States," the institution of slavery prospered in Northern and Southern states. Contrary to popular belief, some in the Northern states were as complicit in the slave trade as the Southern states. New England merchants profited from the importation of slaves, while Southern planters profited from the continued enslavement of Africans. Regardless of the degree to which one state versus another state benefited from slavery, without doubt, the institution of slavery and a substantial number of founding institutions greatly benefited from years of free labor, revenue, power, and social class stratification at the detriment of the enslaved. Additionally, the institution instilled a belief of superiority of one race over another, and perhaps more significant, it instilled a belief of *inferiority* among many African Americans who were acculturated immediately thereafter slavery was abolished, during the Jim Crow years, the civil rights movement, and even into the 21st century.

Although the movement toward reparations for African Americans has wavered during the past eight years, it has picked up substantial momentum with the election of the nation's forty-forth president—Barack Obama. This time, however, the issue of reparations is not being connected to monetary compensation to the descendents of African American slaves but more so to a "formal apology" to African Americans, thereby allowing state governments, individual companies, and religious organizations to be "officially" forgiven for their role in the institution of African American slavery.

So is this the major reason why states such as Maryland, Virginia, Alabama, North Carolina, New Jersey, and Florida along with the U.S. House of Representatives in 2008 "officially apologized" to black Americans for the "fundamental injustice, cruelty, brutality and inhumanity of slavery and Jim Crow" segregation?[33] Additionally, corporations such as Wachovia, J. P. Morgan Chase and Co., R. J. Reynolds, Aetna, Inc., and CSX Corporation, as well as prestigious universities such as Yale and Brown, also have come forth and issued apologies to the descendants of enslaved Africans.[34] Thus, it becomes apparent that the best move with regards to reparations for African American slavery is for corporations, universities, state governments, and the federal government is to issue a formal apology. Will the federal government follow suit and officially issue a formal apology during the Obama administration?

Well, if we consider the statements provided by the then-presidential candidate Barack Obama in August 2008, it would appear that the first African American president will *not* support any formal federal reparations program or apology to the descendants of enslaved Africans in America. As President Obama stated, I have said in the past—and I'll repeat again—that the best reparations we can provide are good schools in the inner city and jobs for people who are unemployed.[35]

When pressed for his position on apologizing to blacks or offering reparations at a conference of minority journalists during the presidential campaign, then-presidential candidate Obama said he was *more* interested in taking action to help people struggling to get by. Because many of these people who are struggling are minorities and that these efforts would help the same people who would stand to benefit from reparations.[36]

CONCLUSION

So will President Barack Obama and the new administration go against the current wave of support for an apology to African Americans for the institution of slavery or will they use their newly acquired federal position and status to stop another push for reparations dead in its tracks? Furthermore, will President Obama and the new administration seriously address the *civil rights* issues surrounding the scrupulous loan and mortgage practices made to African Americans over the years, the discriminatory housing practices, the continual disparities in physician care, the disparity of black faculty at mainstream universities, the higher incarceration rates of blacks in jails and federal prisons, the generations of poverty that continue to persist, and proper compensation for the descendants of enslaved Africans in the United States?

Unfortunately, these issues are just a few of the serious issues that President Obama and his diverse cabinet inherited. Nonetheless, these will be the issues that President Obama and his cabinet will be evaluated on throughout the next four and maybe eight years.

Thus, as stated at the beginning of this chapter as it relates to the African American community, this will be the major question for President Barack Obama during his time in office: Will President Obama take the lead in overturning the litany of civil rights cases against blacks in America?

Only time will tell. The consequences of *not* addressing any of these issues, however, may seriously damage and jeopardize President

Barack Obama's image, mystique, connection, prestige, respect, black male role model status, and coolness, and especially his campaign for a second term as president of the United States.

If President Obama's first 100 days in the Oval Office are any indication of his disconnecting policies and initiatives as it relates to African Americans and unresolved civil rights issues, the time is now to start a new movement, which I refer to as a "cultural rights movement" in the United States.

A cultural rights movement is defined as a system of shared beliefs, values, and traditions associated with a group of people of common background that is passed down from generation to generation through the process of learning to assert one's rights as a human being. Although there have been all types of cultural rights movements throughout history, the major components of each cultural rights movement include the following attributes:

- They are learned.
- They are symbolic.
- They add meaning to reality to the group.
- They are differently shared.
- They are integrated.
- They are adaptive.

Being able to assert one's human rights *culturally* is especially important for African Americans at this point in history. Starting a cultural rights movement will serve three major objectives:

1. To embrace, value, and respect African American culture and how it can be integrated into the totality of American culture.
2. To embrace, value, and respect everyone's cultural traditions, values, and history.
3. To start a regional, national, and global movement among all cultures of the world that want to assert their rights as human beings and to change government policies that do not include these cultural rights.

Most important, a cultural rights movement is an inclusive agenda that mandates that each and every group not only has the right to express its uniqueness, history, values, and traditions but also has equal rights simply because its members are human beings. Societies that do not recognize or embrace the culture of its people at all levels are not being truthful to their mandate—that is to *serve the people.*

African Americans must do some serious soul-searching during the next four to eight years. We are still overjoyed and proud to witness the first African American president lead the nation. It is a somewhat unbelievable historic event that Barack Obama was sworn in as the forty-fourth president of the United States. Yet, as Michael Eric Dyson, well-known author, scholar, and professor of sociology at Georgetown University, reminded viewers during the inauguration on NBC television, "Barack Obama is a politician not a prophet." Therefore, if President Obama and his administration do not seriously confront the inequities in health disparities, discriminatory housing practices, and the inequities in the judicial system, as well as the decline of the public school systems, the disparity of black professionals in higher education, the astronomical incarceration rates of blacks in prisons, and the long-overdue reparations initiative as they relate to African Americans and all citizens of the United States, then a cultural rights movement is inevitable.

Yes, we can start a cultural rights movement in these United States.

Chapter 2

Looking Back: Notable Leaders of the Civil Rights Movement

INTRODUCTION

The words "civil rights" suddenly returned to national prominence with the election, inauguration, and the historical implications of the country's first African American president. The jubilation and continuous celebration from the election to the inauguration of the nation's first African American president along with the first African American First Family was heartfelt by millions of Americans. Indeed, most political pundits and academic scholars had to admit that the impact of the civil rights movement of the 1960s in the United States, particularly for African American communities across the country some forty years earlier, resulted in one of its most remarkable achievements—the election of Barack Obama as the forty-fourth president of the United States.

Let us not forget that the words *civil rights* and the *civil rights movement* of the 1960s has had a tremendous impact on each and every U.S. citizen, whether it was in the past or in the 21st century. The very term "civil rights" provides every U.S. citizen the protection and privileges of personal power mandated by U.S. laws. Laws guaranteeing civil rights may be written down, derived from custom, or implied. In the United States, civil rights laws are most often written. Examples of civil rights and liberties include the right to privacy, the right to get redress if injured by another, the right of peaceful protest, and the right to a fair investigation and trial if suspected of a crime, as well as more generally based constitutional rights, such as the right to vote, the right to personal freedom, the right to freedom of movement, and the right of equal protection.[1] When these *civil rights* are not granted to a person or an entire group of people, then a *civil rights movement* can emerge. Such a movement serves to reclaim a groups' civil rights and advocates new laws to restrict the effects of discrimination. Thus, civil rights and a civil rights movement are terms and actions that apply to every citizen of the United States.

If you ask the average U.S. citizen about the civil rights movement in America, they often refer to the African American civil rights movement of the 1950s and 1960s. Yet civil rights movements in America actually began a long time ago. As early as the 17th century, blacks and whites, slaves in Virginia and Quakers in Pennsylvania, protested the barbarity of slavery. Nat Turner, Sojourner Truth, Frederick Douglass, William Lloyd Garrison, John Brown, and Harriet Tubman are but a few of those who started the resistance to slavery before the Civil War. After the Civil War, another battle mounted against slavery's legacy—racism and segregation. For most Americans, however, the civil rights movement began on May 17, 1954, when the Supreme Court handed down the *Brown v. Board of Education of Topeka* decision outlawing segregation in public schools. The Court unlocked the door, but the pressure applied by thousands of men and women in the movement pushed the door open wide enough to allow Blacks to walk through it toward this country's essential prize: freedom.[2]

When I think about the terms civil rights and the civil rights movement particularly as it relates to African Americans, it makes me think about my years growing up in the small rural Midwestern towns of Springfield and Wilberforce, Ohio, during the late 1950s and 1960s with my parents and older brothers. Being born and living in Springfield until I was about seven years old, our family was quite similar to many other young African American families during this time period.

My parents, Jean and Roger, were two hardworking African Americans trying to raise a family consisting initially of five boys (one of my brothers left before I was born and returned to his mother's home) on a federal government salary. Although my parents felt fortunate and blessed to have their jobs and a roof over our heads, a vast majority of African Americans had little choice about where to live in Springfield, Ohio. This probably was one of the reasons why we lived next to, and played in, the town's city dump—an area in which a vast majority of African American neighborhoods existed.

As children, we did not think much about living next to and playing in the city dump. It was a natural place to play, primarily because there were so many items to play with. Therefore, on any day of the week, but particularly the weekend, you could find all types of kids playing in the city dump. Whether it was playing hide and seek or competing in a track-and-field event such as high jump or long jump, the city dump functioned as our primary playground. Of course, as children, we did not think about the health consequences of playing in the city dump on a regular basis, but I am sure our parents did. That is probably one of the major reasons why my parents were one of the first families in the neighborhood to relocate from this lower-income neighborhood to a burgeoning, new black middle-class neighborhood in Wilberforce, Ohio, approximately twelve miles away.

Unknowingly, this 1964 relocation of my family to Wilberforce (along with countless numbers of other African American families) symbolized our own type of civil rights movement. It was quite apparent that many hardworking African American families were no longer going to *accept* and *be confined* to substandard living conditions, such as living around city dumps. That is why African Americans who lived in Wilberforce and particularly the "valley" represented the new wave of middle-class blacks.

The valley was given this name not only because of its actual physical landscape, sitting vastly lower than the main highway road that ran through Wilberforce, but also because the families that lived in this area formed a close-knit neighborhood. The valley had open fields of grass and weeds big enough for regular size baseball and football fields. Interestingly, the valley was actually part of the land originally owned by a local white farmer who decided to sell portions of it to the town of Wilberforce for new home development. So, we actually lived on newly developed farm land. As increasing numbers of families bought lots in the valley, it increasingly became an exclusive middle-class neighborhood for up-and-coming African Americans. This was a far cry from the city dump where my brothers and I used to play in Springfield.

My parents' lot was ideally positioned in the valley. It was located at the end of one of the roads on a small hill. Our home had three bedrooms and a two-car garage along with an outdoor patio flat. We had a nice-size front yard, which ran beyond the length of the home, and a huge back yard that seemed not to end until hitting the creek at the bottom of the hill. Our home was typical of all the other homes in the valley.

As for the families who lived in the valley, they were African Americans who worked in mainstream companies or institutions, made a steady income, interconnected through fellowship, and were proud of their heritage. Families regularly socialized together, the kids went to school and played together, and, on several occasions, families partied together. There was no doubt that the individuals and families living in the valley along with so many other newly arrived African Americans in Wilberforce were more than ready to exert their civil rights to live where they wanted to live—in safe, uncontaminated, environmentally friendly, and rural surroundings.

Far away from all the national civil rights events and civil rights issues during the 1950s and 1960s that have been well documented in the literature and television news, the town of Wilberforce along with its historic roots for fighting for African Americans (the Historically Black Colleges of Wilberforce University and Central State University) and the new influx of middle-class African Americans expressed its own set of civil rights, including the following:

- the right to personal freedom
- the right to freedom of movement
- the right of equal protection

The impact of this local and subtle civil rights movement among African Americans in and around Wilberforce during this time period dramatically changed and improved the race relations (black and white) among residents in the nearby town of Xenia—a traditional Midwestern town. Although it was not an easy transition for the town of Xenia to embrace a new type of race relations, some of which resulted in fights between blacks and whites, protests at the high school, and boycotts of certain businesses, the transition truly benefited economically, educationally, socially, politically, and culturally from the impact of the newly arrived African Americans in Wilberforce and surrounding communities.

Even in Midwestern small towns, such as Wilberforce and Springfield, Ohio, in the 1950s and 1960s, the issues of civil rights and outcome of local and the national civil rights movement directly affected African American lives. Whether it was relocating to a new town to live in less hazardous conditions, purchasing a new home in a middle-class African American neighborhood, or deciding to be treated fairly and equally in all daily interactions with mainstream America, African Americans in this area of the country fought for and achieved their *civil rights* in their own way.

A BRIEF LOOK AT THE 1950s AND 1960s CIVIL RIGHTS MOVEMENT

Dr. Martin Luther King

Every year on the third Monday in January, the United States celebrates the life, achievements, and dreams of Dr. Martin Luther King—a real-life Baptist minister who became one of the most recognized leaders of the African American civil rights movement during the 1950s and 1960s. During his brief life as a civil rights activist, Rev. King led the 1955 Montgomery Bus Boycott, founded the Southern Christian Leadership conference in 1957, received the Nobel Peace Prize in 1964, and delivered the historical "I Have a Dream" speech on August 28, 1963, on the steps of the Lincoln Memorial, which culminated in the national movement for civil rights for jobs and freedom for all people—not just African Americans.

As John Hope Franklin and Alfred Moss Jr. (1988) explained in "From Slavery to Freedom," it was the 1963 demonstrations in which Dr. Martin Luther King and the Southern Christian Leadership joined demonstrators in Birmingham on April 3 to demand for fair employment opportunities and desegregation of public facilities that sparked the national movement and support for their causes.[3] The actions of the Birmingham police in using dogs and high-pressure water hoses on the marchers caused consternation and dismay in many parts of the county where sympathy demonstrations were held. During the week of May 18, the Department of Justice noted forty-three major and minor demonstrations, ten of them in Northern cities. More such demonstrations were held the following month when Medgar Evers, the leader of the Mississippi chapter of the National Association for the Advancement of Colored People (NAACP), was shot in the back and killed outside his home in Jackson.[4]

There were about as many demonstrations in the North and West as in the South. The emphasis was on increased job opportunities and an end to de facto segregation in housing and education. Neither the president nor Congress could be indifferent to the large-scale demonstrations and the resistance of the white segregationists. In February, before the demonstrations reached their peak, President Kennedy sent a special message to Congress recommending legislation to strengthen voting rights. In June, largely because of events in Birmingham and elsewhere, he submitted a new and broadened civil rights program. In a radio and television speech to the American people during this time, President Kennedy said,

> We face . . . a moral crisis as a country and as a people. It cannot be met by repressive police action. It cannot be left to increased demonstration in the streets. It cannot be quieted by token moves or talk. It is time to act in the Congress, in your state and local legislative body and, above all, in all of our daily lives.[5]

As Congress and the nation debated about President Kennedy's civil rights program and bill, the March on Washington for Jobs and Freedom occurred. All of the major civil rights groups were joined by many religious, labor, and civic groups in planning and executing the enormous demonstration. The American Jewish Congress, the National Conference of Catholics for Interracial Justice, the National Council of Churches, and the American Federation of Labor–Congress of Industrial Organizations (AFL-CIO) Industrial Union Department were among the strong supporters of the March. On August 28, 1963, more than 250,000 blacks and whites from across the United States staged the largest demonstration in the history of the nation's capital. It was during this demonstration that Dr. Martin Luther King, along with numerous other speakers throughout the day, delivered his "I Have a Dream" speech.[6]

A few months after the March on Washington and the tragic assassination of President Kennedy, Lyndon B. Johnson, the thirty-sixth president of the United States on November 22, 1963, was quick to make known his strong support of Kennedy's civil rights program. Five days after he took office he told Congress that he desired, "the earliest possible passage of the civil rights bill."[7]

The following year after much debate in Congress and the nation, the Civil Rights Act of 1964 was passed. The Civil Rights Act of 1964 was the most far-reaching and comprehensive law in support of racial equality ever enacted by Congress. It gave the attorney general additional power to protect citizens against discrimination and segregation in voting, education, and the use of public facilities. It forbade discrimination in most places of public accommodation and established a federal Community Relations Service to help individuals and communities solve civil rights problems. It established a federal Equal Employment Opportunity Commission and extended the life of the Commission on Civil Rights. Yet, one of the most controversial provisions required the elimination of discrimination in federally assisted programs, authorizing termination of programs or withdrawal of federal funds upon failure to comply. Finally, the U.S. Department of Education was authorized to provide technical and financial aid to assist communities in the desegregation of schools. Although some African Americans criticized the act for not going far enough, a vast majority were delighted that a semblance of equality might now be attainable.[8]

Following is the specific timeline of political and social events associated with the Civil Rights Act:

> **April 3–May 10, 1963**—A nonviolent protest is launched in Birmingham, Alabama, by the Southern Christian Leadership Conference and Martin Luther King, Jr. Negotiations involved the U.S. Department of Justice. The protest was widely televised, which documented the demonstration and brutality.
>
> **June 11, 1963**—A nationally televised speech was given by John F. Kennedy that called for major civil rights legislation.
>
> **June 12, 1963**—Medgar Evers, an NAACP field secretary, is assassinated.
>
> **June 19, 1963**—The Justice Department completes work on its version of acceptable civil rights legislation, which is sent to Congress.
>
> **June 19–November 20, 1963**—Kennedy introduces civil rights laws to the House of Representatives. A Democrat and Republican work together and gain committee approval in late October.

August 28, 1963—An estimated 250,000 civil rights demonstrators assemble in Washington, D.C., demanding justice and calling for legislation. Martin Luther King delivers his "I Have a Dream" speech.

September 15, 1963—Four little girls are killed when a bomb goes off in the basement of the Sixteenth Street Baptist Church in Birmingham, Alabama.

November 22, 1963—Vice President Lyndon B. Johnson becomes president of the United States after President Kennedy is assassinated in Dallas, Texas.

November 27, 1963—President Johnson calls for early passage of the civil rights bill as a way to honor President Kennedy.

January 9–30, 1964—The House Rules Committee moves the proposed bill to the floor of the House after rigorous opposition from the committee's chair.

February 1964—Herbert H. Humphrey, a Senate Democrat from Minnesota, is appointed floor manager for the legislation. He organizes a bipartisan team with Thomas Kuchel accompanied by Leadership Conference on Civil Rights lobbyist Joseph Rauh and Clarence Mitchell.

February 9, 1964—House Rules Chair Howard W. Smith of Virginia attempts to kill the civil rights legislation by asking the word "sex" be added in the job discrimination section. The amendment is accepted anyway without the provision.

February 10, 1964—The House of Representative approves the civil rights legislation after nine days of debate by a vote of 290–130.

March 1964—Formal consideration of the pending legislation begins by the Senate between March and June 1964. The bill is filibustered by Southern democrats.

April 19, 1964—CBS News reports on progress of the civil rights bill from the steps of the Capitol.

April 19–June 19, 1964—Protestant, Catholic, and Jewish students begin a vigil on the steps of the Lincoln Memorial and stay until the civil rights bill is passed by the Senate.

April 28, 1964—Church leaders hold an interreligious rally at Georgetown University.

June 10, 1964—Evertt Dirksen a Republican senator called for the end of the floor filibuster and passage of the civil rights bill. The filibuster ends with a 71–29 vote.

July 2, 1964—The bill is signed by President Johnson during a White House ceremony. Johnson delivers a televised speech in which he tells the country to "promote a more abiding commitment to freedom" and says that "most Americans are law-abiding citizens." Several leaders attend the signing ceremony, including Martin Luther King and Hubert Humphrey.

March 17–August 6, 1965—Congress passes the Voting Rights Act of 1965 that strengthens voting provisions for the Civil Rights Act. The Voting Rights Act opens a new political era for African Americans. President Johnson signs the bill into law.

June 4, 1965—President Johnson speaks at Howard University and phrases the term "equality of results." Consequently, the term initiates affirmative action approaches under the Civil Rights Act of 1964.[9]

This account of civil rights history is only one of numerous civil rights movements occurring throughout the United States during 1950s and 1960s.[10] So as we continue to celebrate the memory and achievements of Dr. Martin Luther King every year, we are reminded that Dr. King was one of several million people during this time period who believed in and fought for civil rights for all people. In fact, when my family and I visited the Martin Luther King, Jr. birth home in Atlanta, Georgia, in 1993, we were amazed how "typical" and similar his home was to other African American homes in that area during that time period. What I took away from our federally guided tour of his birth home was that Rev. King was just like other Americans. He lived like a normal child. Yet, as he matured, there was no doubt that King had a special calling to serve and become the cultural icon for the civil rights movement of the 1950s and 1960s.

Johnnie Carr

Another person played a significant part in the civil rights movement and worked alongside Dr. Martin Luther King; yet she often has been overlooked by historians, news reporters, and the general public. Mrs. Johnnie Carr, a childhood friend of Rosa Parks, participated in the Montgomery Bus Boycott and helped end school segregation and voting discrimination in Alabama. Carr succeeded Rev. Martin Luther King, Jr., as president of the Montgomery Improvement Association in 1967 and held the post until her death at the age of ninety-seven. It was the newly formed association that spearheaded the boycott of city buses in the Alabama capital in 1955 after Rosa Parks was arrested for refusing to give up her seat to a white person on a crowded bus.[11]

Arlam Carr, son of Johnnie Carr, discussed his mother in an interview with an Associated Press reporter:

One of the things I respect her for is she did not have the rancor and anger that so many local African Americans of the civil rights movement had. . . . She was very willing to build bridges. Montgomery's always been very divisive, and she showed an example of reaching across racial lines.[12]

In another interview about Johnnie Carr, Mayor Bobby Bright of Montgomery, Alabama had this to say:

> She was always an encourager and not a divider. She was just a lov-
> ing person. She was truly the mother figure that we all so desper-
> ately needed in Montgomery during a very trying period of our
> history. She would always say, "It was tough, but we made it and
> we made it better—and we're going to continue to make it better."[13]

Another reporter recounts her interaction with Johnnie Carr after
her passing in the following abbreviated essay:

> I was privileged to meet Mrs. Johnnie Carr more than 20 years
> ago. I was a young journalist on an assignment from UPI radio to
> mark the 30th anniversary of the Montgomery bus boycott. I vis-
> ited her Hall Street home, just across the street from the park
> where years before she wasn't allowed to take her children
> because of their race. The only black women allowed were maids
> caring for their young white charges.
> Mrs. Carr welcomed me into her prim living room and offered me
> a glass of tea. I listened as she took me back in time to a place I'd
> only read about in textbooks. She talked of Martin Luther King, the
> charismatic young minister of Dexter Avenue Baptist Church, the
> Monday night mass meetings where boycott participants rallied for
> the week ahead and the carpool system she helped orchestrate to get
> people to work when they weren't riding the buses. I realized I was
> in the presence of a giant, that the tenacity of this gentle grandmoth-
> erly figure and others like her had literally changed the nation.[14]

Finally, Public Broadcasting Service (PBS) television host Tavis Smiley interviewed Mrs. Johnnie Carr along with Congressman John Lewis
and Rev. Dr. Joseph Lowery in 2005 for a special television tribute for
Rosa Parks and the Montgomery Bus Boycott of 1955. His questions to
Mrs. Johnnie Carr focused on her friendship with Rosa Parks and what
was it like at this time in history in Montgomery, Alabama.
Mrs. Johnnie Carr said the following:

> Back to our school days, number one, I would like to say our
> parents were interested in us trying to get a good education. And
> in that day and time, education for blacks was very, not almost
> existent. And so when our parents found out about this school
> that was for black girls, and they decided to enroll us in this, to
> help us to be able to get a good education. And that is when I
> met Rosa Parks, in this school. A school that was established here
> in Montgomery, Alabama, just for black girls.

It was owned by white teachers who came down from the north, and established this school. And in this school, all the things that were taught to us were things to help us to become the type of women or the type of citizens that should be. Our background teaching, and our rearing that our parents was one of the backgrounds that I feel helped us to be what we are today.[15]

Tavis Smiley concluded the interview with Mrs. Johnnie Carr by asking her, "What lessons ought we learn out of what you all did 50 years ago?"
Mrs. Johnnie Carr responded saying,

Well, the lessons to learn is first of all, you have got to understand what happened 50 years ago. And if you can get an understanding of what happened 50 years ago, after explaining that everything was segregated and nothing was—you didn't have rights and privileges like other people.
    And then when you look today and see where we are, and the things that you are now able to participate, the things that you can enjoy and be a part of, it should give you a good courage. It should give you an understanding of how you should conduct yourself in order to make sure that you are a product, and you will be producing something to help make things like they ought to be.[16]

These highlighted interviews with Mrs. Johnnie Carr conducted over the years provide us with a better understanding and appreciation for what the average individual African American had to endure, sacrifice, and adjust to during the civil rights era. These interviews shed light on how other distinguished individuals perceive Mrs. Johnnie Carr and how they recognized her as a significant person who contributed much to the civil rights movement and race relations.

Barbara Jordan

One of the first African American women who championed the cause of civil rights into her political career was Barbara Charline Jordan. A dynamic orator, legislator, and educator, Jordan left an indelible mark in American history. Her journey—from the segregated Fifth Ward Houston of her childhood to her status as a legendary public figure on the international stage—was filled with a series of "firsts."[17]
    Always mindful of her humble beginnings in Houston's Fifth Ward, Barbara Jordan overcame innumerable obstacles to become a lawyer and win elected office as the first African American since the Reconstruction to serve in the Texas Senate and then as the first African

American woman from the South to serve in the U.S. House of Representatives. With her striking oratory, charismatic leadership, and dedication to public service, Jordan touched countless lives during her years in government and later as a professor at the University of Texas at Austin's Lyndon B. Johnson School of Public Affairs.

Both as a state senator and as a U.S. congress member, she sponsored bills that championed the poor, the disadvantaged, and people of color. As a congress member, she sponsored legislation to broaden the Voting Rights Act of 1965 to cover Mexican Americans in Texas and other Southwestern states and to extend the law's authority to those states where the disenfranchised and underrepresented had been denied the right to vote or had had their rights restricted by unfair registration practices, such as literary tests.[18]

Jordan gained national prominence for her role in the 1974 Watergate hearings as a member of the House Judiciary Committee when she delivered what many considered to be the most powerful speech of the hearings. Impressed with her eloquence and rising stature in the party, the Democrats chose her to deliver the keynote address at the 1976 Democratic National Convention. She was the first woman and the first African American to do so. Her speech, which addressed the themes of unity, equality, accountability, and American ideals, was considered by many to be the highlight of the convention and helped to rally support for Jimmy Carter's presidential campaign.[19]

Upon leaving the U.S. Congress in 1979, Jordan rejected offers to practice corporate law and instead accepted an invitation to teach public affairs and ethics at the Lyndon B. Johnson School of Public Affairs at the University of Texas in Austin. Students loved her sense of humor and distinctive teaching style, but it was her passion for her subject matter that made her seminars among the most sought-after graduate classes on campus. For seventeen years she taught at the Lyndon B. Johnson School until her death in 1996.[20]

Of all her memorable speeches throughout her groundbreaking civil rights, higher-education, and political career, one in particular directly relates to civil rights and the civil rights movement of the 1950s and 1960s, as well as to civil rights issues of today. Following are excerpts from her speech at Northwestern University in 1993:

> Does the American experience of segregation and integration have any lessons to teach us? My proposition is that we have learned from our past. Our experience with race, slavery, civil rights, and the rule of the law is unlike that of any other nation on earth. One distinction is that, notwithstanding our differences, there is homogeneity. We speak of race more than we speak of ethnicity. We don't have deep cultural differences that exist in other parts of the world. In a sense, we are all immigrants.[21]

This particular speech, along with Jordan's achievements, illustrates how one African American woman utilized her skills in politics, academia, and civil rights to provide a foundation in public policy and civil discourse for rights that this nation is still discussing, fighting, and lobbying—civil rights for everyone.

Shirley Chisholm

Although the country now has its very first African American president, it may be shocking for some to believe that he is not the first African American to run for president. Indeed, Rev. Jesse Jackson sought the nomination from the Democratic Party to run for president in 1984 and 1988. Yet there was another pioneer even before Jackson and Obama, and this person was not a man. This person was Shirley Anita St. Hill Chisholm, better known as Shirley Chisholm or *Ms Chis*.

On January 25, 1972, a poised and determined forty-eight year-old Shirley Chisholm, congress member from New York's Twelfth District, announced her decision to run for president of the United States in front of a standing-room-only crowd at a press conference in the elementary school auditorium at Brooklyn's largest Baptist church. She was a relatively small woman who stood barely five feet tall, with a strong, aggressive voice. With great fortitude and a no-nonsense approach, she faced her chief opponents, Edmond Muskie, Hubert Humphrey, John Lindsay, and George McGovern. The thrust of Chisholm's campaign was her moral character. The announcement was the culmination of years of encouragement from many people particularly college students. Dressed in a black and white patterned dress, waving and smiling at the audience and the cameras, the former nursery school teacher turned congress member, began her speech:

> I stand before you today as a candidate for the Democratic nomination for the Presidency of the United States of America. I am not the candidate of black America, although I am black and proud. I am not the candidate of the women's movement of this country, although I am a woman, and I am equally proud of that. I am not the candidate of any political bosses or fat cats or special interests. I stand here now without endorsements from any big name politicians or celebrities or any other kind of prop. I do not intend to offer to you the tired and glib clichés, which for too long have been an accepted part of our political life. I am the candidate of the people of America. And my presence before you now symbolizes a new era in American political history. I have always earnestly believed in the great potential of America. Our constitutional democracy will soon celebrate its 200th anniversary, effective testimony, to the longevity to our cherished constitution

and its unique bill of rights, which continues to give to the world an inspirational message of freedom and liberty.[22]

Shirley Chisholm's speech showed the political establishment that she was running for president of the United States not only because of who she was as a person but also, and more important, because her campaign messages connected to young and diverse voters.

In the book, *Paving the Way for Madam President*, Gutgold states that Chisholm was not demanding her right to get in, but rather she was asserting her right to be in. As the campaign took place in the midst of the women's and civil rights movements, many of the candidates attempted to woo women and black voters. Obviously, their efforts were hampered by Chisholm's appeal to these groups. Some of the candidates, including New City Mayor John Lindsay and George McGovern asked her to drop out of the race, because of the daunting effort required of a national campaign and because they thought she would steal away votes from their campaigns.[23]

The opening of the campaign was the New Hampshire Primary. Edmund Muskie was victorious. Although he won the primary, it was by a smaller margin than originally was anticipated. The next primary was really the major test for her presidency bid. Florida was the second primary, and it was the first state in which Chisholm actively campaigned, largely because it had a large population of African Americans and youth, and had a strong women's movement. Despite large and enthusiastic crowds that gathered for *Ms Chis* when she spoke, she received only 4 percent of the Florida vote.[24]

Chisholm continued her campaign wherever she could get on the ballot and had enough volunteers to set up speaking events. She campaigned in New York, New Jersey, California, Massachusetts, Minnesota, Michigan, and North Carolina. In some states, Chisholm was on the ballot but never had time to visit.

Civil rights for blacks, women, and the poor; reforms in the U.S. judicial system and in prisons; police brutality, gun control, and tolerance of political dissent; and new approaches to drug abuse prevention and treatment were issues that Chisholm consistently addressed during her campaign. After six months of campaigning in eleven primaries, she had twenty-eight delegates committed to vote for her at the Democratic Convention.[25]

The 1972 Democratic National Convention in July in Miami was the first major convention in which an African American woman was considered for the presidential nomination. Although she did not win the nomination, she received 151 of the delegates' votes. She stuck it out until the end, and she did go into the convention with delegates. She wanted to affect political change with the power of her delegates, and she did so. At two different events (women's caucus and black caucus) at the 1972 Democratic National Convention, Chisholm made the following comments:

> I am just so thankful that in spite of the differences in opinions, the differences of ideology, and even sometimes within the women's movement the differences of approaches, that here we are today at a glorious gathering of women in Miami.[26]
>
> My brothers and sisters let me tell it to you this afternoon like it really is. There's only one thing that you my brothers and sisters have going—the only thing you have going is your one vote. DON'T sell that vote out!! The black people of America are watching us. Find out what these candidates who need our votes to get across the top are going to do for us concretely.[27]

After her presidential campaign, Chisholm continued to serve in the U.S. House of Representatives until 1982. As a member of the black caucus, she saw representation grow in Congress and welcomed other black women as U.S. representatives. In 1984, she cofounded the National Political Congress of Black Women and worked vigorously for Rev. Jesse Jackson's presidential campaigns in 1984 and 1988.[28] Several years later, President Bill Clinton nominated her to be ambassador to Jamaica.

When a producer and director of a film about her life asked her how she would like to be remembered, Chisholm said,

> When I die, I want to be remembered as a woman who lived in the 20th century and who dared to be a catalyst of change. I don't want to be remembered as the first black woman who went to Congress. And I don't even want to be remembered as the first woman who happened to be black to make a bid for the presidency. I want to be remembered as a woman who fought for change in the 20th century. That's what I want.[29]

CONCLUSION

It was not too long ago when civil rights was a significant issue in which thousands of people of all walks of life were blatantly denied equal rights on just about everything. Although it may seem to many younger people that these blatant denials of rights happened so long ago, in fact it was only a few decades ago. Surprisingly, with the achievements of African Americans over the decades whether it was through politics, academics, employment, or the sporting world, our society still tends to paint a picture that the issues related to civil rights for African Americans are over now. Unfortunately, that is far from the truth.

For a vast majority of African Americans, including those who live at the upper echelon and earn higher incomes, civil rights remain a significant issue each and every day of their lives. Real life issues—such as the right to get an equitable mortgage to buy a home; the right to live in any area of a town, city, or suburban area that one wants; the right to get a quality public education from kindergarten through high school; the right to go to any of the most prestigious universities in America; the right to get tenure and promotion at mainstream higher education institutions; the right to get an affordable health insurance plan; the right to have a fair trial in our judicial system; the right to be considered as a head football coach in Division I football and professional football; and even the right to ask for reparations from a country that used the free labor and servitude of enslaved African Americans for more than 200 years—need to be reevaluated by the U.S. federal government.

The issues related to civil rights are tangible and real even in the 21st century. What is even more startling today is that these civil rights are no longer just an African American issue, they are an American issue. These are some of the very same issues that President Barack Obama campaigned about during his candidacy and now that he is president, these are the very same issues that many Americans want resolved. So *YES, WE CAN* debate the issues of civil rights today, and *YES, WE CAN* request that our new President Obama and his cabinet help resolve these civil rights issues, particularly as they relate to African Americans today. It is like the old wives' tale, "There is no better time than the present."

Chapter 3

The War on Poverty Revisited

INTRODUCTION

During the 1950s and 1960s American civil rights movement, thousands of local and national leaders, such as Dr. Rev. Martin Luther King, Jr., Rev. Jesse Jackson Jr., Julian Bond, John Lewis, Thurgood Marshall, Barbara Jordan, Shirley Chisholm, and even Johnnie Carr, spoke about a wide variety of inequities affecting African Americans and underserved and underrepresented populations in the United States. One of the inequities that was so devastating to families during this particular time and even more significant in the 21st century is the issue of poverty. As an African American child growing up during this era, I could not help but not become aware of the issue of the *haves* and the *have-nots*. In the early years of my life, up until the age of approximately six, my family and I definitely belonged to the have-nots.

Although both of my parents had steady government jobs and we lived in a small house in Springfield, Ohio, it still seemed like we belonged to the have-nots. As a kid, you knew you had to do without certain things—for example, you wore hand-me-down clothes from your older brothers instead of having new clothes, you rode in your parents' old Buick instead of a new car, you made up toys with the items laying around the house instead having the latest new toys, and you used the city dump as your playground instead of having a safe and secure playground in which to play.

As stated in chapter 2, playing in the city dump was normal, and it is what all kids in the neighborhood did. These are the things that, as a have-not, I realized we had to get use to as part of our day-by-day existence. As hard as our parents worked each and every day, and as many times we had the best of Christmases and Easters, I knew we were missing out on certain things—not major things but certain things that a lot of other people took for granted. It just did not seem fair, for reasons that I could not understand at the time, that we were relegated to have-not status.

My parents, however, never accepted this have-not status imposed on most blacks by mainstream society. Then within a year, we moved from the have-nots to being a part of the haves. The haves at this time were the struggling, black middle class.

As an adult, I look back on this time period and speculate on how my parents truly adapted to some tough socioeconomic conditions in which so many African American families got trapped and seemingly had no way out. It was not like they wanted to stay in this lower socioeconomic situation. It is more like society forced certain populations, such as African Americans, to believe that they had to accept this lower status, thereby losing the collective motivation and individual belief that one could improve their status in these United States.

Because of my childhood situation, in every city and state that I have lived since pursuing my doctoral degree in anthropology, I have conducted fieldwork in and paid more attention to those populations categorized as living in poverty. Yet, what are we really referring to when we categorize individuals or families living in poverty?

According to the federal government, the United States determines the official poverty thresholds that are issued each year by the Census Bureau. The thresholds represent the annual amount of cash income minimally required to support families of various sizes. The methodology for calculating the thresholds was established in the mid-1960s and has not changed in the intervening years. The thresholds are updated annually to account for inflation.[1] A family is counted as poor if its pretax money income is below its poverty threshold. Money income does not include noncash benefits such as public housing, Medicaid, employer-provided health insurance, and food stamps.

A sampling of the poverty thresholds for 2007 is included in Table 3.1. Reviewing this table shows that two parents with three children are considered to be living in poverty if they make $24,744 or less.[2] For 2009, the federal poverty level was $22,050 for a family of four. Children living in families with incomes below the federal poverty level are referred to as poor. But research suggests that, on average, families need an income of about twice the federal poverty level to meet their basic needs.[3]

During the past few years, and particularly in 2009, the nation failed to recognize the plight of the poor and impoverished in the United States. All attention is placed on the middle class and how to help the middle class out of this devastating economy. But what about the poor and the impoverished, particularly as it relates to African Americans?

To *not* forget all of the millions of individuals and families who are categorized as poor in our United States, following is a brief survey of the demographics of poor children who reside in the states in which

Table 3.1 2007 Poverty Thresholds, Selected Family Types

Single Individual	Under 65 years	$10,787
	65 years and older	$9,944
Single Parent	One child	$14,291
	Two children	$16,705
	No children	$13,884
Two Adults	One child	$16,689
	Two children	$21,027
	Three children	$24,744

Source: Carmen DeNavas-Walt, Bernadette D. Proctor, and Jessica C. Smith, "Income, Poverty, and Health Insurance Coverage in the United States: 2007," U.S. Census Bureau, Current Population Reports, P60-235 (Washington, DC: U.S. Government Printing Office, 2008).

I conducted my fieldwork and have lived since pursing my degree (see Table 3.2).

Not surprising, yet disappointing, the percentage of black children who are poor in these states is two to four times higher than the percentage of white children. These disparity rates show that Latino children are more likely to be poor than white children. What is even more disturbing about this disparity rate among poor black and Latino children in comparison to white children is that their poverty is even worse in the major U.S. cities than in other countries.

A 1987 *New York Times* article entitled "Black Poverty Spreads in 50 Biggest U.S. Cities" brought attention to the severity of black poverty and poor children. In this article, reporter John Herbers visited Toledo, Ohio, interviewed a hard-working African American, and compared his plight with those of other African Americans nationally. Herbers wrote

> When the Rev. H. V. Savage established his Kitchen for the Poor in 1969, he envisioned the free food center in the heart of Toledo's black district as a temporary measure until economic gains took root from civil rights laws and Government antipoverty programs. Almost two decades later, Mr. Savage, surrounded the other day by mounds of unpeeled potatoes, volunteer workers and street people waiting for a noon meal, acknowledged that many Toledo blacks had indeed moved up the economic ladder and out of poor neighborhoods. But he said that black poverty had nevertheless spread, both in numbers and in the area in which it is concentrated. Mr. Savage said, "It is worse, not better," an opinion echoed by many white and black leaders and substantiated by census figures in this industrial city, which, like many others, is struggling to adjust to a service economy.[4]

As Herbers excellently illustrated in his article, Mr. Savage's observation and comments about blacks in Toledo was typical of other black

Table 3.2   Fieldwork Sites—States: Demographics of Poor Children

States	Poor Children
Michigan	All—17 percent (418,943) White—11 percent (184,699) Latino—32 percent (45,258) Black—40 percent (170,343)
Texas	All—23 percent (1,495,683) White—8 percent (197,233) Latino—32 percent (987,216) Black—34 percent (274,022)
Indiana	All—17 percent (272,779) White—12 percent (143,417) Latino—30 percent (37,765) Black—47 percent (84,517)
Georgia	All—21 percent (500,758) White—11 percent (133,166) Latino—30 percent (72,635) Black—35 percent (278,342)
Arkansas	All—21 percent (147,239) White—15 percent (69,659) Latino—31 percent (16,764) Black—43 percent (58,528)
Maryland	All—12 percent (163,307) White—7 percent (47,192) Black—20 percent (90,748)
California	All—18 percent (1,712,807) White—8 percent (246,854) Latino—26 percent (1,145,552) Asian—12 percent (110,186) Black—28 percent (184,846)
North Carolina	All—20 percent (437,182) White—10 percent (127,591) Latino—34 percent (70,561) Black—37 percent (205,654)

Source: Author's compilation.

populations in the United States. Not surprising, the poverty rate data from the U.S. Census Bureau in 1980 are similar to the demographics associated with poor children highlighted in Table 3.2. So why is it that we are still startled when we hear about the continual higher poverty rate among blacks in the 21st century, even while it continues to be a lower priority for the federal government? In fact, in 2006, although the overall poverty rate declined to 12.3 percent, blacks continued to have the highest poverty rate at 24.3 percent. Blacks also have the highest rate of people living in severe poverty (less than half the current poverty threshold): 10.9 percent of blacks were in severe poverty, compared with 7.7 percent of Latinos, 5.1 percent of Asians, and 3.5 percent of non-Hispanic whites.[5]

As for the poverty rate for children, blacks continue to have the highest percentage of children in poverty of any group (33.4 percent). This is more than three times the rate for non-Hispanic whites (10 percent). A similar difference is also seen when we look at the elderly. Those who are sixty-five years and older continue to have the lowest overall poverty rate at 9.4 percent, yet this rate is also higher for blacks (22.7 percent) than for any other group.[6]

Finally, in 2006, median household income increased for all groups except non-Hispanic whites. For blacks, however, the 2006 median household income was 8 percent lower than in 2000. In 2006, Asians had the biggest annual increase in median income (+1.8 percent), followed by Latinos (+1.7 percent), blacks (+0.3 percent), and then non-Hispanic whites (−0.05 percent). When looking specifically at different income groups, blacks continue to have far higher percentages of people living at the lowest incomes (less than $15,000 a year) than non-Hispanic whites or the nation as a whole, and far fewer blacks are in the top income range of more than $100,000.

When all is said and done about poverty in America today, blacks consistently (on average) have lower incomes, more children living in poverty, and three times the amount of poverty than whites. Census numbers do not lie: a marked and continual disparity persists in poverty rates between blacks and whites, and it appears that no national initiatives will address this basic civil rights issue.

Because a major federal agency does not appear to be taking the lead to combat poverty in America, our best strategy is to reexamine a past federal initiative for the purpose of developing some solutions for the have-nots and all those who are living in poverty in the 21st century. The federal initiative that directly addressed poverty was called the War on Poverty.

THE BEGINNING OF THE WAR ON POVERTY

In the late 1950s, the poverty rate for all Americans was 22.4 percent, or 39.5 million individuals. These numbers declined steadily throughout the 1960s, reaching a low of 11.1 percent, or 22.9 million individuals, in 1973. Over the next decade, the poverty rate fluctuated between 11.1 percent and 12.6 percent, but it began to rise steadily again in 1980. By 1983, the number of poor individuals had risen to 35.3 million individuals, or 15.2 percent.[7]

The poverty rate for African Americans, however, is quite different in comparison to poverty rates for all Americans. Blacks consistently have represented a disproportionately higher percentage of the nation's poor over the past four decades. Beginning at approximately 26 percent, the poverty rate for blacks actually increased from the 1950s to 1970s. In both 1959 and 1974, the poverty rate for blacks was about three times that for whites.[8]

A real problem reflecting the economic crisis facing African Americans is found in the large numbers of long-term, persistently poor, and immobile blacks that remain from one generation to the next (which we refer to as generational poverty). Although reports note a decrease in black unemployment during 1959–1969, improving on a condition in which better than one out of every two blacks (55 percent in 1959) was poor, in 1969, one of every three blacks still remained poor. In addition, the proportion of blacks remaining in poverty showed little or no change between 1969 and 1974.[9]

Unfortunately, the particular segment of the black population that remains in poverty year after year, generation after generation is now classified as the "black underclass." The term "underclass" has slowly eased its way back into the nation's vocabulary, subtly conveying the message that another problematic group is emerging that needs society's help. Although still somewhat unclearly defined—and thought by some not to be deserving of serious attention—a permanently entrapped population of poor persons, unused and unwanted, accumulated in various urban areas of the United States during the 1950s and 1960s. Although the underclass included individuals of all ethnic and racial backgrounds, a higher percentage of the underclass located specifically in urban inner cities was black. Thus, the black underclass that included a significant number of African Americans trapped and isolated in their poverty status finally was recognized by mainstream America and the federal government. In fact, a war against poverty was launched with the view that, in but a few years, the condition would be eradicated.

The War on Poverty is the name for legislation first introduced by President Lyndon B. Johnson during his State of the Union address on January 8, 1964. This legislation was proposed by Johnson in response to the difficult economic conditions associated with a national poverty rate of around 19 percent. The War on Poverty speech led the U.S. Congress to pass the Economic Opportunity Act of 1964, a law that established the Office of Economic Opportunity (OEO) to administer the local application of federal funds targeted against poverty.[10]

Congress Member Adam Clayton Powell, Jr.

One of the most fascinating aspects of the Economic Opportunity Act of 1964 was the hearings before the subcommittee on the War on

Poverty Program of the Committee on Education and Labor. The committee, which debated the need for this new bill—H.R. 10440, was presided over by the Hon. Adam Clayton Powell, Jr.

Before becoming chair of one of the most powerful and influential House of Representatives subcommittees, Adam Clayton Powell, Jr., became the first African American elected to Congress from New York, a position he held between 1945 and 1971. As one of only two black congress members, Powell challenged and boycotted many discriminatory practices.

For example, in Harlem, Powell organized mass meetings, rent strikes, and public campaigns, forcing companies, utilities, and Harlem Hospital to hire black workers. He organized a picket line during the 1939 New York World's Fair at the executive offices in the Empire State Building, which resulted in the increased hiring of black employees from about 200 to 732.[11] Thus, as his career illustrates, Powell became an ideal chair to preside over the bill that was designed to mobilize the human and financial resources of the U.S. government to combat poverty in the United States.

The testimony from Powell helps one grasp the significance of bill H.R. 10440—the Economic Opportunity Act of 1964. Here is his verbatim testimony given on Tuesday, March 17, 1964, before the Subcommittee on the War on Poverty Program:

Today marks a historic day in the life of our American society. At last we are coming to grips with one of the most important and crucial issues of our time. Today we are recognizing that all American citizens must have equal access to freedom, justice, and the right to work and make a living. Today we are concerning ourselves about one-fifth of our Nation's population who have been left out of the flowing stream of prosperity. Today we are admitting that America cannot be the great Nation which it is possible of becoming unless we provide for all of its citizens. In our actions at this point, we are rededicating ourselves to the proposition that all men are created equal and reaffirming our belief in the Declaration of Independence and the inalienable rights which it guarantees.

It is really paradoxical that millions of Americans now live in poverty and deprivation in the midst of a general prosperity enjoyed by the majority of citizens in a nation that is considered the richest and most fortunate Nation in the history of the world. It seems incredible that of the 47 million families in the United States in 1962, some 9.3 million or one-fifth of these families— containing more than 30 million persons—had total money incomes below $3,000. Even though mass poverty as it once existed in this country, and still exists in many parts of the world, has been eliminated in the United States due to the combination of steadily rising productivity, higher levels of educational attainment and other welfare and insurance practices, there still remains the hard core of poverty among Americans.[12]

This opening statement by Powell was significant because he wanted the nation to know that despite the increased prosperity, opportunities, and yearly income for more people, millions of Americans still were trapped in severe poverty. It was apparent to him that it was time for Congress to step up and support President Johnson's War of Poverty initiatives.

Powell further stated:

A closer examination of the statistics regarding poverty shows the scars of discrimination, lack of education, and broken homes. Of the poor, 22 percent are nonwhite and nearly one-half of all nonwhites live in poverty. The heads of over 60 percent of all poor families have only a grade school education. Of the poor, 54 percent live in cities; 16 percent on farms, and 30 percent are rural, nonfarm residents. Over 40 percent of all farm families would be considered poor according to American standards of living.[13]

In this part of the testimony, Powell eloquently provides the specific data on those who are in poverty and those who are affected. Here he highlights the very high percentage of nonwhites who live in poverty, where they live and how it affects their education attainment.

Finally, Chairman Powell made the final key statements regarding Bill H.R. 10440:

Any war on poverty must include opportunities to build individual earning power, increase the level of educational accomplishment, provide improved health conditions, extend community programs to embrace all areas of the population and provide equal opportunity in all facets of American life.

The bill that we have before us today, H.R. 10440, the Economic Opportunity Act of 1964, would provide an opportunity:

1. To give almost half a million underprivileged young Americans the opportunity to develop skills, continue education, and find useful work.
2. To provide an opportunity for American communities to develop comprehensive programs designed specifically for the peculiar problems of poverty which they face.
3. To give rural communities an opportunity to raise the economic standards within their geographical confines.

4. To provide an opportunity for employment for larger numbers needing work.

5. To give dedicated Americans the opportunity to enlist as volunteers in the war against poverty.

6. To help families become united through occupational opportunities.

This antipoverty program which we prefer to call by its more positive name—the Economic Opportunity Act—is designed to lift people out of conditions of poverty and raise their educational, health, and skill levels to increase their opportunities. The war against poverty, while a national effort, will be carried out through community action. This will call not only for coordination and cooperation among the departments and agencies of the Federal Government, but also participation of State agencies and full participation by the private sector of the community. **Poverty can and must be eliminated.**[14]

This powerful, opening statement by Powell not only solidified its support among the House of Representatives but also connected all Americans regardless of socioeconomic, educational, political, and racial background to the importance of this bill to each and every underprivileged person in the United States. If anyone was just right for the moment, it was Chairman Adam Clayton Powell, Jr.

After days of testimony from experts, leaders and average citizens from all parts of the United States, Bill H.R. 10440 passed. The result of Bill H.R. 10440 was the creation of the OEO.

The OEO was the agency responsible for administering most of the War on Poverty programs created during the Johnson's Administration, including VISTA, Job Corps, Head Start, Legal Services, and the Community Action Program. Although the OEO received much criticism from both political parties, Democrats and Republicans alike, it still launched one of the most successful programs during its time—Project Head Start.

Initially launched as an eight-week summer project in 1965, Project Head Start was designed to help end poverty by providing preschool children from low-income families with a program that would meet emotional, social, health, nutritional, and psychological needs. The following year, it was authorized by Congress as a fully funded year-round program.

Today, Head Start is the longest-running program to address systemic poverty in the United States. It is a program of the U.S. Department of Health and Human Services within the Administration for Children and Families (ACF) that provides comprehensive education, health, nutrition, and parent involvement services to low-income children (ages three to five) and their families.

The major programs of Head Start include the following:

- **Early Head Start**—Promotes healthy prenatal outcomes, promotes healthy family functioning, and strengthens the development of infants and toddlers beginning as young as newborn infants.

- **Head Start**—Helps to create healthy development in low-income children ages three to five. Programs offer a wide variety of services, which depend on a child's and each family's heritage and experience, to influence all aspects of a child's development and learning.

- **Migrant and Seasonal Program Branch**—Provides the children of migrant and seasonal farm workers who meet income and other eligibility guidelines with Head Start services.

- **American Indian-Alaska Native Program Branch**—Provides Native American and Alaskan Native children and families with services such as health care, education, nutrition, socialization, and other services promoting school readiness. Services are primarily for disadvantaged preschool children, and infants and toddlers.[15]

As of late 2005, more than 22 million preschool-age children have participated in Head Start. The more than $6.8 billion dollar budget for 2005 provided services to more than 905,000 children, 57 percent of whom were four years old or older, and 43 percent three years old or younger. Services were provided by 1,604 different programs operating more than 48,000 classrooms scattered across every state (and nearly every county) at an average cost of $7,222 per child.[16]

In 2007, Head Start's enrollment was approximately 908,412 children with a budget of $6.88 billion. Interestingly, the racial and ethnic composition has changed dramatically from its early beginnings. Table 3.3 shows the racial and ethnic composition.

Although the OEO and the War on Poverty was dismantled under President Nixon's administration during the early 1970s, at least one of its major programs—Head Start—continues to fulfill the legislation, policy, and mission of the War on Poverty started by President Johnson and enacted by Chairman Powell through the Bill H.R. 10440—the Economic Opportunity Act of 1964.

THE 21ST-CENTURY WAR ON POVERTY

It has been more than forty-five years since the War on Poverty initiative. Although many critics felt that this federal government's initiative had no chance to succeed, the fact that several of its programs,

Table 3.3 Head Start's Racial and Ethnic Composition: 2007

Race/Ethnicity	Percentage
Native American/Alaska Native	4.0 percent
Black/African American	30.1 percent
White	39.1 percent
Asian	1.7 percent
Hawaiian/Pacific Islander	.8 percent
Biracial/Multiracial	4.9 percent
Unspecified/Other	18.8 percent
Hispanic/Latino	34.7 percent

Source: Administration for Children and Families, Head Start Program Fact Sheet, http://www.acf.hhs.gov/programs/ohs/about/fy2008.html (accessed October 3, 2009).

such as Head Start, improved and changed the lives of thousands of children and families for the better should be enough evidence in itself. This is evidence that a federally initiated program with the support of the president (that is, Lyndon B. Johnson) and Congress worked then and is still working in the early 21st century.

The Obama Administration

Do any major new federal initiatives specifically target those who are impoverished in America? Moreover, does the new Obama administration have a plan to fight poverty? These are fair questions, particularly as the country as a whole is going through some tough economic times.

According to the White House Web site on February 13, 2009, President Obama has been a lifelong advocate for the poor. It specifically states

As a young college graduate, he rejected the high salaries of corporate America and moved to the South Side of Chicago to work as a community organizer. As an organizer, Obama worked with churches, Chicago residents, and local government to set up job training programs for the unemployed and after-school programs for kids. As president, he will use his life experiences to fight poverty and improve opportunities for poor families all across America's high- poverty areas, an approach that facilitates the economic integration of families and communities with efforts to support the current low-income residents of those areas.[17]

President Obama's administration will address poverty in five major areas.

They are as follows:

1. Expanding access to jobs
2. Making work pay for all Americans

Table 3.4 Obama Administration Poverty Initiatives

Expand Access to Jobs	• Help Americans Grab a Hold of and Climb the Job Ladder • Create a Green Jobs Corps • Improve Transportation Access to Jobs • Reduce Crime Recidivism by Providing Ex-Offender Supports
Make Work Pay for All Americans	• Expand the Earned Income Tax Credit • Raise the Minimum Wage to $9.50 an Hour by 2011 • Provide Tax Relief
Strengthen Families	• Promote Responsible Fatherhood • Support Parents with Young Children • Expand Paid Sick Days
Increase the Supply of Affordable Housing	• Supports Affordable Housing Trust Fund • Fully Fund the Community Development Block Grant
Tackle Concentrated Poverty	• Establish 20 Promise Neighborhoods • Ensure Community Based Investment Resources in Every Urban Community • Invest in Rural Areas

Source: White House Web site, "Poverty," www.whitehouse.gov/agenda/poverty (accessed October 3, 2009).

3. Strengthening families
4. Increasing supply of affordable housing
5. Tackling concentrated poverty

But what exactly are these specific strategies to each of these poverty-focused Obama administration initiatives? Table 3.4 highlights the specific initiatives. In addition to these initiatives, President Obama's 2009 Stimulus Plan provided specific funding to aid the poor in the form of $40 billion to provide extended unemployment benefits through December 31, 2009, and $20 billion to increase food stamp benefits by 14 percent, and provided an additional $3 billion in temporary welfare payments along with $2 billion for Head Start.

The next question is will these Obama administration initiatives designed specifically to address poverty be enough and make a difference on America's ongoing War on Poverty? These poverty-focused initiatives simply do not go far enough in addressing the massive problem of poverty in America because poverty, particularly in today's economic troubled times, affects many more American citizens than ever before, and the ethnic composition of those who are categorized as poor and impoverished is diverse.

Perhaps one of the most puzzling aspects regarding how the new Obama administration will address poverty in America is the fact that the word "poverty" and those who are "in poverty" have not been mentioned by any of the political candidates during the election and since the president's election. It is like poverty in America no longer exists, and therefore, those who are living in poverty or are considered poor do not exist either.

For example, in a 2008 Huffington Post report, Sam Stein explains that as the country was coping with a massive financial crisis, the presidential campaign witnessed the second of its three debates. With the nation's economic woes firmly on their minds, John McCain and Barack Obama engaged on topics from job creation, tax relief, and the utility of the market bailout. The word poverty was not mentioned once.

Stein specifically stated in his report the following:

> Indeed, as economic observers fret that the ripple effects of the market meltdown could result in greater numbers of underemployed and unemployed, the focus of the campaign remains firmly on businesses and the middle class. During the first debate, when the financial crisis was first coming into focus, "poverty" went similarly unmentioned. It is in many ways, regrettable. Not simply because the number of those living in poverty—37.3 million in 2007 demands more attention. But because those who have studied poverty-eradication programs say that Barack Obama has a plan that could be historic in its reach and innovation.[18]

So why is it that U.S. politicians, whether during the recent national presidential campaign and even now during the Obama administration, fail to mention the word "poverty" and to directly legislate initiatives to fight this new War on Poverty? For some reason, U.S. political leaders are avoiding this serious American and, dare I say, African American issue.

One major politician has championed the continual War on Poverty. That national politician is Rep. Barbara Lee of California.

Rep. Barbara Lee

As a U.S. House of Representative of the Ninth District (Oakland, Berkeley, Emeryville, Fairview, Cherryland, Ashland, and Castro Valley) in California and now chair of the Congressional Black Caucus (CBC), Rep. Barbara Lee has always been a consistent voice and leader for civil rights issues for all people, particularly for African Americans. Born in El Paso, Texas, Lee came to California in 1960 with her military family parents and attended high school at San Fernando High School in San Fernando, California.

While attending Mills College in California, a nationally renowned liberal arts women's college founded in 1852, Lee was in the audience of a speech that Shirley Chisholm gave in 1972. At the time, Lee, who was president of the Black Student Union, was a mother of two children and was receiving financial assistance. When she heard Chisholm's words of inspiration, Lee was swept away by the charismatic role model speaking in front of her, and she wanted to get involved in Chisholm's presidential campaign. After Lee approached Chisholm and told her of her interest in volunteering on her presidential campaign, Chisholm told her that the first thing she could do was register to vote. Lee took her advice and eventually became the Northern California Chair of the Chisholm Campaign.[19] Lee's political career was actually inspired by one of her mentors—presidential candidate Shirley Chisholm.

Her other mentors included U.S. Rep. Ron Dellums and Bobby Seals of the Black Panther Party. With the Black Panther Party, Lee was primarily a community worker and organizer. With Ron Dellums, she became his administrative assistant and ran his campaign on several different occasions.[20]

Lee's willingness to stand on principle earned her international acclaim when she was the only member of Congress to vote against giving President Bush a blank check to wage war after the September 11 attacks. In addition to being one of Congress's most vocal opponents to the war in Iraq, Lee has been a leader in promoting policies that foster international peace, security, and human rights. In 2006, she successfully blocked funds from being used to establish permanent military bases in Iraq. She sponsored legislation disavowing the doctrine of preemptive war and has been a leader in the bipartisan effort in Congress to end the ongoing genocide in Darfur, Sudan, including the passage of legislation she authorized to allow divestment from companies doing business in Sudan.[21]

As co-chair of the Out of Poverty Caucus in 2008, Lee was committed to eradicating poverty, fostering opportunity, and protecting the most vulnerable in society. In January 2008, Lee introduced House Concurrent Resolution 198 to get her colleagues on record saying that the United States should set a national goal of cutting poverty in half over the next ten years. The resolution stated that "policy initiatives addressing poverty have not kept pace with the needs of millions of Americans," and "[t]he United States have a moral responsibility to meet the needs of those persons, groups, and communities that are impoverished, disadvantaged or otherwise in poverty."[22] The resolution passed, affirming the goal of cutting the poverty rate in half in ten years.

Lee specifically stated the following during the 2008 presidential primaries:

Of course, I'm an Obama person. Every chance I get I'm pushing (his campaign) to talk about poverty in a direct way. And I assume the Clinton people are talking to their candidate about this . . . We've always talked about the middle class—which is fine, we want to make sure the middle class stays strong. But we never seem to fix our mouths to talk about the poor and low-income individuals. And, of course, when you talk about poor people there may be some negative connotations about that. You know, maybe there's a messaging issue. But when people are poor, they're poor. When they don't have any money, they don't have any money.[23]

Without doubt, other national politicians are championing the cause for the poor, but congress member and chair Barbara Lee has not only consistently fought and lead legislation for the poor and underprivileged in state and federal government systems but also understands on a community, cultural, and personal level how individuals, particularly African Americans, have to adapt their lifestyle when they are poor and underserved.

War on Poverty Florida, Inc.

Interestingly, because no "official" federal government agency is leading a War on Poverty initiative, individual states have established their own program. The state of Florida is one of the strongest examples.

The War on Poverty Florida, Inc. (WPF) is a nonprofit organization started in March 2007, which embarked on a journey to lay the groundwork for revitalization of minority communities throughout the state of Florida. Utilizing a collaborative approach, the WPF is dedicated to reducing poverty and racial inequality, increasing opportunities for asset accumulation for minority families, and ensuring that their voices are heard in major policy debates.[24]

Led by Executive Director Karen Landry, the WPF develops local boards and partnerships to assist in the creation of a comprehensive approach to fighting poverty in their communities through economic development, workforce development, and housing and financial literacy. The community is empowered to transform spectators to players and to become active participants and stakeholders in the design and development of the future of their community and the neighborhoods where they live, work, and raise and educate their children.

Because of the poor condition of the United States and state economies in 2009, the WPF partnered with several local community-based organizations to host clinics specifically on foreclosure prevention. These clinics were designed to provide struggling homeowners with financial education opportunities, foreclosure prevention specialists, and access to local lenders.

Additionally, the WPF partnered with the Miami Job Corp to assist local small businesses in their early development. The success of this partnership is expressed in the following statement from Zuba's Bakery—a small business in Miami:

> We are thoroughly enjoying our experience with the program as well as the activities we participate in. We are very fortunate to have War on Poverty helping us with workshops, activities, field trips and creating our small business, Zuba's. The experience and the knowledge we gain is invaluable. Thank you War on Poverty.[25]

New York City Center for Economic Opportunity

The New York City Center for Economic Opportunity (NYC CEO) is one of the most innovative, city-based programs that specifically targets poverty-related issues in their area. The NYC CEO was established by Mayor Michael Bloomberg on December 18, 2006, to implement ways to reduce poverty in New York City. The CEO works with NYC agencies to design and implement evidence-based initiatives aimed at poverty reduction and manages an Innovation Fund through which it provides NYC agencies annual funding to implement such initiatives. The CEO oversees a rigorous evaluation of each program to determine which are successful in demonstrating results toward reducing poverty and increasing self-sufficiency among New Yorkers.[26]

The NYC CEO is led by Executive Director Veronica White and reports directly to Deputy Mayor Linda Gibbs. Along with its partner agencies, the center will continue to put into action the recommendations that the CEO has made.

Interestingly, the CEO published a 2006 report on the state of poverty in the city. The report stated that, in spite of great economic growth and expansion in NYC, one in five New Yorkers and one-third of New York's children continue to live in poverty. The following highlights a few of the major issues in the report:

- **Poverty is pervasive**—More than 1.5 million people live below the poverty line. This represents 19.1 percent of NYC residents.
- **Poverty disproportionately affects children**—More than 185,000 children five years old or younger are being raised in a family living below the federal poverty line.
- **Poverty is tied to the condition of our families**—The poverty rate for single female-headed households is 41 percent as compared with 11 percent for married couples with children.
- **A disproportionate share of New York's immigrant workers earn low wages**—In 2000, 19 percent of native-born workers earned

less than $10 an hour. On the other hand, almost 35 percent of foreign-born workers earned an hourly wage under $10.

- **Our nation's legacy of racial discrimination endures**—The poverty rate for African Americans and Hispanics is higher than the city average—21.4 percent for African Americans and 28.6 percent Hispanics.
- **Poverty is clearly related to education**—Almost one-third of those who lack a high school or General Educational Development (GED) diploma live below the federal poverty line.
- **Many of the poor are employed**—In more than 46 percent of households living below the poverty level, the head of household is working.
- **Poverty is concentrated geographically**—In New York City, 248 census tracts are classified as in "extreme poverty" in which more than 40 percent of the population lives below the poverty line.
- **A significant number of New Yorkers live on the borderline of poverty**—While just over 19 percent of New Yorkers live below the federal poverty line, another 19 percent are considered low-income because their earnings are between 100 and 199 percent of the poverty line.[27]

Following are a few of the Commission for Economic Opportunity's recommendations to address poverty in New York City:

- Recommend an approach that concentrates efforts first on communities of highest need.
- Encourage managers to adopt an approach that strongly values civic engagement at the community level.
- Adopt program initiatives at the community level and build on and support community networks and resources.
- Tailor each recommendation to appropriate scale with the goal of maximizing effectiveness.
- Leverage existing services, motivate maximum participation, and convince the greatest number of poor New Yorkers to join in this new approach.[28]

Interestingly, one of the latest antipoverty programs from the NYC CEO and Mayor Bloomberg, which has received a lot of national attention, is the Cash-for-Good-Behavior program. Funded by $53 million in private donations, including from billionaire Mayor Bloomberg, this Cash-for-Good-Behavior program pays parents and children for saving money. New York wants poor people to save money, so it is offering a big incentive to encourage them to do so—a 50 percent match of up to $250 if families put money from their federal earned-income tax credit into a savings account and keep it there for one year.

New York's savings plan is the newest way the city is trying to reduce poverty by offering poor residents cash for good behavior. Improving the health, education, and job qualifications of poor families, as well as their savings rate, will help "break cycles of poverty." So says Deputy Major Linda Gibbs, who oversees the program.[29] Time will tell whether it works, but without doubt, the NYC CEO and Mayor Michael Bloomberg are fighting their War on Poverty using a wide variety of innovative government and private partnership strategies.

CONCLUSION

In 21st-century America, it seems the nation has forgotten about the poor and those who are living in poverty. The poor are the ones who are least represented, lobbied for, and blatantly ignored when it comes to state and national political campaigns. It appears as if this growing number of individuals, children, mothers, fathers, and families of all racial and ethnic backgrounds do not exist. How can this happen in this great nation?

A majority of Americans really do care for their neighbors and, yes, U.S. citizens are known to help each other in times of need. Examples of the American Spirit continue to amaze, particularly when tragic events occur, such as the terrorist attacks of September 11, 2001, and the aftermath of Hurricane Katrina.

So why is it that we can come together to help each other during tragic events, but somehow cannot come together to help those who are in need on a year-round basis, like the poor? At one time in the United States, the poor were predominately African Americans; however, now the poor include every racial and ethnic group, whether a new immigrant to the country or a native-born American.

As I sat in front of the television set like millions of other Americans to hear President Obama give his economic agenda speech on February 24, 2009, it felt good to see an African American man lead our nation for a change. I also felt somewhat disappointed, however, primarily because in his speech on the economy President Obama did not mention one word about communities of color in economic need, the poor, or the impoverished here in America. It was not that he had to mention the words, it was the simple fact that when the country is going through such tough economic disparity, the poor, the impoverished, and communities of color like African Americans are the first to be affected. There is no other way to get around it, yet once again, U.S. leaders avoid the issue. One day soon, we *all* will have to come together to revisit and fight the War on Poverty.

Chapter 4

Reforming the U.S. Education System

INTRODUCTION

As I look back at my years in primary and secondary schools during the 1960s and 1970s in Springfield, Xenia, and Wyoming, Ohio, I honestly can say that I was a kid who definitely loved going to school. Whether it was starting kindergarten and first grade in Springfield, or going to elementary school in Xenia for three years, or moving sixty miles away for a year to attend fifth grade in Wyoming (outside of Cincinnati), or returning to Xenia's public school system to complete the rest of my primary and secondary education, I loved practically every aspect of my school experience. Granted, some days, weeks, and even one year I struggled to maintain above-average grades and I desired to be more popular among my classmates, but no doubt, I felt comfortable just being in school.

For me, school was a place that I could learn about the world, be rewarded for just giving the effort to learn, and I could become somebody. I did not know what I was going to become in these early years, but I knew that this was the place that was going to make me become that somebody in this world.

What is even more fascinating about my experience in grade school, middle school, and high school is the fact that I, along with other African Americans students, were bused every day from our black middle-class neighborhoods to attend the predominately white schools. Therefore, we always were the minority in numbers at each primary and secondary school.

That said, I still felt comfortable being in school. My classmates and friends were white and black children. Although I was aware that I was usually the only African American or part of a small group of African Americans in my classes, I did not allow it to affect my love for school. Even during the tumultuous times of local race relations between black and white students during the early 1970s in Xenia, I somehow maintained my love for school.

Fortunately for me in junior high school, I was somewhat insulated from much of the racial tension and confrontations that occurred in the Xenia school system at that time. My brother Dwight, who was four years older, was not.

When I was in seventh and eighth grades (1971 and 1972), Dwight was in eleventh and twelfth grade. As a junior and senior high school student and starting wide receiver on Xenia's varsity football team, Dwight became involved in a number racial confrontations, fights, and boycotts. In fact, the black football players on the team boycotted the homecoming king and queen halftime event, simply because no African American young women or young men presided on the king and queen courts. Apparently, my brother's African American classmates and football players had enough of the blatant discriminatory practices and demonstrated their right by boycotting the event. Finally, the school administrators recognized how important this right was to African American Xenia high school students and football players, thereby changed this practice.

Whether my experience was similar to or different from other African Americans during this time period, it was no less an African American experience—one that was molded, guided, and inspired by my mom and dad on a daily basis. My parents, just like so many other African American parents, stressed the *family value* of an education and wanted all their children to receive their education.

In the years to follow my primary and secondary years of schooling, I was fortunate to attend college (Central State University and Miami University, Ohio), earn my bachelor's and master's degrees, and follow up these degrees up with a doctorate in anthropology (Wayne State University, Detroit, Michigan), and a master's of public health (Emory University, Atlanta, Georgia). I was then employed as a college professor at various universities, including the University of Houston, Indiana University at Indianapolis, the University of Arkansas Medical Sciences, Charles R. Drew University, and East Carolina University, for more than twenty years in higher education institutions. One would think that by 2008, our nation would have experienced increased numbers of African Americans and persons of color in higher educational institutions. Yet this escalating trend has not happened.

Unfortunately, the generational gains in postsecondary education appear to have stalled and, for far too many people of color, the percentage of young adults with some type of postsecondary degree compared with older adults has actually fallen.[1] For example, in 2006, among Hispanics, 18 percent had at least an associate degree, but just

16 percent of young Hispanics had reached that same education threshold. Among Native Americans, 21 percent of older adults had at least an associate's degree compared with 18 percent of young adults.

The postsecondary education attainment rates of African Americans remained relatively the same for both age-groups, at approximately 24 percent. Asian Americans and whites were the only two groups for which young adults were more educated than prior generations. Sixty-six percent of young Asian Americans had at least an associate's degree compared with 54 percent of older Asian Americans. The percentages of whites were 41 percent for young adults and 37 percent for older adults.[2]

How could this disturbing trend have happened? From 1994 to 2004, overall higher education enrollment increased by 3 million students (or 21 percent) to reach 17.3 million students. According to the American Council on Education (ACE), the tremendous growth of students with unknown race or ethnicity and a sizeable increase in minority enrollment accounted for 50 percent, whereas whites experienced only a modest increase of 6 percent (or nearly 600,000 students) during the decade. Minority students made dramatic gains, increasing by more than 1.6 million students (or 49 percent), and students with unknown race or ethnicity increased by nearly 700,000 (or 144 percent).

Despite making substantial increases in enrollment, African Americans and Hispanics continue to trail whites in the percentage of eighteen- to twenty-four-year-old high school graduates enrolled in college, commonly referred to as the college participation rate. Between 1993–1995 and 2003–2005, the white college participation rate increased from 43 percent to 48 percent. During the same period, college participation rates for African Americans increased from 35 percent to 41 percent. Despite having a greater increase in college participation rates than whites, African Americans still trail whites in the percentage of college-age students who enroll in college. In 2006, 61 percent of Asian Americans ages eighteen to twenty-four were enrolled in college, compared with 44 percent of whites, 32 percent of African Americans, and 25 percent of Hispanics and Native Americans, respectively.[3]

Additionally, the Hispanic college participation rate showed little improvement between 1993–1995 and 2003–2005. This is primarily a result of the growth in the number of Hispanics ages eighteen to twenty-four who were enrolled in higher education not increasing as fast as the growth of the general Hispanic population.[4]

As for completing college and degrees conferred, minorities outpaced whites in the percentage change in total degrees awarded at all levels over the past decade. Minority women showed stronger gains than minority men at all degree levels. Following are some additional trends in degrees conferred:

- The number of minorities earning associate degrees between 1995 and 2005 grew 84 percent to just over 201,000. The number of minorities earning bachelor's degrees over the same period grew 65 percent to 355,000.
- Hispanics nearly doubled the number of bachelor's degrees received over the last decade to more than 105,000. Hispanics also made dramatic gains in doctoral degrees earned, rising form 950 in 1995 to more than 1,700 in 2005, an increase of 83 percent.
- During the last decade, the number of Asian American men receiving doctoral degrees dropped by 10 percent, whereas the number of Asian American women receiving these degrees increased by 74 percent.
- African Americans more than doubled the number of master's degrees earned from nearly 25,000 in 1995 to nearly 53,000 in 2005. During the same period, the number of doctoral degrees earned by African Americans increased 84 percent from nearly 1,600 to nearly 2,900.[5]

With regard to the increased numbers of African Americans in graduate school, a new report by the Council of Graduate Schools found that African Americans continue to make good progress in enrollments in master's and doctoral degree programs. Specifically, the data show that, in 2007, 170,167 African Americans were enrolled in graduate education in the United States. They made up 13 percent of all graduate students. Therefore, in terms of enrollments in graduate programs, black Americans have reached parity in comparison to the black percentage of the U.S. population.[6]

In looking at the number of minorities employed in higher education, a major disparity persists in the areas of college faculty, administrators, and presidents among minorities and whites. Although minorities have made gains as college faculty, administrators, and presidents over the last decade, whites still fill the overwhelming majority of these positions. For example, in 2005, minorities represented 17 percent of all college administrators; 16 percent of full-time faculty, and 13 percent of college presidents.[7]

In regards to black faculty in higher education, nationwide just over 5 percent of all full-time faculty members at colleges and universities in the United States are black. This percentage has increased only slightly over the last decade. But the percentage of black faculty at almost all the nation's high-ranking universities is significantly below the national average of 5.2 percent. The two universities that ranked the highest in percentage of black faculty were Emory University in Atlanta at 6.8 percent and Mount Holyoke College in Massachusetts at 9.7 percent.[8]

Now that I have been a professor in academia for the past twenty years, I can say with certainty that institution always have had a problem with finding and retaining black faculty at each university that I worked for. Whether as a candidate for a faculty position or as a professor serving on faculty search committees, selecting and hiring black faculty always has been a fascinating social, political, and cultural challenge for the selection committee. From the search committee's perspective, it always was difficult to find that "right" black faculty who could fit within the social, political, intellectual, and cultural dynamics of a department. Overall, from my experience, I can see why black professionals have had a difficult time being considered as a qualified professional, let alone being hired for a full-time faculty position.

There is little doubt that the United States has continued to have a serious problem with providing a quality and equitable public education for all people throughout history. Since the landmark decision in the case of *Brown v. Board of Education of Topeka* of the U.S. Supreme Court on May 17, 1954, which ruled unanimously that "separate educational facilities are inherently unequal," thereby paving the way for the full integration of all public schools, one would think that, by now, the U.S. education system would have implemented a well-designed equitable school system serving the needs of all people. Although blacks and whites can go to school together now and most school districts have a student population that is multiethnic and vastly much more diverse than in the 1950s and 1960s, it seems like so many school districts across the country still struggle with such issues as race relations, dropout rates, education achievements, and graduation rates, particularly as these issues relate to African American students. How and why are these problems occurring in our America today? They simply should not happen.

Moreover, why do we not have a more diverse faculty at all the major colleges and universities across the country? Now that our major colleges and universities have substantially increased the diversity of their student populations, major colleges and universities have no excuse but to do the same for its faculty. The faculty at each college and university must reflect in percentages the demographics of its student population. Unfortunately, most major colleges and universities are not fulfilling this mission. Again, this simply should not happen.

The problems and solutions in today's primary and secondary school systems and higher education institutions can be better understood if we look back at a particular event in one of our major cities—Chicago—to see how it was resolved. In this case, it highlights the problems that Chicago African Americans experienced with the blatant discriminatory practices in the public school system and illustrates how African Americans mobilized themselves with the help of the Black Power movement to reform the education system that was supposed to be adhering to the federal mandate of an equitable education for blacks in the city.

Chicago Public Schools: A Cultural Historical Review

The history of blacks in Chicago extends to Chicago's very beginnings when Jean Baptiste Pointe DuSable, a black trader from Santo Domingo, became the first permanent settler of Chicago in 1790. By 1900, there were 30,150 blacks in Chicago (1.9 percent of the total population), up from 14,271 just ten years previous. This drastic increase was due to a large influx of migrants from other states. In 1900, more than 80 percent of Chicago's black population had been born out of state. In 1920, there were 109,458 blacks; by 1930, there were 233,903, making blacks account for 6.9 percent of the total Chicago population. Black migrants primarily settled on the city's South Side in an area known as the "Black Belt."[9]

The Black Belt was a narrow strip that stretched over thirty blocks southward along State Street. It was only a few blocks wide except at its northern end. In 1910, 78 percent of the city's black population lived in the Black Belt. The rest of Chicago's blacks were scattered throughout the city on the West Side, Englewood, the Near North Side, and the North Side.[10]

In 1916, 91.3 percent of black Chicago attended integrated schools. There were all-white schools, but virtually all of the schools attended by African Americans had white students. By 1930, 63.2 percent of the city's African Americans lived in areas that were nine-tenths black. However, 82.4 percent of African Americans were attending schools with a 90 to 100 percent black population.[11]

Although Chicago's black schools looked physically better than black schools in the South, the schools were still grossly inferior to white schools. During the Depression years and beyond, black schools were extremely overcrowded with double-shift assignments. That meant that students went to school for three or four hours, instead of five hours to accommodate overcrowding. Other elements that factored into the overcrowding were that blacks relied heavily on the public schools and black teens were remaining in school longer as a result of the diminishing job market during the Depression. With the advent of the Depression, school construction ended, except for the completion of four white elementary schools. Many in the African American community were furious about their children's inadequate education.[12]

During and after World War II, a second wave of migrants entered Chicago's city limits, and the wave continued well into the 1960s. By then, Chicago became known as the nation's most segregated large city.[13]

Although organizations in the Chicago African American community, such as the National Association for the Advancement of Colored People (NAACP) and the Chicago Urban League, had long fought for equality, during the civil rights movement, black Chicago organizations came together with civic and religious organizations under the umbrella of the Coordinating Council of Community Organizations (CCCO) to fight for equality and the elimination of discrimination. In the early 1960s, these organizations and other community groups made reports documenting the overcrowded conditions in black schools and the undercrowded condition at white schools. Because of these implications, black organizations in the vein of the civil rights movement demanded first that the space in those schools be filled and second that Chicago schools be integrated.[14]

Mayor Richard J. Daley's city administration and Superintendent Benjamin C. Willis' school administration refused to budge despite the pressure from civil rights groups, massive boycotts, and the Title VI complaint, which led to the city's federal education funds being temporarily withheld. Chicago was Daley's city and, as one of the most powerful politicians in the nation, what he wanted usually happened.

At this time as well, Chicago was still going through some massive changes. In 1964, the black population of Chicago increased to 930,000, up 65 percent from the previous decade. At the same time, Chicago's white population decreased by 399,000 residents, most opting to escape city life in the suburbs. Chicago's population decreased for the first time in decades in the 1960s. The South Side's ghetto expanded, at times block by block, while the West Side expanded to become a second black ghetto.[15]

With the enormous population increases, overcrowded schools became a significant problem. The biggest issue with overcrowding was that while many black schools were on double shift and extremely over capacity, in neighboring white schools, classroom space was available.[16]

After a long fight under the banner of civil rights and Dr. Rev. Martin Luther King's failure to make the sweeping slum reform in Chicago, black Chicagoans picked up the banner of Black Power and Black Pride and demanded that changes be made at the schools in their communities. The shift to Black Power followed a national trend as black people nationwide found that perhaps they had been asking for the wrong things.[17]

In fact, black community organizations, students, and teachers changed their focus from asking the city school administrators for change to focusing their efforts on community control of institutions within the black community instead of desegregation. Education was one such institution where African Americans galvanized, risking suspension, expulsion, job loss, arrest, and prosecution for community control of schools.[18]

The significance of the Black Power and the Black Pride national movement during the 1960s and 1970s particularly as it relates to the City of Chicago was that it supported the notion that blacks should control the institutions in their communities. Through the creation of manifestos, weekly boycotts, sit-ins, and other organizing tactics, black students, teachers, and community organizations demanded that blacks be in decision-making administrative positions, curricula be utilized that would be relevant to their needs, and the community have input in school decisions. Black teachers organized against Chicago Teachers Union's policies that were not supportive of black teachers' certification. Black Power calls for community control differs from civil rights cries for desegregation in the early 1960s because Black Power reformers demanded education improvement in schools that blacks already attended.[19] This is exactly the type of education reform (not necessarily under the same name as Black Power) that is needed in the 21st century.

THE U.S. EDUCATION SYSTEM

Now that I am a parent with three children, it has become quite apparent to my wife and I that the school systems in which our children have had to attend from state to state struggle with providing quality and equal education for all children. From Indiana to Georgia to Arkansas to Maryland to California and now to North Carolina, our children have had to adjust to the county and state public education requirements in various grades for their education advancement. For them not only to meet their grade school requirements but also to excel, my wife and I had to be proactive within every school district to ensure that our children receive the quality and equal public education that they deserve.

Unfortunately, however, many parents and children have been unable for a variety of reasons to receive a quality and equitable education regardless of their socioeconomic standing. This is the major problem that haunts our national, state, and county public education systems today.

In recent years, the nation's commitment to equal educational opportunity has been bolstered by the realization that, in addition to being a moral and constitutional imperative, equal education opportunity is critically important to America's continued political and economic vitality. Responding to the nation's commitment, nearly every state has adopted standards-based reforms based on the premise that, with proper resources and supports, virtually all children can meet challenging academic standards. Although the actual quality of the standards varies significantly from state to state, some parents feel that these reforms have raised academic expectations for America's children.[20]

The federal No Child Left Behind Act (NCLB), signed into law in 2002, expands the equity imperatives of Title I and combines them with education reforms emerging from the state standards movement into a potent package that promises, a half century after *Brown v. Board of Education*, that equal education opportunity and universal student proficiency actually will be achieved. Specifically, NCLB mandates as America's fundamental national educational policy that:

1. All children will reach academic proficiency by 2014.
2. Proficiency will be defined by each state in accordance with challenging state academic standards containing rigorous content.
3. All children will be taught by "highly qualified teachers."
4. States and school districts will be accountable for ensuring that all schools have the instructional capacity to make certain that their students advance in accordance with specifically defined annual progress expectations. There will be specific consequences and sanctions for schools and school districts that do not meet these expectations.
5. Student progress will be measured through validated annual assessments that are aligned with the state standards. Results will be reported in disaggregated form by racial, ethnic, disability, and income groupings to ensure that the needs of all students are being met.[21]

Yet according to Rebell and Wolff's book *Moving Every Child Ahead: From NCLB Hype to Meaningful Educational Opportunity* (2008), in spite of this historic commitment, seven years after its enactment, NCLB is failing to achieve any of these objectives:

1. No state is on track to reach the full proficiency goal by 2014. Overall, progress on standardized reading and math tests has been minimal, and wide achievement gaps persist between low-income and minority students and their more affluent white peers.
2. Most states have not set academic standards that are "challenging," and a number of states have lowered their proficiency criteria in response to NCLB pressures.
3. At best, the law has ensured that more children are being taught by minimally qualified teachers, but large numbers of poor and minority students with the greatest education needs are still assigned the most inexperienced and least qualified teachers.

4. Many of the increasing numbers of "schools in need of improvement" lack the resources and instructional capacity to bring
larger percentages of their students to proficiency, and few are
obtaining effective assistance from state departments of education
or school districts. In many cases, state education departments
and school districts also lack the required resources and capacity.

5. Many of the state tests used to measure adequate yearly progress
are not valid in accordance with established psychometric standards, and most state tests are not fully aligned with the state's
academic standards.[22]

In addition, Rebell and Wolff (2008) state that Congress knows that
it is impossible to achieve the 100 percent proficiency and therefore it
should establish as its mandatory goal for 2014 the more achievable
aim of providing meaningful education opportunity for all children by
that time. Furthermore, the term proficiency should be redefined to
emphasize consistent progress toward high levels of achievement,
rather than absolute attainment of a concrete level of performance at a
definite point in time.

Finally, and most important, particularly as it relates to African
American children, each state's adequate yearly progress should be
judged in terms of the extent to which the achievement gaps between
advantaged and disadvantaged groups of students are reduced. This is
a mechanism for ensuring that the twin goals of advancing excellence
and equity are both served.[23]

To further emphasize the importance of reforming our education
system now whether it is through the NCLB initiative or another more
practical initiative, a 2008 report entitled *Measuring Up 2008* shows
how our nation's children compare with children in other countries as
it relates to education achievement. *Measuring Up 2008* is the most
recent in the series of national and state-by-state report cards for higher
education that was inaugurated in 2000. The key findings revealed that
the nation and most of the fifty states are making some advances in
preparing students for college and providing them with access to
higher education. Other nations, however, are advancing more quickly
than the United States, which continues to slip behind other countries
in improving college opportunities for our residents. In addition, large
disparities in higher education performance by race and ethnicity, by
income, and by state limit the nation's ability to advance the education
attainment of its workforce and citizenry—and thereby remain compet-
itive globally.[24]

The Measuring Up 2008 report stated further that the likelihood that
a high school freshman will enroll in college by age nineteen has
improved modestly in this decade, from 39 percent to 42 percent, and

that the proportion of eighteen to twenty-four year olds enrolled in college has grown even more modestly. Meanwhile, the enrollment of working-age adults in college-level education or training has been declining since the early 1990s. The indicators show that access to college is fairly flat in the United States, with mostly small improvements in some states and declines in others.[25]

The report also compares the U.S. rates with other countries. *Measuring Up 2008* specifically states that the United States' world leadership in college access has eroded steadily, as reflected in the international comparisons of the proportion of eighteen to twenty-four year olds enrolled in college. In college completion, which has never been a strength of American higher education, the United States ranks fifteenth among twenty-nine countries. The U.S. adult population ages thirty-five and older still ranks among the world leaders in the percentage who have college degrees—reflecting the education progress of earlier times. Among twenty-five to thirty-four year olds, however, the U.S. population has slipped to tenth in the percentage who have an associate degree or higher. This relative erosion of our national "educational capital" reflects the lack of significant improvement in the rates of college participation and completion in recent years.[26]

Finally, *Measuring Up 2008* suggests that to make significant headway in increasing the education attainment of its population and thereby its comparative standing internationally, the United States must address disparities in education opportunity and achievement among all Americans. The report specifically states that "[t]hese persistent gaps must be closed if the United States is to meet its workforce needs and compete globally."[27]

THE OBAMA ADMINISTRATION

As with every administration, major agenda items are highlighted during the president's term in office. For President Barack Obama, education is definitely one such item. So what are the major objectives from the Obama administration regarding the country's educational system?

According to the White House Web site (March 10, 2009), President Obama and Vice President Joe Biden believe that the nation and its children cannot afford four more years of neglect and indifference. It specifically states:

Obama and Biden are committed to meeting this challenge with the leadership and judgment that has been sorely lacking for the last eight years. Their vision for a 21st century education begins with demanding more reform and accountability, coupled with the resources needed to carry out that reform; asking parents to take responsibility for their children's success; and recruiting, retaining, and rewarding an army of new teachers to fill new successful schools that prepare our children for success in college and the workforce. The Obama-Biden plan will restore the promise of America's public education, and ensure that American children again lead the world in achievement, creativity and success.[28]

The Obama-Biden plan will address education in the following four major areas:

- Early Childhood Education
- K–12
- Higher Education
- Students with Disabilities

So what are the specific strategies for each of the major education-focused Obama administration initiatives?

Table 4.1 shows the Obama administration's specific initiatives. In addition to these initiatives, President Obama's Stimulus Plan (2009) provided approximately $141.6 billion dollars for education. Here is the breakdown of the stimulus money:

- $62 billion: To school districts through various programs, including $21 billion for school modernization
- $39 billion: State aid to school districts and public colleges and universities to prevent cutbacks to key services
- $15.6 billion: To states for hitting performance measures
- $25 billion: Fund to help states to prevent layoffs of "critical" public employees, including teachers

Obviously, the next question is, "Will these Obama administration initiatives designed specifically to address education be enough and make a difference for kids going to public education (K–12) and higher education (colleges and universities)?

In my opinion, in many ways definitely, yes, and other ways definitely, no. The Obama-Biden plan states that it will reform the NCLB initiative, which primarily puts pressure on school districts, school administrators, teachers, and students to perform to a given state requirement at each grade level instead of improving the assessments used to track student progress to measure readiness for college and the workplace. The key word here is "readiness" and that suggests that

Table 4.1 Obama Administration Education Initiatives

Early Childhood Education	• Zero to Five Plan • Expand Early Head Start and Head Start • Provide Affordable, High Quality Child Care
K–12	• Reform No Child Left Behind • Support High-Quality Schools and Close Low-Performing Charter Schools • Make Math and Science Education a National Priority • Address the Dropout Crisis • Expand High-Quality After School Opportunities • Support College Outreach Programs • Support College Credit Initiatives • Support English Language Learners • Recruit Teachers • Prepare Teachers • Retain Teachers • Reward Teachers
Higher Education	• Create the American Opportunity Tax Credit • Simplify the Application Process for Financial Aid
Students with Disabilities	• Increase Funding and Effectively Enforce the Individuals with Disabilities Education Act • Early Intervention Services

Source: White House Web site, "Education," http://www.whitehouse.gov/agenda/education (accessed October 3, 2009).

the Obama administration will support and reward school systems that will assist students in being "ready" for college or the workplace. This is quite different than just achieving a certain standardized number from testing by the end of the year.

Nonetheless, the Obama administration will not effectively address the education problems in the primary or secondary school years (K–12) and higher education (colleges and universities) if it continues to avoid one of the key issues related to education, which is *culture.* Unfortunately, there is not one word in the administration's initiative for education on culture or the extreme multiracial and multiethnic diversity of our public school systems across America, whether at the primary or secondary school level and particularly at the college and university level. Somehow the words "culture," "diversity," and "ethnicity" are being omitted from the dialogue, planning, and discussion associated with our public school systems yet again.

How and why is this occurring in 2009, when in fact our country is exploding with such new diversity (students, administrators, and teachers) within our public school systems?[29] It simply is not right when *cultural rights* are ignored once again under a new administration that symbolizes diversity in its most visible and subtle ways.

Culturally Competent Schools

One of the most effective strategies in fulfilling our racially and ethnically diverse student populations' needs (educationally, socially, economically, historically, and politically) in America is to make our public school systems and public colleges and universities *culturally competent*. A culturally competent school is generally defined as one that honors, respects, and values diversity in theory and in practice and in which teaching and learning are made relevant and meaningful to students of various cultures.[30] A culturally competent school is exactly what the parents, teachers, and children wanted in the Chicago Public School system during 1960s and 1970s. Although the time period was different socially, politically, and racially, the issue was not—they wanted *culturally competent* schools just as much as Americans today deserve *culturally competent schools*.

Whether we use the term *culturally competent education* or *multicultural education*, we are seeking to extend the ideals that were meant only for an elite few. It is about embracing that ideal that all students should have an equal opportunity to learn in school regardless of their gender, socioeconomic status, ethnicity, religion, physical or mental abilities, or other cultural characteristics.[31] This is exactly what is missing from our national and local public education initiatives today.

In fact, principals of culturally competent schools should encourage understanding and respect for individual differences and strive for high education standards and levels of achievements for all students. Student problems should be examined within the context of environmental factors, including prior educational experiences, instruction, second language acquisition, and culture.[32] Table 4.2 outlines strategies and procedures that are essential to creating a culturally competent school environment.

THE BLACK MALE INITIATIVE: A CULTURALLY COMPETENT EDUCATION INITIATIVE

Now that I have been a college professor for more than twenty years, I definitely have noticed a significant problem in U.S. colleges and universities. From one mainstream university to another, this problem is growing each and every year. That problem is this: Where are the African American male college students? It seems like every year, the number of African American male college students in my classes and on campus continues to dwindle as though we do not even exist anymore. I am sure others have noticed this trend, yet very few educators are doing something about it. Why is that?

Table 4.2 Culturally Competent School Strategies and Procedures

Staff Development	• Ensure that all professional development opportunities are culturally sensitive and inclusive. • Teach all staff members the distinction between the second language acquisition process and language differences and learning disabilities. • Recruit qualified school personnel who represent the cultural and ethnic makeup of the communities being served.
Early Intervention and Assessment	• Use a team problem-solving model to address student achievement or behavior problems and provide early intervention support. • Match students with appropriate mentors or life coaches from similar cultural backgrounds. • Include English as a Second Language (ESL) teachers and other staff members who have a background in cultural differences and second language acquisition issues on the general education problem-solving team. • Use assessments that are unbiased, culturally sensitive, and advocacy-oriented. • Use outcome-based data for decision making and planning.
Instruction and Curriculum Selection	• Give all students the same enriching, evidence-based educational opportunities. • Offer a culturally inclusive curriculum that encourages cultural inquiry. • Encourage teachers to hold cultural sensitivity discussions with students when literary selections or references present negative stereotypes. • Explicitly teach and model important values and appropriate classroom behavior.
Community and Parent Involvement	• Ensure that communications from the school are available in languages other than English, as appropriate. • Have childcare available at parent meetings. • Help students develop a sense of civic responsibility toward their immediate community, the nation, and the world. • Collaborate with parents and other community members and invite them to share their home cultures with the school.

Source: Mary Beth Klotz, "Culturally Competent Schools: Guidelines for Secondary School Principals," National Association of School Psychologists, http://www.nasponline.org/resources/principals/Culturally%20Competent%20Schools%20NASSP.pdf, March 2008.

Of course, I'm personally and culturally concerned because I want everyone to succeed and get a college education and degree, particularly those who have been neglected in U.S. society—the black male. The numbers speak for themselves with regards to this discouraging trend in higher education.

Between 1980 and 2000, the number of black men who enrolled in college in the fall semester grew by 37 percent—climbing from 464,000 in 1980 to 635,000. For black women, however, the number grew by 70 percent—climbing from 643,000 to 1.1 million in 2000. That means that roughly 450,000 more black women were enrolling in college in 2000 than black men. This wide disparity within the African American student population was not found in any other minority group according to ACE annual report of 2006.

Equally alarming was the actual number of black men graduating from college over the last twenty years. In 1980, according to the ACE report, 24,511 black men earned bachelor's degrees, compared with 36,162 black women—a difference of 11,651. By 2000, that gap more than *tripled* when only 38,103 black men earned four-year degrees compared with 73,204 black women. Thus, nearly 70 percent of black students who earned bachelor's degrees in 2000 were women.[33]

Some of the causes for this drastic decline in black men in higher education relate to their high school years. Among the causes are the following:

- The type of academic and career counseling black males receive in high school
- The expectations high school teachers, counselors, parents, and other adults have of black men
- Lack of exposure to college-preparatory curriculum
- The preparation of their teachers
- Their family's financial standing
- Their self-identity and overall attitude toward education and scholarship
- Their assessment of jobs and pay available with a high school degree or less, in comparison to a college degree.[34]

One public university that took on this charge to address the disparity of black males in higher education is City University of New York (CUNY). Starting the Black Male Initiative in 2005, CUNY developed programs such as counseling programs for black men; the creation of new centers to help black men deal with academia, financial, and personal issues; recruitment programs in top high schools and in prisons;

and efforts to help faculty members—male and female, of all racial backgrounds—better reach black students.[35]

In particular, the Medger Evers College Male Development and Empowerment Center guides students through elementary and secondary schools into higher education. By building on collegewide initiatives and programs, the Center implements a systematic approach that addresses the causes of male education underachievement and not simply the symptoms. Because dis-identification with education goals occurs relatively early in the primary school years, the Center has created a holistic approach that delivers intentional interventions throughout the life span of a typical urban male.[36] Overall, the mission of the Male Development and Empowerment Center is to maximize the involvement of males in their community by increasing their knowledge and understanding of self, promoting leadership, encouraging education and personal pursuits, and enhancing the level of economic sufficiency.[37]

Recently, however, the federal Department of Education opened an inquiry into the program to determine whether the Black Male Initiative violated federal laws prohibiting race or gender discrimination. It was unclear whether any CUNY students have complained about the program to the federal Department of Education or to the state or city agencies whose task is to enforce various antidiscrimination laws. Programs similar to the initiative exist in a handful of public universities across the country, but this was the first to receive scrutiny from civil rights investigators at the federal Department of Education.[38]

Imagine that, a public education program designed to assist an underrepresented segment of the student population, African American males, being scrutinized by the federal Department of Education. This is another example as to why the U.S. public education system continues to fail miserably in giving all citizens a fair chance to obtain a quality education and to exercise *cultural rights* as human beings. This is yet another reason why we need to reform the U.S. education system right now.

CONCLUSION

Getting an education is still an important value and achievement in U.S. society in the 21st century. Whether it is grade school education, a middle school education, a high school education, a college education, or vocational school education, education of any type is an achievement to cherish simply because not everyone in America can get a quality education even today.

In the African American community, education was and still is a precious accomplishment for the individual and the entire extended family. It represents the individual and familial sacrifice that loved ones made for that one individual to be recognized as a high school graduate or college graduate. So, when someone gets a degree in the African American family, everyone—and I do mean everyone—gets that degree in their own way as well.

My parents always told me that education is a great equalizer in society. They told me and my brothers, "if you get your education, you can achieve anything." I sincerely believe that even today and that belief keeps me in the field of education. I know it has to change for all of us—not just for the select few.

Chapter 5

Expanding U.S. Medical and Health Models

INTRODUCTION

Ironically, one of the unfortunate memories that I have when growing up in Springfield, Ohio, during the late 1950s and early 1960s was the fact that I spent several different occasions in the local hospital. By the age of six, I had to be admitted to the hospital at least two different times for what appeared to be very serious health conditions. As my mother explained to me recently, I was admitted to the hospital for two medical situations—the first was mononucleosis and the other was double pneumonia.

According to my mother, I contracted mononucleosis (mono) as an infant because too many relatives and neighbors "kissed" me as a baby, thereby exposing me to too many germs and saliva from their kisses and causing me to contract mono. That was what my mother *believed* to be the cause of my mono.

In fact, my mother's belief system as to the cause and the route of transmission agrees with the medical definition of mononucleosis. According to Medline Plus, infectious mononucleosis is defined as:

An infection caused by the Epstein-Barr virus. The virus spreads through salvia, which is why it's sometimes called "kissing disease." Symptoms of mono include—fever, sore throat, and swollen lymph glands. A blood test can show if you have mono. Most people get better in two to four weeks. However, you may feel tired for a few months afterward. Treatment focuses on helping symptoms and includes medicines for pain and fever, warm salt water gargles and plenty of rest and fluids.[1]

Interestingly, my mother's *belief system* also came into play when I was hospitalized for double pneumonia in first grade. My mother's belief was that my double pneumonia was caused by my exposure to other people's germs that I somehow contracted at the elementary school or elsewhere. These germs infected my lungs causing extra mucus and making it difficult for me to breathe. At the time, she did not know what was exactly wrong with me, but she knew I needed serious medical help. Once seen by our doctor, my mother and father were informed that I needed to be admitted to the hospital.

Again, my mother's belief system as to the cause and route of transmission agreed with the medical definition of pneumonia. According to Medline Plus and Teen Health, pneumonia is defined as:

> An infection of the lungs. When a person has pneumonia, lung tissue can fill with pus and other fluid, which makes it difficult for oxygen in the lung's air sacs to reach the bloodstream. Pneumonia is commonly caused by viruses, such as influenza virus (flu) and adenovirus. Other viruses, such as respiratory syncytial virus (RSV), are common causes of pneumonia in young children and infants. Double pneumonia simply means that the infection is in both lungs. It's common for pneumonia to affect both lungs so don't worry if your doctors says this is what you have—it doesn't mean you're twice as sick. When pneumonia patients are hospitalized, treatment may include intravenous (IV) antibiotics (antibiotics that are delivered through a needle inserted into a vein) and respiratory therapy (breathing treatments). This is a good time to sleep, watch TV, read, and lay low. If you treat your body right, it will repair itself and you'll be back to normal in no time.[2]

What I remember most from my double pneumonia experience was that I missed a couple of weeks from my first grade class. For a kid who always loved school, this was devastating. I could not imagine missing so many days of school even in first grade.

Fortunately, my mother and father worked out an arrangement with my elementary school in Springfield in which my first grade teacher voluntarily visited me at my hospital room at the end of the school day to provide me with my lesson plan. As I laid there in the bed each day getting the rest that I needed, I also thought about how much I couldn't wait to see my teacher. By the end of the day, she arrived with a smile and then proceeded to tutor me in my hospital bed. I knew then that my first grade teacher was very special and for some reason she treated me like a special kid. This was particularly unusual during this time in the early 1960s because my teacher was a young white woman and I was this young Negro kid (those where the terms used in the 1960s for African Americans and Caucasians).

The major reason for highlighting my two serious health conditions is to demonstrate that people often have *belief systems* about illnesses and diseases that may be similar or dissimilar to mainstream society's medical belief system. In the case of my mother, she had a *belief system* that was different from yet connected to the belief system of mainstream medical society. In addition, a vast majority of African Americans adhere to varying health beliefs and treatment systems that are distinctively different from mainstream medical society's belief system yet connect in varying ways as well.[3]

MEDICAL BELIEF SYSTEMS

In the field of medical anthropology, an individual's or groups' health belief system and the means by which they seek treatment is called "ethnomedicine." These differing ethnomedical health and medical belief systems between blacks and mainstream medical society is an issue that's vastly overlooked and continues to be a contributing factor for the cause of the epidemic health disparity rates between blacks and whites for a countless number of diseases. If you do not believe that this is a significant issue, then let's look at some cold hard medical and health data.

In 2003, the death rate for African Americans was higher than whites for heart disease, stroke, cancer, asthma, influenza and pneumonia, diabetes, HIV/AIDS, and homicide. According to the Office of Minority Health (2008) at the Department of Health and Human Services, the following are quick facts associated with each health disparity issue:[4]

Cancer

- In 2003, African American men were 1.4 times as likely to have new cases of lung and prostate cancer compared to non-Hispanic white men.
- African American men were twice as likely to have new cases of stomach cancer as non-Hispanic white men.
- African American men had lower five-year cancer survival rates for lung and pancreatic cancer compared to non-Hispanic white men.
- In 2004, African American men were 2.4 times as likely to die from prostate cancer compared to non-Hispanic white men.
- In 2003, African American women were 10 percent less likely to have been diagnosed with breast cancer; however, they were 36 percent more likely to die from breast cancer compared to non-Hispanic white women.

- In 2003, African American women were 2.3 times as likely to have been diagnosed with stomach cancer, and they were 2.2 times as likely to die from stomach cancer, compared to non-Hispanic white women.[5]

Diabetes

- African American adults were 1.8 times more likely than non-Hispanic white adults to have been diagnosed with diabetes by a physician.
- In 2002, African American men were 2.1 times as likely to start treatment for end-stage renal disease related to diabetes compared to non-Hispanic white men.
- In 2003, diabetic African Americans were 1.8 times as likely as diabetic whites to be hospitalized.
- In 2004, African Americans were 2.2 times as likely as non-Hispanic Whites to die from diabetes.[6]

Heart Disease

- In 2004, African American men were 30 percent more likely to die from heart disease compared to non-Hispanic white men.
- African Americans were 1.5 times as likely as non-Hispanic whites to have high blood pressure.
- African American women were 1.7 times as likely as non-Hispanic white women to be obese.[7]

HIV/AIDS

- Although African Americans make up only 13 percent of the total U.S. population, they accounted for 47 percent of HIV/AIDS cases in 2005.
- African American males had more than eight times the AIDS rate of non-Hispanic white males.
- African American females had more than twenty-three times the AIDS rate of non-Hispanic white females.
- African American men were more than nine times as likely to die from HIV/AIDS as non-Hispanic white men.
- African American women were more than twenty-one times as likely to die from HIV/AIDS as non-Hispanic white women.[8]

Stroke

- African American adults were 50 percent more likely than white adult counterparts to have a stroke.
- African American males were 60 percent more likely to die from a stroke than their white adult counterparts.
- Analysis from a Centers for Disease Control and Prevention (CDC) health interview survey reveals that African American stroke survivors were more likely to become disabled and have difficulty with activities of daily living than their non-Hispanic white counterparts.[9]

Infant Mortality

- In 2004, African Americans had 2.4 times the infant mortality rate of non-Hispanic whites.
- African American infants were almost four times as likely to die from causes related to low birth weight compared to non-Hispanic white infants.
- African American mothers were 2.6 times as likely as non-Hispanic white mothers to begin prenatal care in the third trimester, or not receive prenatal care at all.[10]

Immunization

- In 2005, African Americans age sixty-five and older were 40 percent less likely to have received the influenza (flu) shot in the past twelve months compared to non-Hispanic whites of the same age-group.
- In 2005, African American adults age sixty-five and older were 30 percent less likely to have received the pneumonia shot compared to non-Hispanic white adults of the same age-group.
- Although African American children ages nineteen to thirty-five months had comparable rates of immunization for hepatitis, influenza, MMR, and polio, they were slightly less likely to be fully immunized compared to non-Hispanic white children.[11]

Related to many of these diseases affecting African Americans disproportionately in the 21st century is the fact that African Americans are overweight and obese. According to data from the CDC's National Interview Survey, black adults (30.4 percent) were considerably more likely than white adults (20.8 percent) to be obese. In this report, entitled "Health Behaviors of Adults: United States, 1999–2001," researchers found that black men (24.9 percent) were significantly less likely than black women (34.9 percent) to be obese. Additionally, among black adults and Native Hawaiian or other Pacific Islander adults, prevalence of overweight was about the same for men as for women.[12]

The statistical trend showing that African Americans are experiencing higher prevalence of overweight and obesity is illustrated in several other national studies.[13] For example, in a survey of 4,115 adult men and women in 1999 and 2000, the National Health and Nutrition Survey showed that among women, obesity and overweight prevalence were highest among non-Hispanic black women. More than half of non-Hispanic black women age forty years or older were obese and more than 80 percent were overweight.[14]

So what really is behind these health disparity data associated with African Americans in the United States? Is our public health system along with our local, state, and federal government health agencies simply missing a significant component in better understanding African American health beliefs, health care patterns, and health treatment actions? I would have to answer, yes, primarily because the vast majority of U.S. medical and public health initiatives do not truly connect with the health belief system (ethnomedical) shared by many African Americans and most Americans thereby are not *culturally competent*.

In other words, medical practitioners need to use knowledge, attitudes, and skills to better appreciate and understand African American cultural health beliefs and treatment patterns to negotiate effectively and collaborate with patients and groups and to optimize outcomes that work within their world. At this time, that simply is not happening on a regular basis in medical clinics, hospitals, community-based organizations, and public health agencies locally or nationally across our America. Perhaps the best approach to expand the medical and public health model is to evoke an "African American health culture" into this standardized westernized model of medicine.

AFRICAN AMERICAN HEALTH CULTURE

To truly understand African American health culture, we need first to embrace the "cultural history" of African Americans. Only then can we begin to better understand the reasons for the various health disparity issues affecting the African American population today. African Americans are primarily descendants of West African people who share a common history, place of origin, language, food preferences, values, and health beliefs that engender a sense of exclusiveness and self-awareness of being a member of this ethnic group.[15]

As early as the 1500s, West Africans were forcibly transported to South America, the Caribbean, and North America. Over half of the

West Africans came from the coastal areas of what are now Angola and Nigeria. Others came from the regions that are today Senegal, Gambia, Sierra Leone, Liberia, Togo, Ghana, Benin, Gabon, and Zaire. In addition, they belonged to different kinship groups—the Mandingo, Hausa, Efiks, Fanting, Ashanti, Bambara, Fulani, Ibo, Malinke, or Yoruba—and spoke different, though related, languages.[16] In the process of adapting to the new settings, West Africans merged their African cultural traditions with European and American Indian traditions.[17]

With regard to health beliefs and health care practices, African Americans are believed to have retained many of the preventive and treatment practices associated with indigenous West African cultures, primarily because these methods were perceived to be most useful and because they shared similar belief systems of living, health, illness, and spirituality. For example, in the African Living Belief System, living refers to the African emphasis on life as a dynamic, perpetually evolving condition that includes the way in which the ancestors "live" on long after their death. Belief is the thought or rationale behind the African's worldview, customs, and behaviors. Finally, system is the totality of a complex, highly organized structure of ideas and behaviors that is passed on (actively and passively) from generation to generation. Thus, the African Living Belief System encapsulates a holistic quality whose emphasis equally relates community, man and woman, deity, and natural elements for living out the system of belief.[18]

These shared belief systems of living, health, illness, and spirituality that many African Americans have in common with their West African ancestors, even today, illustrate the power of culture. The word "culture" is used quite often to describe a wide array of human behavior patterns. In this book, culture is defined as a system of shared beliefs, values, customs, and behaviors that are transmitted from generation to generation through learning.

Culture is a learned process. African Americans learn certain health beliefs and practices from their extended familial network. When a health care crisis occurs, African Americans tend first to seek health care information from their extended familial network or a lay health professional, and then opt for professional care.

Culture is transmitted by symbols verbally and nonverbally. African Americans are acutely aware of nonverbal body language that indicates whether a health care provider is comfortable or not comfortable in treating an African American person. If the African American patient perceives the nonverbal language as positive, he or she most likely will return for care. If the African American patient perceives the nonverbal body language as negative, however, he or she most likely will not return for care and will not adhere to the prescribed regimen.

Culture is integrated. Like all Americans, African Americans are connected to the social, economic, political, and health care fabric of our society. Yet once an economic or health care crisis occurs in U.S. society, as it presently has, African Americans often are affected first primarily because one-third of the population are considered to be the working poor.

Culture adds meaning to reality. African Americans respect and honor those who train, graduate, and serve in the health professional fields. Often, African American health care professionals feel a commitment to serve their community. Because of the low numbers of African American physicians and health care specialists, African Americans frequently choose to work in underserved communities of color as opposed to communities with relatively low numbers of persons of color. African Americans' commitment to work and to serve those who are underserved adds meaning to their profession of the health care field.

Culture is differently shared. African Americans perceive health and the health care system differently. Although African Americans have many common traits and patterns, there remains a high degree of diversity within the African American population. For instance, intergenerational health care issues differ among African Americans as they relate to perceptions of the health system and health belief system. Additional sociodemographic factors, such as gender, region of the country, income level, and education level may also cause differing perceptions of health care issues in the African American population.

Culture is adaptive. Traditionally, African Americans have had to adapt to social, economic, political, and health care barriers to mainstream society. Whether the barriers are actual or perceived, African Americans learn alternative patterns of utilizing the local medical and public health systems.

Thus, the African American health culture framework expands the traditional medical and public health models in such areas as disease causation, illness perception, treatment practices, preventative care, and health practitioners. In fact, the African American health culture framework fits more with the medical anthropological approach to health and disease—a biopsychosociocultural perspective—than the traditional medical and public health approaches.

With the "biopsychosociocultural perspective," biology, psychology, sociology, and culture are combined in this holistic approach for the purpose of diagnosing and treating an individual from a comprehensive perspective. This approach emphasizes that each factor—*biology, psychology, sociology, and particularly culture*—are evaluated equally to determine an individual's state of health or illness. Moreover, the key element to this approach, *culture*, has played a significant role in modifying and changing how we as public health researchers and practitioners must engage, treat, and develop new public health and medical programs for all segments of the U.S. population, particularly African Americans.

THE OBAMA ADMINISTRATION

It was quite apparent from the start of his administration that President Obama was going to make health care a major priority item during his presidency. In fact, within the first fifty days of his administration, President Obama stated to the country and to Congress that he wants a health care reform and a new national health care plan for the country.

According to the White House Web site (March 22, 2009), the administration's plan provides affordable, accessible health care for all Americans, builds on the existing health care system, and uses existing providers, doctors, and plans. Under the Obama-Biden plan, patients will be able to make health care decisions with their doctors, instead of being blocked by insurance company bureaucrats. It specifically states:

> Under the plan, if you like your current health insurance, nothing changes, except your costs will go down by as much as $2,500 per year. If you don't have health insurance, you will have a choice of new, affordable health insurance options.[19]

The Obama-Biden health plan will address health care in four major areas. They are as follows:

- Provide Health Insurance
- Reduce Medical Costs
- Promote Public Health
- Commit to Fiscal Health Care Responsibility

Upon further investigation of the Obama-Biden health plan, an interesting paragraph discusses how this plan will address health disparities. In the area of reducing medical costs, the Obama-Biden plan states the following with regards to tackling disparities in health care:

> Although all Americans are affected by problems with our health care delivery system, an overwhelming body of evidence demonstrates that certain populations are significantly more likely to receive lower quality health care than others. Barack Obama and Joe Biden will tackle the root causes of health disparities by addressing differences in access to health coverage and promoting prevention and public health, both of which play a major role in addressing disparities. They will also challenge the medical system to eliminate inequities in health care by requiring hospitals and health plans to collect, analyze and report health care quality for disparity populations and holding them accountable

for any differences found; diversifying the workforce to ensure culturally effective care; implementing and funding evidence-based interventions, such as patient navigator programs; and supporting and expanding the capacity of safety-net institutions, which provide a disproportionate amount of care for under-served populations with inadequate funding and technical resources.[20]

Quite interestingly, this is the only place in the health plan that mentions disparities and disparity populations.

The federal government agency responsible for implementing the Obama-Biden plan is the U.S. Department of Health and Human Services (DHHS). Although the original nominee to head DHHS, former senator Tom Daschle, had to withdraw his name because of back tax revelations, President Obama's 2009 budget allocated $76.8 billion in support of the department's mission.

According to DHHS, following are the funding highlights for 2009:

- Accelerates the adoption of health information technology and utilization of electronic health records.
- Expands research comparing the effectiveness of medical treatments to give patients and physicians better information on what works best.
- Invests more than $6 billion for cancer research at the National Institutes of Health as part of the administration's multiyear commitment to double cancer research funding.
- Strengthens the American Indian health system with sustained investments in health care services for American Indians and Alaska Natives to address persistent health disparities and foster healthy Native communities.
- Invests $330 million to increase the number of doctors, nurses, and dentists practicing in areas of the country experiencing shortages of health professionals.
- Supports families by providing additional funding for affordable, high-quality child care, expanding Early Head Start and Head Start, and creating the Nurse Home Visitation program to support first-time mothers.
- Strengthens the Medicare program by encouraging high-quality and efficient care, and improving program integrity.
- Invests more than $1 billion for Food and Drug Administration food safety efforts to increase and improve inspections, domestic surveillance, laboratory capacity and domestic response to prevent and control food-borne illness.[21]

Other than supporting cancer research at the National Institutes of Health and strengthening the American Indian health system for American Indians and Alaska Natives, the Obama administration and the DHSS have not publicly announced any new mandate or initiative to address health disparity issues for specific ethnic and health disparity groups, such as African Americans, Hispanic/Latinos, Asian and Pacific Islanders, women, men, elderly, gay, lesbian, transgender, urban, rural, mentally challenged, or physically challenged groups. As mentioned earlier in this chapter, all of these groups, and so many more, desperately need specific budgetary support from the new administration to address their specific health disparity issues.

Therefore, the major question is as follows: "Will the Obama administration's Initiatives make a significant impact in reducing health disparity for specific ethnic and health disparity groups in the United States?"

In its present form, I have to say, no. The health plan simply does not have enough substance or include specific initiatives directly targeted toward the wide array of health disparity problems facing many groups in our country. For some reason, very little language is included recognizing ethnicity as well as culture. Obviously, from my perspective as a medical and cultural anthropologist with a public health focus, this is a major concern.

RECOGNIZING AND ADDRESSING ETHNIC HEALTH DISPARITY GROUPS

Perhaps one way that the Obama administration can become aware of these massive health disparity problems in America is to highlight the major ethnic and health disparity groups' culture and health issues. Although America promotes this country as a melting pot in which all of the ethnic groups come together to live as one, we still are having serious problems recognizing the equal legal, social, economic, housing, judicial, and in this case, health rights of all Americans. The next sections of this chapter highlight the sociodemographics and health culture associated with the three other major racial and ethnic groups in the United States.

Hispanic/Latino Health Culture

The Hispanic/Latino American population is the largest ethnic minority group. The term "Hispanic" is an umbrella term used to conveniently describe a large and diverse population. Hispanics/Latinos represent almost 15 percent of the population. A person with a Hispanic/Latino background is one whose conditions and events surrounding and influencing his or her life, including education, language, experiences, and health beliefs are associated with Spanish civilization.[22] We must realize that each Hispanic/Latino group is distinct and unique, with its own history. Each group has its own relation to this country, and each tends to be concentrated in different geographic areas of the United States.[23]

The Hispanic/Latino racial group includes any person of Cuban, Mexican, Puerto Rican, South or Central American, or other Spanish culture or origin, regardless of race. According to the 2006 U.S. Census Bureau population estimate, roughly 44.3 million Hispanic/Latinos live in the United States. In 2004, among Hispanic/Latinos subgroups, Mexicans rank as the largest at 66 percent. Following Mexicans are Central and South Americans (13 percent), Puerto Ricans (9.4 percent), Cubans (3.9 percent), and the remaining 7.5 percent are people of other Hispanic/Latino origins. States with the largest Hispanic/Latino populations are California (13 million), Texas (8 million), New York (3 million), Florida (3.6 million), and Illinois (1.9 million). Another significant issue is that, in 2004, 34.3 percent of Hispanics/Latinos were under the age of eighteen in comparisons to 22.3 percent of non-Hispanic whites. Among Hispanics/Latinos, Mexicans have the largest proportion of people under age eighteen, at 36 percent.[24]

A 2002 study conducted by the Pew Hispanic Center concluded that language fluency varies among Hispanic subgroups who reside within the mainland United States. The numbers for Hispanics/Latinos who speak only English at home are as follows: 3.9 million for Mexicans, 763,875 for Puerto Ricans, 163,599 for Cubans, and 1.8 million for other Hispanic/Latino groups.[25] The numbers for Hispanics/Latinos who speak Spanish at home are as follows: 14.5 million for Mexicans, 2.3 million for Puerto Ricans, 1 million for Cubans, and 6.7 million for other Hispanic/Latino groups.[26]

Because of the lack of specific cultural health data associated with Hispanics/Latinos, this section will summarize the major traditional health beliefs and treatment actions that have been documented in various medical anthropological and public health documents. Although we need to continue to recognize extreme diversity in these health beliefs and treatment practices among Hispanics/Latinos, this overview provides a general framework for health providers and public health administrators to better understand the broad-based health disparity issues associated Hispanics/Latinos.

According to the Hippocratic theory, the body humors (blood, phlegm, black bile, and yellow bile) vary in both temperature and moistness. In this system, health is conceived as a state of balance among the four humors that manifests itself in a somewhat wet, warm body. Illness, on the other hand, is believed to result from a humoral imbalance that causes the body to become excessively dry, cold, hot, wet, or a combination of these states. Food, herbs, and other medications, which are classified as wet, dry, or cold, are used therapeutically to restore the body to its supposed natural balance. Thus, according to the system, a "cold" disease, such as arthritis, is cured by administering "hot" foods or medications.[27] However, there is no general agreement as to what is a hot disease or food and what is a cold, disease or food. In addition, the classification varies from person to person, and what is hot to one person may be cold to another.[28]

The hot-cold system stems from the Hippocratic humoral theories of disease, which were carried to the Western Hemisphere by the Spanish and Portuguese in the 16th and 17th centuries.[29] Medical schools established in Mexico and Peru in this period taught the system, and its tenets were embodied in household medical references and Aztec beliefs, which were used throughout Spanish America by priests and others who provided European medical care to the indigenous populations.[30] Through these channels of influence, the humoral theory became an integral part of Mexican American folk medical practice, where it persists today.[31]

The hot-cold syndrome in Latin America has been reported for Mexico, for Mexican American communities, for the Guatemalan Highlands, for coastal Colombia, for the Colombian Highlands, and for coastal Peru and coastal Chile.[32] For example, cold foods include most fresh vegetables, the ancient Indian staples (maize, beans, and squash), most tropical fruits (including citrus fruits), dairy products, and low-prestige meats such as goat, fish, and chicken. Hot foods include most (but not all) chili peppers, most temperate-zone fruits, goat's milk, cereal grains, and high-prestige meats such as beef, waterfowl, most oils, hard liquor, and aromatic beverages. A given food stuff is often both hot and cold, depending on whether and how it is cooked. Foods that can be either hot or cold include beans, rice, wheat, pork, and peaches.[33]

The qualities of hot and cold are related to aspects of life other than those of nutrition and disease. In these other contexts, the symbolic meanings of warmth and cold are most clearly revealed: cold is associated with threatening aspects of existence. While warmth is associated with reassurance.[34]

In sum, the traditional framework of knowledge about health and disease of Mexican Americans is integrated by a conceptualization of the individual as a sum of balanced parts and qualities.[35] A healthy individual is one whose entire being is in balance. This concept relates to the set of contrasting qualities, hot and cold, wet and dry. Conceptually, individuals and parts of their body are conceived as having a specific place and function; a change in the manner in which any of these parts relates to the whole is presumed to cause illness.

Mexican American folk medicine classifies disease mainly according to cause rather than symptoms. The primary classification of disease distinguishes three major categories:

1. Natural and supernatural forces
2. Imbalances of hot and cold
3. Emotions as a cause of disease[36]

Natural and supernatural forces cause diseases either by an individual's violating the balance of the natural world controlled by God or by a bewitchment sent by human adversaries utilizing evil, satanic forces. A natural illness is corrected by restoring the particular balance that was disrupted. Bewitchment is cured by counter magic or by removing the immediate source of harm.[37]

For example, exposure to the forces of nature, such as moonlight, eclipses, cold, heat, air, wind, sun, and water, is believed to cause illness.[38] "Mal aire" is a folk belief in which "bad air" affects children and adults, causing pain and cramps. "Bad air" may enter the body of a child or an adult, producing aches in the particular area where it lodges. Thus, it is a health belief to protect oneself from cold winds and night air.[39]

In terms of the supernatural forces, some people believe that some ailments are caused by magical powers such as the "evil eye." If someone with "strong vision" admires someone else's child without actually touching him or her, the child may fall ill—the evil power is transmitted through the gaze of that person. Symptoms of this illness include insomnia, aches and pains, excessive crying, fever, severe headache, and restlessness. All individuals are regarded as susceptible to the virulence of "evil eye" (*mal ojo*) but women and children are more vulnerable than men.[40]

Imbalances of hot and cold are the second major cause of disease among Mexican Americans. The state of health is seen as demanding a balance between the hot and cold and maintaining a strong defense against outside forces. Some diseases are hot, and some are cold. In addition, foods and herbs are classified into hot and cold treatments. Sickness that enhances the cold within the body requires a hot treatment to restore the balance, and vice versa. To avoid a hot sickness, the person must not become cold; therefore, the individual must not walk barefoot on cold tiles for fear of catching tonsillitis. Moreover, people are given chili, a hot food, or chicken soup for a cold disease such as pneumonia or a common cold.

Finally, emotions as a cause of disease are the third major category. An example of an emotionally based illness is called *susto*. Susto (fright) is usually the result of a traumatic experience that may result from witnessing an accident or death to a simple scare at night.[41] It afflicts many people—males and females, rich and poor, rural dwellers and urbanites. It involves "soul loss": the soul is able to leave the body and wander freely. This can occur when a person is dreaming or when a person experiences a particularly traumatic event. Often, the susto syndrome will appear in an individual who is unable to meet the expectations of his or her society for a social role for which he or she has been socialized.[42] The symptoms of the disease are as follows:

1. The person is restless while sleeping.
2. When awake, the person is listless, anorexic, and disinterested in personal appearance, which includes both clothing and personal hygiene.
3. The person experiences a loss of strength, is depressed, and becomes introverted.[43]

The types and sources of treatment actions among Mexican Americans, Puerto Ricans, and Cuban Americans are likely to vary according to gender, age, class, region of the United States, and degree of assimilation to mainstream society. In the United States, most ethnic groups have the option of selecting from the variety of sources listed earlier.

In addition to the variety of home remedies or patent medicines used among Mexican Americans, a variety of alternative health practitioners serve the Mexican American community: (1) sobador, (2) curandero, (3) yerbero, (4) espiritisa, and (5) santero. Each alternative health practitioner uses different treatment actions.

For example, the sobador (massager) is usually a woman who gives therapies rather than medicines.[44] She is needed in cases of indigestion, infection (empacho), or counseling. The curandero, on the other hand, is a full-time or part-time specialist who heals by virtue of a "gift from God," typically revealed and confirmed in dreams and often involving a close association with the spirit of a renowned predecessor. Curanderos, who may be male or female (curandera), often see themselves as having unusual qualities, thereby obtaining a high status within the community. Curanderos also rub, massage, and otherwise manipulate the body (for example, "lifting" the fontanel back into place). Still other curanderos have occult powers, including the ability to bewitch as well as to cure.

The yerbero (herbalist), espiritisa (practitioner of Espiritism, a religious cult concerned with communication with spirits and the purification of the soul through moral behavior), and santero (practitioner of Santeria, a religious cult concerned with teaching people how to control or placate the supernatural) are the other major alternative health practitioners serving the Mexican American community. Each of these alternative health practitioners plays an important role in the Mexican American community.

Finally, many Mexican American alternative treatment patterns do not require alternative healers or home remedies. For many illnesses,

Mexican Americans frequently seek the intervention of saints, the Virgin Mary, or Christ, lighting candles and praying at their alters. Often, vows or solemn promises are made to "miraculous" images of Christ or the Virgin. Christ and the Virgin are only advocates who intercede for their human clients; God, in the final analysis, decides on the outcomes.[45]

This brief review of the Hispanic/Latino health culture reflects a broader understanding of the factors that influence their health care action. Moreover, the cultural-historical analysis of Hispanic/Latino traditional health beliefs and practices provides special insight regarding the ethnic and sociocultural bond an individual may develop toward his or her health beliefs and practices.

As former DHSS director, Louis Sullivan stated at the 1992 National Workshop on Hispanic/Latino Health that there are five major areas that we need to focus on if we are going to improve the health and health status of the Hispanic/Latino community:

1. We need to enhance access to health care.
2. We need to improve the data collection on the Hispanic/Latino population.
3. It is imperative that we increase Hispanic representation in the sciences and health professions.
4. We need to focus greater attention and resources on health promotions and disease prevention.
5. We need to emphasize calls for comprehensive and relevant research for the Hispanic/Latino populations.[46]

Asian and Pacific Islander Americans Health Culture

Asian Americans are defined as people having origins in any of the original peoples of the Far East, Southeast Asia, or the Indian subcontinent. Pacific Islander Americans are defined as individual who are descendants of the original residents of the Pacific Islanders under the jurisdiction of the U.S. government.

Asian Americans include specific ethnic groups such as Asian Indians, Cambodians, Chinese, Filipino, Hmong, Japanese, Korean, Laotian, Thai, Vietnamese, and "other Asian." Pacific Islander Americans include specific ethnic groups such as Chamorro, Hawaiians (Kanaka Maoli), Melanesians, Micronesians, Polynesians, Samoans, and "other" Pacific Islanders (Chamorros are the people indigenous to Guam and Kanaka Maoli are the indigenous Hawaiians).

According to the 2006 Census Bureau, 14.9 million Asian Americans are living in the United States. Asian Americans account for 5 percent of the nation's population. This number represents an increase of 63 percent from the 1990 census, thus making Asian Americans the fastest growing of all major racial and ethnic groups. The following states have the largest Asian American populations: California, New York, Hawaii, Texas, and New Jersey. The percentage of persons five years or older who do not speak English at home varies from Asian American groups: 62 percent of Vietnamese, 50 percent of Chinese, 24 percent of Filipinos, and 23 percent of Asian Indians are not fluent in English.

In addition, according to the 2006 Census Bureau, roughly 1,007,644 Native Hawaiians/Pacific Islanders reside within the United States. This group represents about 0.1 percent of the U.S. population. Out of that number, approximately 27 percent Native Hawaiians or Pacific Islanders reside in Hawaii. Some other states that have a significant Native Hawaiian/Pacific Islander population are as follows: California, Washington, Texas, New York, Florida, and Utah. It is significant that 30 percent of this group is under the age of eighteen.

Because of the lack of specific cultural health data associated with Asian and Pacific Islanders, this section will summarize the major traditional health beliefs and treatment actions that have been documented in various medical anthropological and public health documents. Although we need to continue to recognize extreme diversity in these health beliefs and treatment practices among Asians and Pacific Islanders, this overview provides a general framework for health providers and public health administrators to better understand the broad-based health disparity issues associated with Asians and Pacific Islanders.[47]

Chinese medicine, for example, may be divided into three distinct, but related, types: classical Chinese medicine, medicine in contemporary China, and Chinese alternative medicine. Classical Chinese medicine is a doctrine based on ancient texts and the principle of the yin and yang. Chinese medicine in contemporary China draws ideas from both classical and folk traditions but is a pragmatic and progressive system. Finally, Chinese medicine as it is practiced in Chinatowns in the United States is probably closer to folk medicine than to any other system. It is a medicine in practice, administered by practitioners who differ widely in background, knowledge, and skill and who are virtually free of the constraints of official supervision.[48]

The evaluation of symptoms and illness occurs against a background body image: what is in the body, what it looks like, how it functions, and how it is affected by the outside world. For some organs, such as the heart and bowels, a patient has sounds or sensations that help to locate the organ in the body. For others, like the gallbladder, one does not have evidence of the existence of such an organ or of its functioning: as a result, body image is largely a symbolic system with a tenuous connection to anatomy.

Symptoms and disease are most often explained by reference to wind, hot, and cold. A diagnosis of fright may be used to explain why a child is listless, cries at night, refuses food, or has a slight fever. Although this often is a problem related to magic in Asia, in America, fright is treated by giving the child "protect-infant-pill," a patent medicine readily available in herbal shops and Chinese grocery stores.[49]

The recommended treatment for a symptom or even the diagnostic procedures indicated may deter patients from treatment and cause them to tolerate their symptoms. Some Chinese are afraid of blood loss, hospitalization, and surgery. Many older people regard the hospital as a place to die, and they confirm that view by waiting until the point of death to go there. The association of the hospital with surgery and death as well as the problems of cost, language, and food all contribute to the practice of delaying hospital care.[50]

In traditional Hawaiian culture, illness and other misfortunes are thought to be caused by an imbalance of *mana* (energy that permeates and links all things) or loss of *pono* (rightness or proper order). Dreams are considered important sources of information, used to solve problems and to forecast events and behaviors.

Home preventive treatment, for example, is performed by Chinese Americans as a matter of routine. In hot weather, people drink cooling teas and eat more "cold" and cooling foods; in cold weather, they consume tonics in the form of soups and special dishes with herbs such as chicken or pork cooked with herbs, dragon eye, and red dates. Other "hot" foods include broccoli, rice wine, liver, mushrooms, ginger, black vinegar, peanuts, and any form of pepper. These usually are taken with the evening meal.

In addition to herbs and plants, Chinese Americans use other products with medicinal and healing practices. Some of these products were used in ancient Europe and are still used today. Other popular traditional Chinese remedies include the following: deer antlers (used to strengthen bones, increase a man's potency, and dispel nightmares), lime calcium (used to clear excessive mucus), turtle shells (used to stimulate weak kidneys and to remove gallstones), snake flesh (eaten as a delicacy to keep eyes healthy and vision clear), and seahorses (pulverized and used to treat gout).[51]

Alternative or native practitioners among Asian Americans are numerous. For example, all the major Chinatowns have numerous traditional practitioners, all of them called (in Chinese) "Chinese doctor." A "Chinese doctor" can do one or more of the following: sell herbs, diagnose minor problems from the patient's appearance and history, make pulse diagnosis, perform acupuncture, and set bones. The flood of immigrants, not only Chinese but also Thai, Korean, and Vietnamese, has provided a demand for traditional practitioners.[52]

Alternative or native practitioners vary greatly in their style and methods. For instance, traditional Chinese methods for the treatment of illness include acupuncture, moxibustion (described later), respiratory therapy, remedial massage, exercises, treatment of fractures and injuries, and herbal medicine. Although all these methods are used in contemporary China, Taiwan, and Hong Kong (China), only herbal medicine and acupuncture are common in the United States. Religious and magical healing methods, so common in Hong Kong and Taiwan, are not conspicuously present in Mainland China and the United States.[53]

Typically, the practitioner writes a prescription that the patient fills at an herbal shop. A common prescription consisting of a mixture of drugs of plant, animal, and mineral origin is boiled in a specified amount of water, and the concoction is taken internally. Sometimes practitioners prescribe patent medicines, particularly those manufactured in China in recent years.

Acupuncture is an umbrella term that includes many techniques such as acupressure, laser acupuncture, scalp acupuncture, Korean hand acupuncture, moxibustion, electro-acupuncture, and more.[54] Most acupuncture techniques involve the use of needles with mystic rituals explained by metaphysical concepts derived from ancient practices of traditional Chinese medicine. The procedure consists of puncturing the body to cure disease or relieve pain. The body is punctured with special metal needles at precise points for the treatment of specific symptoms. The most important aspect of the practice of acupuncture is the acquired skill and ability to know precisely where to puncture the skin.[55] Nine needles are used in acupuncture, each with a specific purpose. The following is a list of the needles and their purposes:

1. Superficial pricking: arrowhead needle
2. Massaging: round needle
3. Knocking or pressing: blunt needle
4. Venous pricking: sharp, three-edge needle
5. Evacuating pus: sword like needle
6. Rapid pricking: sharp, round needle
7. Puncturing thick muscle: sharp, round needle
8. Puncturing thick muscle: long needle
9. Treating arthritis: large needle[56]

Moxibustion has been practiced for as long as acupuncture. Its purpose, too, is to restore the proper balance of yin and yang. Moxibustion is based on the therapeutic value of heat, whereas acupuncture is a cold treatment. Acupuncture is used mainly in diseases in which there is an excess of yin. Moxibustion is performed by heating pulverized wormwood and applying this concoction directly to the skin over certain specific sites. Moxibustion is believed to be most useful during the period of labor and delivery, if applied properly.[57] Alternative therapeutic practices and native health practitioners play an important role in the Asian American community.

This brief review of the health culture in the context of Asian and Pacific Islander American cultures reflects a broader understanding of the factors that influence their health action. Moreover, the cultural-historical analysis of Asian and Pacific Islander American traditional health beliefs and treatment actions provides insight into the cultural bond an individual may develop toward his or her health beliefs and treatment actions.

American Indian and Alaskan Native Health Culture

American Indians and Alaskan Natives include people having origins in any of the original peoples of North, South, and Central America, who maintain tribal affiliation or community attachment. As of 2006, an estimated 4.5 million people were classified as American Indian and Alaskan Native alone or American Indian and Alaskan Native in combination with one or more other races. This racial group accounts for 1.5 percent of the total U.S. population.[58]

Approximately 1.8 million American Indians and Alaskan Natives (AI/AN) live on reservations or other trusted lands. Fifty-seven percent of AI/ANs live in metropolitan areas, and 1.3 million AI/ANs are under the age of eighteen, which accounts for one-third of this racial group.[59]

Currently, there are 561 federally recognized AI/AN tribes, and more than 100 state-recognized tribes. There are also tribes that are not state or federally recognized. Federally recognized tribes are provided with health and education assistance through a government agency called Indian Health Service, U.S. Department of Health and Human Services. The Indian Health Service operates a comprehensive health service delivery system for approximately 1.8 million AI/ANs. The majority of those who receive these services live mainly on reservations and in rural communities in thirty-five states, mostly in the western United States and Alaska, Thirty-six percent of the service area population resides in non-Native areas.[60]

Historically, the earliest accounts of AI/ANs in North America date to approximately 30,000 years ago. Archaeological evidence indicates that a small number of American Indian hunting groups filtered gradually into North America.[61] AI/ANs began to diversify as they adapted to new conditions. Despite the numerous disruptions and dislocations from their native habits, AI/AN ancient cultural traits have survived for centuries, such as the predominance of tribal or group councils, tribal languages, hunting ceremonialism, and a deeply spiritual religious and health belief system.[62]

Many AI/ANs with traditional orientations believe there is a reason for every sickness or pain. They believe that it is a price that is being paid, either for something that happened in the past or for something that will happen in the future. In spite of this conviction, a sick person must still be cared for. Everything is seen as being the result of something else, and this cause-and-effect relationship creates an eternal chain. AI/ANs do not subscribe to the germ theory of modern medicine. Illness is something that must be. Even the person who is experiencing the illness may not realize the reason for its occurrence, but it may be the best possible price to pay for the past or future.[63]

According to Navajo belief system (southwest American Indians), disease may be contracted by five basic methods:

1. Soul loss
2. Intrusive object
3. Spirit possession
4. Breach of taboo
5. Witchcraft[64]

The notion of soul loss is not a major means by which specific diseases are caused, yet there is reason to believe that the concept is important to AI/ANs. The soul, or wind, as it is most often called, enters the body soon after birth and forms the individual's basic personality. At death, the soul leaves the body and proceeds to the afterworld. Faintness and suffocation are signs that the wind-soul is leaving the body and signal the final stage of an illness.[65]

In addition, some form of breach of taboo is the most frequently reported kind of diagnosis among the Navajo. Breach of taboo is not only the commission of prohibited acts but also coming into contact with a dangerous object. The responsibility for breaking a taboo may lie with someone other than the afflicted. Thus, a pregnant woman may breach a taboo and cause her child to become ill later.[66]

There are variations in the healing procedure from tribe to tribe in different culture areas. However, some methods are nearly universal. For instance, the traditional healer of AI/ANs is the medicine man, and Natives have maintained their faith in him over the ages. He is a person wise in the ways of the land and of nature. He knows well the interrelationships of human beings, the earth, and the universe. He knows the ways of the plants and animals, the sun, the moon, and the stars. The medicine man takes his time to determine the cause and treatment of an illness and then the proper treatment. To determine the cause and treatment of an illness, he performs special ceremonies that may take up to several days.[67]

There is also a diagnostician. The function of the diagnostician is first to determine the cause of the illness and then to recommend the treatment, that is, the type of chant that will be effective and the medicine man who can best do it. The diagnostician may suggest one of three types of divination: motion in the hand (the most common form and often practiced by women), stargazing (prayers to the star spirit asking it to show him the cause of the illness), and listening (cause of the illness is determined by the sound that is heard).[68]

AI/ANs rely on the extensive use of herbal remedies. There are specific rituals to be followed when herbs are utilized and gathered. Each plant is picked to be dried for later use. No plant is picked unless it is the proper one, and only enough plants are picked to meet the needs of the patient. Timing is crucial, and procedures are followed.[69]

Various plants are thought to be good for treating a large variety of symptoms. AI/ANs who have knowledge of these plants and who are able to obtain them use them much as the general population uses aspirin.[70]

For example, the native medicines commonly included leaves, flowers, fruits, barks, seeds, or roots used for their astringent effect in diarrhea and hemorrhage. In several tribes, the root bark of dogwood is a diarrhea remedy, while the dried bark of sweet gum, often mixed with red-oak bark, is used against dysentery.[71]

In the early 21st century, AI/ANs are faced with a number of health-related issues. Many of the old ways of diagnosing and treating illness have been modified and changed. Yet it is still important to understand the framework of AI/AN traditional health culture for any intervention to truly have a long-lasting impact and positive change in their overall health status.

NEW NATIONAL ETHNIC HEALTH AND HEALTH DISPARITIES INITIATIVES

Two particular issues can make a significant impact in not only reducing health disparities but also eliminating health disparities. These two national ethnic health and health disparities initiatives are as follows:

- Bicultural health initiative
- Initiative to use technology to teach health disparities

These two initiatives are designed to address the growing diversity and lifestyles of our communities and to educate others and ourselves about the critical real-life issues affecting specific ethnic and health disparity groups in the United States.

Bicultural Health Initiative

One of the major ethnic health and health disparities issues dramatically overlooked for decades and particularly since the U.S. Census Bureau and the Center for Health Statistics have been collecting data on the U.S. population is the fact that our country consists of millions of biracial and bicultural people. In fact, the 2007 U.S. Census stated that more than 4 million people have identified themselves as belonging to more than one race.[72]

These 4 million individuals who have identified themselves as belonging to one or more race have now become the third most populous racial and ethnic group in the United States, surpassing Asian and Pacific Islanders and AI/AN populations. This number is not only remarkable but it is indication that people today feel more comfortable about acknowledging their biracial heritage than ever before. Therefore, it is time for our government and our society to give the proper attention, respect, and support for all those who decide to identify themselves as biracial.

On a personal level, many of my close family members are biracial and, at times, it is an issue that we have avoided to address simply because it is a touchy, sensitive issue for some family members. Often my relatives are pressed to answer the following question posed to them by strangers or some friends: "Do you consider yourself African American or do you consider yourself Caucasian?"

It really should not matter, but in American society, which still wants to categorize individuals based on physical traits such as skin color, that is often the question asked of a biracial individual.

To answer this question and to allow individuals who consider himself or herself as biracial, I propose not a biracial initiative but a bicultural initiative. I believe that this is perhaps the most appropriate time to propose such an initiative simply because we have a biracial president.

As the offspring from a white Kansan woman and a black Kenyan man, President Obama has had to deal with the racial categorization of his identity all his life. Debate over whether to call this son of a white Kansan and a black Kenyan biracial, African American, mixed-race, half-and-half, multiracial—or, in Obama's own words, a "mutt"—has reached a crescendo since Obama's election shattered assumptions about race.[73]

Obama has said, "I identify as African American—that's how I'm treated and that's how I'm viewed. I'm proud of it."[74]

Thus it appears that the world gave Barack Obama no choice but to be black.

Fortunately, times have changed and now individuals such as President Obama can make their choice, if they chose to decide. This is the reason why a bicultural initiative is needed now.

A bicultural health initiative is an agenda to encourage researchers, administrators, and directors of all various disciplines to learn about the specific health cultural issues associated with biracial individuals. As I presented earlier in this chapter with the other major ethnic groups, investigating one's health culture means to investigate a groups' health beliefs, values, history, and treatment practices patterns along with their sociodemographic factors. In essence, it involves taking a comprehensive, biopsychosociocultural perspective on their basic health beliefs and patterns. This type of critical health information is lacking for all those who categorize themselves as biracial. Whether through holding conferences, forums or funding new research programs, the bicultural initiative would become a significant strategy in answering health disparity issues associated with more than 4 million individuals in the United States.

Using Technology to Teach Ethnic Health and Health Disparities

One of the major pedagogical challenges in higher education related to ethnic health and health disparities is figuring out how to teach this topic to health professionals, public health administrators, and the general public who are interested and new to this field of research and public health initiative. Instead of the face-to-face traditional lecture approach, instructors and professors would use the online, distance education infrastructure within each university or college to reach more of the community at large.

These new university and college courses would be entitled "Ethnic Health and Health Disparities." Whether taught at the undergraduate or graduate level, these new online, distant education courses would accomplish the following objectives:

1. Identify and assess the major health issues associated with specific ethnic and health disparity populations
2. Describe ethnic health and health disparity cultural issues
3. Apply principles and strategies derived from public health and medical anthropology toward planning, implementing, and evaluating specific ethnic health and health disparities intervention programs in a culturally competent approach

In fact, I have been successful in implementing this very type of online, distant education course at East Carolina University for the past three years. Students used the university's Blackboard software not only to hear and view my audio podcast and webcam lectures but also to respond to the discussion board and chatroom sessions online. Since the course is entirely online, students feel less inhibited to share sensitive issues and discuss many of their concerns related to ethnic health and health disparity.

The success of this new online course not only has enabled health professionals and public health administrators to acquire new public health skill-sets that will assist them in working with and developing culturally competent health programs but also has helped to create the design of a new online twelve-credit graduate certificate program in Ethnic Health and Health Disparities at East Carolina University. The graduates who complete this certificate program will become part of the new culturally competent specialists in public health to eliminate ethnic health and health disparities in eastern North Carolina.

CONCLUSION

Now that the country has a new administration within the White House, there are high expectations that our health care crisis will soon come to an end. In fact, within the first fifty days of the Obama administration, President Obama signed legislation to reauthorize the State Children's Health Insurance Program (SCHIP), which provides an additional $32.8 billion to preserve health insurance coverage for about 7 million low-income children currently enrolled and extending coverage to an additional 4 million previously uninsured kids. President Obama also signed an executive order to allow federal taxpayer dollars to fund significantly broader research on embryonic stem cells, which could uncover cures for serious ailments, such as diabetes, paralysis, Parkinson's disease, and maybe even Alzheimer's disease.

Finally, President Obama and his administration set out to overhaul the U.S. health care system by getting the country to hold townhall meetings on health care reform. Beginning at the end of 2008 and continuing throughout 2009, townhall meetings to address health care reform throughout the United States were held by governors in several states, professional organization conferences, various federal public health agencies, and even the White House. The primary purpose of all of these meetings was not only to receive feedback from Americans and produce official documents on health care reform but also to get buy-in from Americans, because this new health care reform leading to a national universal coverage for all Americans will cost more than $634 billion over the next ten years. As President Obama stated on March 5, 2009:

We cannot delay this discussion any longer. Health care reform is no longer just a moral imperative, it is a fiscal imperative. If we want to create jobs, rebuild our economy, and get our federal budget under control, then we must address the crushing cost of health care this year.[75]

I wholeheartedly agree that something needs to be done about health care costs and health insurance for all Americans. No one in America should be without health insurance period.

Nonetheless, the strategy needed to achieve universal health care coverage in the United States is debatable. The fact that all Americans will have to pay for new universal health care coverage, particularly those who are in poverty or barely struggling to make ends meet, seems to punish them more than those who are well-off and who can pay more for a national health insurance coverage. Indeed, paying for this new universal health insurance coverage and determining which segment of the U.S. population will most likely pay more than others for their coverage will be an ongoing debate among many households, groups, agencies, media outlets, and political organizations in America. Yet, what is still missing in the current discussion of health care reform and a new universal health care coverage are the issues of *health care disparities* and *health disparities*.

As discussed, health care disparities are defined as differences in the access, use, quality, or outcomes of health care services received by racial or ethnic populations.[76] Examples of health care disparities are as follows:

- Racial and ethnic minorities have significantly *worse access* to health care compared with nonminorities.
- Racial and ethnic minorities have *lower rates* of health care services compared with whites.
- Racial and ethnic minorities are more likely *not* to have a usual source of care.
- Racial and ethnic minorities tend to receive *lower quality* of care.
- Racial and ethnic minorities are *more* likely to experience *communication problems* with their health care provider.
- Racial and ethnic minorities are *more likely* to feel *uncomfortable* asking their health care provider questions.[77]

Of course, connected to health care disparities are health disparities—in essence, the direct outcome of health care disparities. Health disparities are defined as differences in the incidence, prevalence, mortality, and burden of disease and other adverse health conditions that exist among specific population groups in the United States. At the beginning of this chapter and within each ethnic group, I highlighted the numerous and significant number of health disparities data affecting all ethnic and minority communities in the United States, particularly in the African American population.

Therefore, we must ask: Will our new national universal health care plan reduce, solve, and eliminate the health care disparities and health disparities as we know it today? I would have to say, absolutely not.

As long as we continue to avoid talking about and understanding the importance of "culture," one's specific "ethnic health culture," and "cultural competency" then all our good intentions and billions of dollars will go to waste once again. Someone must stand up and support *culture* particularly as it relates to our overall well-being, health status, life expectancy, and quality of life.

I am ready to stand up, how about you?

Chapter 6

Justice for All

INTRODUCTION

It is quite obvious that my early years growing up in rural Springfield, Ohio, made a major impression on me then and now as an adult. As a child, you think that this is how everyone in the country lived. You considered your lifestyle and living situation typical to most Americans living in the 1950s and 1960s. Living with two parents and my older brothers in a cozy small home was something that I thought all children experienced.

Since I was the youngest of the family, I was naturally protected from a lot of the social ills of society and the neighborhood. It did not take me long to understand that my parents and particularly my older brothers protected me from bullies and fights in the neighborhood, the drinking of hard liquor that occurred in the neighborhood, and the cops that patrolled our streets.

For some reason at this age, I was taught not to trust police officers. I was not taught this by my parents, because my parents always taught us to respect authority figures and obey the law. They were proud law-biding Americans and so were all of my brothers and relatives. In fact, a vast majority of my family members worked for the federal government and served in the armed services. So it was a part of our cultural history to be proud of and to serve our country.

Yet this type of respect for authority figures was not the same for police officers. The major reasons for my disconnect with police officers at this early age (five to seven years of age) had to do with what I saw on television, what I experienced in terms of how the police officers treated us in the neighborhood, and what I witnessed during a gun-fire confrontation of police officers with a neighbor. These three major incidents therefore caused me to view police officers as a threat and as a uniformed officer to fear—not as a uniformed officer who could protect me and my family.

Although my parents tried to protect us from the social ills and events of society, they could not stop us from seeing how blacks were sometimes treated by police officers on the television. One has to remember, during the late 1950s and early 1960s, there were major confrontations nationally and regionally between blacks and "the system" as a result of the changing segregation and Jim Crow laws throughout our country. On our small black-and-white television, I occasionally would see and remember how blacks were treated by police officers (the "man" or the "system") when the national or local news television program aired. I was shocked and startled to see people like me being treated so badly. I could not believe what I was seeing—blacks being beaten by cops for a wide variety of situations. From a child's perspective, after seeing these incidents repeatedly on television, you tend to build up a dislike and fear for police officers. You think that it can happen to you or a family member, so therefore you take no chances when a police officer comes in your neighborhood.

What I also remember at this age was the fact that police officers patrolled our neighborhood frequently. From a child's perspective, I could not really understand why the police cars regularly drove through our neighborhood. We had an active neighborhood in which a vast majority of folks got along well together and did not bother each other too much. Although at times, the neighborhood would get fairly lively in occasional fights and altercations and the fact that my "green tricycle" (first bike) was stolen (something I could never forget), I still did not think that it was necessary for the police to regularly patrol our neighborhood.

As stated in an earlier chapter, much of our neighborhood entertainment revolved around athletics particularly our make-shift track-and-field events in the city dump, boxing in the backyard, and playing basketball in the driveway. These were the activities that my friends and I (boys) regularly played as well as older kids—my brothers' age-group (ten to eighteen years old). So when police officers drove their cars through our neighborhood, it had to be for other reasons—not monitoring the kids' activities, but actually monitoring other people's activities.

Although we did not know the actual reasons for the police officers patrolling our neighborhood, my friends and I did not like it. In fact, I can vividly remember running away and hiding from police cars with my friends as they came patrolling down the street. In our kids' world and what we saw on television, the police officers were perceived as the "outsiders" who potentially could harm, not protect, us. The fact that the police officers were always white did not help the situation either. So, therefore, we did not trust them, which unfortunately caused us not to see police officers as human beings but as officials who represented "the system." Most blacks were not a part of this system, and at the time, this influenced us to purposely stay away from "the system." It was our way to survive in our little rural neighborhood of Springfield.

The final and most startling incident that caused me to view police officers as a threat and as uniformed officers to fear occurred the day that a whole bunch of police officers and their cars arrived at a neighbor's house just a couple of houses over across the street. The officers started shooting their guns directly into our neighbor's house. Once the gun-fire started, my mother pulled my older brothers and I down to the floor where we stayed for several minutes. There was nothing that we could do but to protect ourselves the best way that we could—stay low and don't move!

I cannot recall how long this moment lasted, whether it was seconds, minutes, or an hour or two, but I definitely can say that it made a significant and unforgettable negative impact on my childhood. I was shell-shocked and stunned that a person in our neighborhood was fired upon by police officers in such a direct confrontational way. Although I am sure that my parents told us the reason why this confrontation between police officers and a neighbor resulted in gun-fire, from a young child's perspective, it was just another reason to fear and dislike police officers. It seemed like whenever I had encounters with them or saw them on television, they always treated blacks unjustly. It just didn't seem right—even from a child's perspective.

Despite my parents' effort to protect my brothers and I from experiencing any discriminatory events during the 1950s and 1960s as it relates to the criminal justice system or experiences with the local police, to a certain extent, we knew what was going on between blacks and the criminal justice system. As children, we did not understand all the reasoning and the facts behind the national and local confrontations, yet we knew something was wrong. Additionally, it was not that we did not respect authority figures and officers of the law, we were just uncertain as to how they were going to treat us. Were we going to be treated poorly and unjustly like we heard and saw occasionally on television, or were we going to be treated like ordinary citizens? As a child, you just didn't know. That probably is the reason why I can remember vividly running and hiding from the police cars as they patrolled our neighborhood. The only thing that you did know was that people who looked like you were not treated fairly, and sometimes they got sent to jail or prison.

RACIAL DISPARITY IN THE CRIMINAL JUSTICE SYSTEM

The criminal justice system is a process of a series of points through which system personnel make decisions that result in introducing a person to the system, continuing or discharging that person from the system, and determining what will be done with the person while under supervision. Decision points range from police decisions regarding the enforcement of specific laws to parole decisions that may terminate state supervision of an offender. Virtually all of these decisions permit at least some discretion to the decision maker. The exercise of that discretion can produce racial disparity to the extent that the factors that influence the decision have a disproportionate impact on particular racial groups.

Racial disparity in the criminal justice system exists when the proportion of a racial and ethnic group within the control of the system is greater than the proportion of such groups in the general population. The causes of such disparity may be varied and include differing levels of criminal activity, law enforcement emphasis on particular communities, legislative policies, and decision making by criminal justice practitioners who exercise broad discretion in the justice process.[1]

CULTURAL HISTORY

From the beginning of our history in the United States, African Americans raised critical issues concerning the criminal justice system: procedural fairness in trials of blacks, the inequities in administration of justice (from arrest to sentencing after trial to post conviction remedies), the punishment of whites for mistreatment of blacks, and the sentences blacks and whites received for the same offense. African Americans questioned whether economic conditions were more important than race in determining treatment and whether black-on-black crime was punished.[2]

For example, the disparity in number of years sentenced to blacks versus whites for similar crimes has a long-standing history. An analysis of sentencing in the southern district of New York from May 1, 1972, to October 31, 1972, found that white-collar defendants, predominantly white, received more lenient treatment as a general rule than defendants charged with common crimes, largely unemployed and undereducated blacks, who were more likely to receive prison sentences. There was little differentiation in sentencing between blacks and whites charged with the same offense. However, most whites were charged with white-collar crime, and the only certain punishment even after conviction was a suspended sentence or a short prison term. The same criminal justice mandates certain incarceration for the so-called common crimes, with which most blacks were charged.[3]

A contemporary example of this inequity of sentencing for virtually the same offense (tax problems) between blacks and whites can be illustrated by actor Wesley Snipes and the new secretary of treasury, Timothy Geithner. African American actor Wesley Snipes was sentenced in April 2008 to three years in prison for three misdemeanor counts of failing to file tax returns—the maximum requested by federal prosecutors. Assistant Attorney General Nathan J. Hochman of the Justice Department's Tax Division said,

> Snipes' long prison sentence should send a loud and crystal clear message to all tax defiers that if they engage in similar tax defier conduct, they face joining him. There is no secret formula that eliminates a person's tax obligation, nor are there any special exceptions. The majority of Americans pay their taxes timely and accurately. Those who willfully violate the law must be held accountable.[4]

Before the sentencing, Wesley Snipes asked the court to show mercy and offered three checks totaling $5 million as a gesture of good will. Actors Denzel Washington and Woody Harrelson, as well as television judges Joe Brown and Greg Mathis, submitted letters to the judge on Snipes' behalf. This, however, wasn't enough. Federal prosecutors diverted the checks to the U.S. Treasury, which accepted the payment as a down payment.[5]

On the other hand, President Obama's secretary of treasury, Timothy Geithner, whose position includes directing $350 billion in bailout money to Wall Street, and billions more to the major banks, the automobile industry, financial institutions, and insurance companies, was discovered not to have paid $35,000 in self-employment taxes for several years. In a statement to the Senate panel considering his nomination, Geithner called the tax issues, "careless," "avoidable," and "unintentional" errors, and he said he wanted to "apologize to the committee for putting [them] in the position of having to spend so much time on these issues." Additionally, Geithner said that he was always under the impression that he was an employee, not a self-employed contractor while he served as director of the Policy Development and Review Department of the International Monetary Fund. Geithner's comments are contradicted by the Senate report that showed he not only was informed of his status, but also actively applied for the allowance.[6]

On January 26, 2009, the U.S. Senate confirmed Geithner's appointment by a vote of 60–34. Geithner was sworn in as treasury secretary by Vice President Joseph Biden and witnessed by President Barack Obama.

In both cases—Secretary Timothy Geithner and actor Wesley Snipes—confessed to making a mistake with their taxes yet one received a three-year prison term whereas the other received a new job and works with President Obama. Although the individual circumstances in these two cases were different, there is still this sense of leniency more so for whites as opposed to blacks when being judged for criminal activity.

After Emancipation in 1865 for blacks, the statistics reported by the U.S. Census Bureau indicated an increase in black criminality. This was predictable. No longer valuable property, the former slaves became despised free blacks. The criminal law was used to control and harass them. For example, in the state of Georgia, there were only 183 prisoners confined in the penitentiary in 1858, all of whom were white. In 1870, there were 393 persons confined, of whom fifty-nine were white and 334 were black.[7]

According to the U.S. Census, the total number of blacks confined in southern federal and state prisons in 1870 was 6,031; ten years later the number had increased to 12,973; twenty years later there were 14,244; and in 1904, there were 18,550. The commitment rate for blacks in 1904 was higher than that for whites; the rate for whites was 187 per 100,000 population and for blacks 268 per 100,000 population. For certain immigrants, however, the rate was higher than for blacks. Interestingly, the commitment rate for immigrants declined as they became absorbed into American life, whereas blacks remained unassimilated and with a higher commitment rate.[8]

The criminal justice system reinforced the oppression of blacks in other ways. Large numbers of black workers signed contracts to work for white planters who underpaid, overcharged, and cheated them and then prosecuted them for contract violations when they attempted to leave the plantation. Many black workers appealed to the Justice Department to protect them. Despite the federal antipeonage law of 1867, the Justice Department failed to abolish debt slavery, which continued to flourish until the 1940s.[9]

From the 1920s through the 1950s, arrests and sentencing of blacks increased dramatically. Black crime rate was consistently higher than that of whites. For instance, in the first half of 1924 in Philadelphia, blacks, who made up 7.4 percent of the population, accounted for 24.4 percent of the arrests. During the first six months of 1926 in Detroit, the black crime rate was 3.9 per 10,000 as opposed to 1 per 10,000 for whites. In the superior courts of North Carolina in 1922–1925, there were 4.65 indictments per 1,000 for whites and 8.71 per 1,000 for blacks. Nationwide, the U.S. Census Bureau reported in 1923 that blacks formed 31.3 percent of the total prison population and 23.3 percent of the commitments, in contrast to only 9.3 percent of the total adult population.[10]

Conviction and sentencing patterns gave even stronger evidence of disparity in the criminal justice system. In a 1926 Detroit study, 48.6 percent of black defendants compared with 43.8 percent of whites were convicted of felonies. Of the blacks, only 7.1 percent were given the alternative of a fine or prison sentence, compared with 13.5 percent of whites. Only 7.2 percent of blacks were given probation, while 12.2 percent of the whites received it. Altogether, 30.9 percent of the blacks and 15.5 percent of the whites were sentenced to imprisonment.[11]

Blacks not only were convicted more often than whites but also received longer sentences. For example, a 1927 study of 1,521 chain-gang prisoners in North Carolina found that 7 percent of the white prisoners and 11 percent of the blacks were serving sentences shorter than three months. On the other hand, 6 percent of the white prisoners and 11 percent of the blacks were serving sentences of three years.[12]

Finally, several events occurred in the criminal justice system to focus increased public concern on black crime rates by the 1960s. First, the Supreme Court rendered a series of decisions that served to apply most of the due process requirements of federal criminal procedures to state criminal justice systems. Because the Tenth Amendment to the Constitution left the punishment of crimes to the states, enjoining federal constitutional procedures in the state criminal justice system was a matter of great controversy.

Second, the climate of law enforcement abuse in the streets of Selma, Montgomery, and other cities was blatantly obvious and controversy was continuous over police brutality, dragnet arrests, and discriminatory official conduct. The rebellions, riots, and insurrections in the cities, carried out by blacks in reaction to the failure of both the legal civil rights changes and the Johnson administration's War on Poverty to improve their social and economic condition, usually erupted in response to perceived police brutality. As defenders of the social order, police were in the most exposed position among blacks in the cities and thus were more likely to have their activities become the precipitating cause of any rebellion.[13]

In Detroit, for example, police efforts to close a "blind pig," an illegal after-hours drinking establishment, resulted in a large-scale riot; in Watts, it was the arrest of a black man in the midst of a crowd; and in other cities, it was the shooting of black suspected criminals. During the rebellions, blacks destroyed and appropriated the property of businessmen and store owners in what many whites regarded as needless, irrational rage. The spectacle reinforced the notion that blacks were likely to be criminals, violators of law and order.[14]

Finally, in the 1960s and 1970s, blacks viewed the police as a white alien army occupying their neighborhoods. Statistics supported this characterization. For example, in 1970 blacks made up between 27 and 63 percent of the total population of Detroit, Atlanta, Chicago, and Washington, D.C., but represented only between 5 and 21 percent of the police forces in those cities.[15]

Even in my small town of Springfield, Ohio, I felt the same way in that our neighborhood was constantly monitored by white police officers. Eventually, this constant monitoring, confrontations with local neighbors, and the lack of seeing any black police officers caused me as well as many of my friends to resent police officers during this time period.

Overall, this brief cultural historical review of the African American relationship with the criminal justice system shows a pattern of injustice, discrimination, and racism in each major component of the system. Whether it is through the enactment, enforcement, or sentencing of the laws, African Americans have had just reasons to distrust the criminal justice system. Oftentimes, these experiences of the past significantly influence how African Americans perceive and interact with the 21st-century criminal justice system.

CONTEMPORARY CRIME AND INCARCERATION DATA

Since the early 1970s, the prison and jail populations in the United States have increased at an unprecedented rate. The more than 500 percent rise in the number of people incarcerated in the nation's prisons and jails has resulted in a total of 2.2 million people behind bars.[16]

The national incarceration rate for whites is 412 per 100,000 residents, compared with 2,290 for African Americans and 742 for Hispanics/Latinos. These figures show that 2.3 percent of all African Americans are incarcerated compared with 0.4 percent of whites and 0.7 percent of Hispanics/Latinos. In total numbers, African Americans now constitute 900,000 of the total 2.2 million incarcerated population.

While these overall rates of incarceration are all at record highs, they fail to reflect the concentrated impact of incarceration among young African American males in particular, many of whom reside in disadvantaged neighborhoods. One in nine (11.7 percent) African American males between the ages of twenty-five and twenty-nine currently are incarcerated in a prison or jail. Moreover, the uneven geographic distribution of incarceration in communities of color means that the effects of this situation radiate beyond the individual to the broader community.[17]

For example, the black rate of incarceration ranges from a high of 4,710 per 100,000 (4.7 percent of the population) in South Dakota to a low of 851 (0.85 percent of the population) in Hawaii. Comparing the rates of incarceration for African Americans with those for whites reveals profound patterns of racial disparity. The state with the lowest rate of incarceration for African Americans—Hawaii, at 851 per 100,000 population—maintains a rate 15 percent higher than the state with the highest rate for whites—Oklahoma, at 740 per 100,000 population. While more than 1 percent of African Americans in forty-nine states and the District of Columbia are incarcerated, not a single state in the country has a rate of incarceration that high for whites.[18]

Furthermore, an examination of the ratio of black-to-white incarceration rates by state illustrates not only the heightened use of imprisonment for African Americans, but also regional differences in how incarceration policies produce disparities. While the national black-to-white ratio of incarceration is 5.6, among the states, the ratio ranges

from a high of nearly 14:1 in Iowa to a low of less than 2:1 in Hawaii.
In seven states—Iowa, Vermont, New Jersey, Connecticut, Wisconsin,
North Dakota, and South Dakota—the black-to-white ratio of incarcera-
tion is greater than 10:1.[19]

One of the major reasons for the increased incarceration of blacks
was the change of sentencing policies for drug offenders. In the 1970s,
blacks accounted for less than 25 percent of drug arrests in the United
States. By the late 1980s, this had increased to 42 percent. Between
1976 and 1980, the percentage increase in drug arrests for whites was
70 percent compared with 450 percent for blacks. Currently, black
males incarcerated for drug offenses outnumber white males by a factor of between four and eight.[20]

In 1984 Congress directed the U.S. Sentencing Commission to create
sentencing guidelines and policies that would be "blind" to the
offenders' race, sex, national origin, creed, and socioeconomic status
and treat all offenders the same regardless of family, community, occupation, or education. This resulted in mandatory sentencing that restricted parole and limited judicial discretion at the federal level. This
new approach to sentencing included longer sentences for specific
offenses and offenders, mandatory sentences for drug and weapons
offenses, three-strike laws that imposed life sentences on repeat
offenders, and more recently truth-in-sentencing laws that require
offenders to serve at least 85 percent of their sentences. In addition,
federal-level sentencing guidelines penalized the possession of crack
cocaine, which is more likely to be used by African Americans, more
heavily than powered cocaine in a 100:1 ratio.[21]

The racial disparity in incarceration rates is also reflective in other
areas of the criminal justice system. Disparities in the system can be
seen in the following:

- The widely discussed phenomenon of "driving while black" illustrates the potential abuse of discretion by law enforcement. Traffic
  stops recorded on Interstate 95 in Maryland over a two-year period revealed that African Americans represented 70 percent of
  drivers stopped and searched by police, while only 17.5 percent of
  all drivers—as well as speeders—were black.

- A New York state study found that minorities charged with felonies were more likely to be detained than whites. The researchers
  concluded that 10 percent of minorities detained in New York
  City and 33 percent in other parts of the state would have been
  released before arraignment if minorities were detained at the rate
  of comparably situated whites.[22]

- African American youths represent 26 percent of juvenile arrests;
  31 percent of referrals to juvenile court; 46 percent of waivers to

adult court; and 58 percent of juveniles sentenced to adult prison.[23]

- A black male born in 1991 has a 29 percent chance of spending time in prison at some point in his life, a Hispanic/Latino male 16 percent, and a white male 4 percent.[24]

What is truly disturbing about much of this racial disparity data is that, on one hand, blacks are committing more criminal activity at an earlier age and thereby are becoming more susceptible to being jailed or imprisoned and, on the other hand, blacks are being wrongly convicted and imprisoned for crimes that they simply did not commit.

Homicide Rates and Blacks: The Facts

One of the most discouraging and depressing issues continuing to plague the African American community is that we have and continue to experience extraordinary high rates of homicide in our community. Whether it is in the small rural towns, the suburban sprawls, or the inner cities across America, homicide affects all of us, particularly the African American community. The fact that we have been perpetrators and victims of homicide activity makes this racial disparity issue even more perplexing.

In 1995, the homicide rate for young African American males was eight times the rate for young European American males.[25] To examine the problem of homicide in the African American population, Whitman, Benbow, and Good conducted an epidemiological review of homicide data in Chicago. In 1993, there were 850 homicides in Chicago. Whitman, Benbow, and Good stated that this number corresponds to a crude rate of 31.2 per 100,000 population.[26] The 1992 rate of 34.3 was the highest in the history of Chicago. The epidemiological analysis of the homicide rate, however, revealed some interesting tendencies.

For example, Whitman, Benbow, and Good found that homicide tends to be perpetrated on members of one's own racial or ethnic group: 93 percent of homicides committed by non-Hispanic blacks were against non-Hispanic blacks; 74 percent of homicides committed by non-Hispanic whites were against non-Hispanic whites; and 78 percent of homicides by Hispanics were committed against Hispanics. Therefore, Whitman, Benbow, and Good suggested that their study contradicted the popular image of homicide. That is, the greatest threats come not from strangers ("stranger danger") but from those we know, even those we love, and from people of the same race and ethnicity.[27]

Finally, Whitman, Benbow, and Good stated that "homicide is connected directly to poverty and disenfranchisement, through their proxy measure of race, and it must be understood that these factors, and many more, cannot be abstracted from the context of the society in which they exist.".[28] Thus, the more a population experiences increased poverty and disenfranchisement, the more likely it will experience increased homicide rates.

That is why it is so significant and revealing to examine current homicide rates and attempt to determine whether these homicide rates are a reflection of the current downturn of the economy or the result of a wide array of sociocultural factors affecting the African American family and particularly young African American men. According to the U.S. Bureau of Justice Statistics for 2005, the following current homicide trends are connected to black males:

- Black males eighteen to twenty-four years old have the highest homicide offending rates. Their rates are more than three times the rates of black males fourteen to seventeen years old and almost five times the rates of black males age twenty-five and older.

- For black males eighteen to twenty-four years old, offending rates declined after 1993 reaching a low in 2004. The rated increased in 2005.

- For black females of all age-groups, offending rates declined since the early 1990s.

- Homicide victimization rates for blacks were six times higher than the rates for whites.

- Offending rates for blacks were more than seven times higher than the rates for whites.

- Black victims are over-represented in homicides involving drugs.

- Ninety-four percent of black victims were killed by blacks.[29]

In addition to these disturbing trends, a 2008 study conducted by criminologists James Alan Fox and Marc Swatt at Northeastern University in Boston found that the number of young black men and teenagers who either killed or were killed in shootings has risen at an alarming rate since 2000. For example, in 2007, 426 black males between the ages of fourteen and seventeen were killed in gun crimes. That marked a 40 percent increase from 2000. Similarly, an estimated 964 in the same age-group committed fatal shootings in 2007—a 38 percent increase from seven years earlier.[30]

Although nationwide, the overall number of murders and violent crimes dropped, according to the Federal Bureau of Investigation (FBI), it is not dropping for black males in particular. Fox and Swatt emphasized that the racial gap will continue to grow without new countermeasures like restoring police officers in the streets and creating social programs for poor youths. They further stated that "the landscape is

quite different for countless Americas living, and some dying in vio-
lence-infested neighborhoods."[31]

The facts are the facts. Blacks are not only victims of homicide and
criminal activity, we are also the offenders. So, I pose the following
straight-forward question: What should we do and what can the government do about the homicide and criminal activities occurring at alarming rates in the African American communities throughout America?

Wrongful Imprisonment: The Facts

During the past eight years, an interesting phenomenon has been
occurring within the judicial and prison system that has directly
affected all long-term convicted prisoners who contend their innocence
particularly among black males. That phenomenon is the overturning
of criminal court decisions on individuals who were innocent and sent
to prison wrongfully. One recent wrongful conviction case in 2008
highlighted this trend.

Three times during his twenty-seven years in prison, Charles Chatman went before a parole board and refused to admit he was a rapist.
His steadfastness was vindicated when a judge released him because
of new DNA (deoxyribonucleic acid) evidence showing that, indeed,
he was not guilty of rape.[32]

The release of Chatman (forty-seven) added to Dallas County's
(Texas) nationally unmatched number of wrongfully convicted inmates.
Chatman became the fifteenth inmate from Dallas County since 2001 to
be freed by DNA testing. He served more time than any of the other
inmates, four of whom were in court to show their support. Overall,
the state of Texas leads the country in prisoners freed by DNA testing,
releasing at least thirty wrongfully convicted inmates since 2001.[33]

One of the biggest reasons for the large number of exonerations is
the crime lab used by Dallas County, which accounts for about half the
state's DNA cases. Unlike many jurisdictions, the lab used by police
and prosecutors retains biological evidence, meaning DNA testing is a
viable option for decade's-old crimes. District Attorney Craig Watkins
attributes the exonerations to a past culture of overly aggressive prosecutors seeking convictions at any cost.[34]

Fortunately in Charles Chatman's case, the Innocence Project helped
to review new DNA evidence that proved he was not involved in the
crime. What is the Innocence Project?

The Innocence Project

The Innocence Project was founded in 1992 by Barry C. Scheck and
Peter J. Neufeld at the Benjamin N. Cardozo School of Law at Yeshiva
University (New York) to assist prisoners who could be proven inno-
cent through DNA testing. To date, 237 people in the United States

have been exonerated by DNA testing, including seventeen who served time on death row. These people served an average of twelve years in prison before exoneration and release.[35]

The Innocence Project's full-time staff attorneys and Cardozo clinic students provide direct representation or critical assistance in most of these cases. The Innocence Project's mission is nothing less than to free the staggering numbers of innocent people who remain incarcerated and to bring substantive reform to the system responsible for their unjust imprisonment.[36]

For example, the efforts of the Innocence Project helped to overturn and exonerate two imprisoned African Americans—Charles Chatman and Alan Crotzer. In both cases, DNA evidence and additional testimonies were reexamined, allowing both African Americans to be freed after spending more than twenty years in prison.

The major reasons for highlighting these two Innocence Project cases of two innocent black males is to illustrate how the criminal justice system can get it totally wrong, even with the latest technology available for collecting and analyzing forensic evidence. As I have learned from not only reviewing the number of cases from the Innocence Project but also providing an overview of the criminal justice system, there is potential for error at every stage. Not surprisingly, the potential for errors dramatically increases when black males are involved in the crime. Whether the errors happened during testimonies of the victims and accused assailants, collection of forensic evidence, or attorneys representing the accused, something is seriously wrong with the U.S. criminal justice system.

Finally, what should our criminal justice system in each state do for those who are wrongly convicted and imprisoned for years? Are they liable particularly in some cases in which the evidence to convict was not reliable and exhibited a high degree of uncertainty?

So what is the right thing to do when the U.S. criminal justice system continues to send mostly black men to prison for crimes that they did not commit? In cases like that of Crotzer and Chatman, monetary compensation and a free education should be supported legislatively so that the criminal justice system in every district of all fifty states will more meticulously try every serious criminal case.[37] If this legislative act is instituted in all states, the number of innocent black males sent to prison would decrease significantly not increase as it has for several years.

THE LEGISLATURE AND THE CRIMINAL JUSTICE SYSTEM

An effective way to reduce racial disparity in the criminal justice system, particularly that of innocent individuals being sentenced to prison, could be achieved through the legislature. Legislatures at the federal, state, and local levels create the criminal justice system by passing laws that define prohibited behavior, the penalties to be imposed for violating those laws, and the processes by which cases are to be disposed and sentences are to be determined. Even county and city legislatures frequently pass local ordinances that are enforced by the police and the criminal courts. Many of these laws have a disproportionate impact on communities of color, which could have been foreseen before the laws were passed.[38]

The political furor over crime during the last fifteen years has driven legislatures to pass ever-more punitive laws resulting in enormous growth in prison and jail populations. The vast majority of inmates are people of color, and as a whole, they have been offered little in the way of training, education, and meaningful drug treatment during periods of incarceration. This enormous increase in the use of jails and prisons has taken place without persuasive evidence indicating that incarcerative strategies are the only, or even the most effective, approach to controlling crime.

This suggests the need for legislatures to treat proposed criminal legislation with the same care many now accord to other legislation. Thorough legislative impact analyses would identify probable disproportionate racial impacts and signal the need to seek alternative problem-solving strategies to eliminate or significantly lessen such effects. Indeed, a requirement to perform such analyses would slow the legislative rush to simple punishment, provoke a more deliberative strategy development process, and encourage extensive and effective use of the range of public and private resources for ensuring public safety.[39] This is precisely the place where our federal legislatures and federal justice initiatives can have a direct impact on our country's criminal justice system, particularly as it relates to the African American population.

The Obama Administration

So do any federal initiatives in the Obama administration address the racial disparity issues in the criminal justice system? The fact that criminal activity continues to increase in so many African American communities throughout the United States and those who are perpetrating these crimes are African American is still a major problem. The data speak for themselves, particularly the homicide rates for young black males. Yet for all the crimes committed by African Americans, just as many individuals would choose not to live a life of crime if given an opportunity to redirect their lives in constructive areas. The federal government can play a significant role in helping individuals to change their lives for the better by funding more crime-fighting programs.

According to the White House Web site (2009), President Obama intends to lead the nation in criminal justice reform. The site specifically states:

The President will lead the fight to build a more fair and equitable criminal justice system. He will seek to strengthen federal hate crime legislation and will work to ensure that federal law enforcement agencies do not resort to racial profiling. He supports funding for drug courts, giving first-time, non-violent offenders a chance to serve their sentence, if appropriate, in drug rehabilitation programs that have proven to work better than prison terms in changing behavior. President Obama will also improve ex-offender employment and job retention strategies, substance abuse treatment, and mental health counseling so ex-offenders can successfully re-join society.[40]

The federal agency responsible for instituting President Obama's criminal justice reform is the U.S. Department of Justice (DoJ) headed by the new Attorney General Eric Holder. The president's 2009–2019 Budget for the DoJ is $26.5 billion. The budget addresses the key priorities of the president and the attorney general, including those for National Security and crime-fighting programs in the FBI and other DoJ components, such as resources to combat financial fraud and protect the public interest. The budget funds the Community Oriented Policing Services (COPS) hiring program; ensures that prison and detention programs are adequately funded, including prisoner reentry programs; reinvigorates federal civil rights enforcement; and increases border security.

In particular, the budget provides $6 billion for the Bureau of Prisons and $1.4 billion for the Office of the Detention Trustee to ensure that sentenced criminals and detainees are housed in facilities that are safe, humane, cost-efficient, and appropriately secure. Additionally, the budget includes $109 million for prisoner reentry programs, including an additional $75 million for the Office of Justice programs to expand grant programs authorized by the Second Chance Act that provides counseling, job training, drug treatment, and other transitional assistance to former prisoners.[41]

In the budget for fiscal year 2010 released on May 7, 2009, President Obama requested $212 million for prisoner reentry programs, including $100 million for Second Chance Act programs administered by the DoJ and $112 million for Second Chance Act programs administered by the U.S. Department of Labor. The Second Chance Act programs address the issues of prisoner recidivism.

Ironically, the Second Chance Act bill was signed by former president George Bush in 2008 and developed by the chief architect Rep.

Danny Davis (D-Ill.). The measure provides more than $180 million a year in 2009 and 2010 for prisoner reentry services to curb a recidivism rate that has held steady at about 66 percent, meaning that two-thirds of all inmates released annually from state and federal prisons reoffend or violate the conditions of their release within three years and are locked back up.[42]

Among the services it calls for is help for inmates in obtaining identification documents, such as birth certificates and social security cards, before release from prison. In addition, it provides federal funding for the development of programs that deal with substance abuse, family stability, and job training and that offer financial incentives to employers who hire former prisoners. One key component at the federal level calls for the Bureau of Prisons to provide inmates with a sufficient amount of medication as they leave the facilities, in addition to connecting them with medical services.[43]

As Davis said in 2008, he hopes the bill, beyond the money, triggers a discussion at the state and local levels about incarceration and alternatives to imprisonment. He further commented:

> We add this up and the impact will be far greater than just the amount of money that gets appropriated. We know it's not a panacea. It's not close to any kind of panacea but our hope is this becomes a sort of trigger for a great deal of additional action.[44]

The Sentencing Project Initiative

One organization that has taken the lead in reducing racial disparity in the criminal justice system is the Sentencing Project Organization. The Sentencing Project is a national organization working for a fair and effective criminal justice system by promoting reforms in sentencing law and practice, as well as alternatives to incarceration. The Sentencing Project was founded in 1986 to provide defense lawyers with sentencing advocacy training and to reduce the reliance on incarceration. Since that time, the Sentencing Project has become a leader in the effort to bring national attention to disturbing trends and inequities in the criminal justice system with a successful formula that includes the publication of groundbreaking research, aggressive media campaigns, and strategic advocacy for policy reform.[45]

The Sentencing Project's publication entitled "Reducing Racial Disparity in the Criminal Justice System: A Manual for Practitioners and Policymakers" provides a final section discussing options for reducing racial disparity. Following a list of the options, they provide examples on how some of the options may reduce disparity and why they are important.

On the issue of law enforcement, the Sentencing Project (2008) suggests six areas to reduce racial disparity:

1. Conduct research and assessment of disparity
2. Develop community policing approaches
3. Monitor and record data on traffic and pedestrian stops
4. Develop alternatives to arrest
5. Develop operations and training
6. Undertake public education regarding approaches to racial disparity.[46]

In developing community policing approaches, the report suggest that police departments should institute public feedback forums to create awareness among the public and the police about cultural and racial issues, and to provide opportunities for discussion. From the law enforcement agency perspective, the forums could be designed with a "human relations approach" by using Police Advisory Boards to open lines of communication to the public; from the public's perspective, they could assess how law enforcement strategies are developed to ensure that they are the result of an assessment of constructive approaches. In addition, law enforcement agencies should launch public campaigns, in conjunction with representatives of underserved communities of color, to educate the public and members of the department on the importance of racial sensitivity and fairness in law enforcement and criminal justice, to describe what the department is doing in that regard, and to highlight the successes that have been achieved.[47]

Perhaps the most interesting aspect of this report has to do with their use of the words "cultural acclimatization." Cultural acclimatization can be part of the effort to strengthen the bonds between the police and the community. In each precinct, or community where the underserved and communities of color are prominently represented, cultural familiarity programs can be constructed for all police personnel (regardless of rank) serving that area. Such programs should be designed and implemented with representative of the community to:

- Introduce the officers to friendly local faces
- Orient them to the language, culture, and traditions of the community
- Introduce them to representatives of local institutions who can assist them in their work
- Identify the kinds of problems about which residents are most concerned, and the kinds of police tactics that are considered unnecessarily intrusive
- Explain to them styles of speech and interaction that are considered respectful and those that are considered insulting

Such orientations can be valuable to police officials who otherwise are exercising discretion in an unfamiliar context, where they do not know the people, the place, or the culture. This can reduce the officer's sense of distance from the community and their belief that the residents perceive them with hostility.[48]

Without doubt, community policing approaches and cultural acclimatization strategies for police officials have significantly helped law enforcement agencies throughout the United States to develop a better connection and rapport with local neighborhoods. It also has helped to reduce the feelings of distrust that many of us in black neighborhoods formed over many years in regards to area police departments.

The Insiders Juvenile Crime Prevention Program

An innovative program called the Insiders Juvenile Crime Prevention Program addresses the very high crime rate among African American adolescents. The Insiders Juvenile Crime Prevention Program was a juvenile delinquency deterrence program that brought youth to the Virginia State Penitentiary and exposed them to the realities of prison life. The Insiders Juvenile Crime Prevention Program was a *Scared Straight*–style program run by the inmates at the Virginia State Penitentiary. The program demonstrated the realities of prison life to youthful offenders to deter them from a life of crime and incarceration.[49]

To be eligible for participation in the Insiders Program, an individual must be between the ages of thirteen and twenty and have been judged guilty of a delinquent offense at least twice. Participants visited the Virginia State Penitentiary in groups of fifteen or fewer. They would be locked in a cell, informed about the daily routine of an inmate, and exposed to explicit lectures from inmates. Inmate lectures focused on such issues as the loss of identity and loss of freedom associated with prison life, as well as the murder, drugs, gangs, and homosexual rape that occur within prison. Lectures included verbal intimidation, harsh language, and harassment (in the form of inmates taking away participants' shirts or shoes and challenging them to retrieve them).

This juvenile crime prevention program actually worked on some of the highest risk African American black males. Although this get-tough approach had many critics, innovative approaches like the Insiders Crime Prevention Program are essential to truly challenge the criminal behavior pattern among some African American youth today.

Prison Ministry: The Tony Dungy Initiative

Former head coach of the National Football League (NFL) team the Indianapolis Colts, Tony Dungy has been on his own mission since his retirement from the NFL. As one of the few African American head coaches in league history and the first to win a Superbowl, Tony Dungy now seeks to motivate and improve the lives of men like the 500 or so felons at Hardee Correctional Institution in Florida.

On April 4, 2009, Dungy spoke to the audience at the optional meeting composed of about one-third of the inmates at Hardee, a prison southeast of Tampa where the population ranges in age from nineteen to seventy-seven. The average sentence here is twenty-nine years; the population includes inmates convicted of first-degree murder, kidnapping, assault with a deadly weapon, and child abuse. Nearly 600 inmates are serving life terms.[50]

Dungy did not merely lecture from arm's length. After his twenty-minute speech on faith and planning one's life, he was swarmed by prisoners and spent a half-hour per inmate in face-to-face conversations. In total, Dungy spent approximately six hours at Hardee Correctional facility, including more than an hour with inmates in solitary confinement. Then he went to the work camp, where he ate the prison food for lunch.

Although Dungy has made about a dozen such excursions to prisons with Tampa-based Abe Brown Ministries, dating to 1997 when he coached the Tampa Bay Buccaneers. He said on this visit:

I saw how young and impressionable a lot of these guys are. We could sit down and talk . . . about life, about sports or whatever. It's deep. The main thing is to give these guys a little hope. But this is also a gospel message. It's changing on the inside.[51]

Although Dungy admires President Obama, he turned down a White House invitation to be on a council for faith-based, neighborhood partnerships. He further stated: "I want to be helpful. If they ask for my opinion on things I'll be glad to give it. But I'm not really looking for a full-time job."[52]

The primary purpose in highlighting former NFL football head coach Tony Dungy is to show that individual, celebrity African Americans really do care about, and are attempting to make a difference for, those many African Americans who are incarcerated in U.S. prisons.

CONCLUSION

Some would say that the U.S. criminal justice system has come a long way since the civil rights years of the 1950s and 1960s. From the days in which police departments, law practices, and the judicial system were staffed predominantly by Caucasians to the early 21st century in which more African Americans are employed at all levels of the system. In fact, more African American chiefs of police, African American police officers, African American attorneys, African American judges, and African American personnel are affiliated with the criminal justice system across this country than ever before. It is as though the criminal justice system has taken an about-face in its inclusion of people of color who represent their system.

Perhaps the most important visual change of the U.S. criminal justice system is the recent presidential appointment of Eric Holder as the country's first African American attorney general and head of the DoJ. As head of the Justice Department, Holder has the opportunity to reshape the department's civil rights division, which lost several long-serving attorneys during the Bush administration, and to weigh in on dramatic racial disparities in convictions and sentencing of criminal defendants.

Interestingly, in his first major speech to the Justice Department, Attorney General Eric Holder was frank, clear, blunt, direct, and sincere about his feelings on the country's failure to address issues of race in the United States. Following are a few exerts from his speech:

> Though this nation has proudly thought of itself as an ethnic melting pot in things racial we have always been and continue to be, in too many ways, essentially a nation of cowards. . . .
>
> On Saturdays and Sundays, America in the year 2009 does not, in some ways, differ significantly from the country that existed some 50 years ago. This is truly sad. . . .
>
> I think if we're going to ever make progress, we have to have the guts. We have to have the determination to be honest with each other.[53]

Not surprisingly, the newly appointed Attorney General Eric Holder received much criticism from various mainstream political pundits, politicians (Republican and Democrat), and the general public. They all were astonished that this black man could say these types of racial things, particularly when the country has just celebrated the election of its first African American president and the appointment of its African American attorney general.

Nonetheless, the vast majority of African Americans knew what he meant by his statement and agreed. In fact, Dayo Olopade, an African American news reporter for the *Root* (an online news journal), said the following about Eric Holder's speech and President Obama's speech on race, which he gave during the 2008 campaign in Philadelphia:

> I watched Obama's 2008 race speech with my white colleagues in a conference room in Washington. It was a spectacular speech. But Holder's comments are a much more productive, proactive take on race in America and, in some ways, can be seen as a critique of the message of Obama's stump pitch. In the Philadelphia speech, Obama prettified the sentencing disparities, employment discrimination and affirmative action battles that are the province of the U.S.

Justice Department. He spent more time explaining Chicago's Trinity United Church, the subject of the uproar that prompted his address. However charming (or disarming) it seemed at the time, Holder's point is more relevant—most churches today are still all black or all white, and in 2009, such voluntary segregation isn't going to move America forward. America has embraced Obama for talking the talk. While Obama may have paved the way for him to do so, Eric Holder is walking the walk.[54]

Indeed, that is how many African Americans felt about Holder's speech. Yet one significant African American disagreed. That person was President Barack Obama. When asked about the attorney general's speech, President Obama said he would not have used the same language that Holder did. Although he understood Holder to be saying the country often is uncomfortable talking about race, Obama is not someone who believes that constantly talking about race can solve racial tensions. To address that problem requires fixing the economy, putting people to work, making sure that people have health care, and ensuring that children are learning.[55] The president also said, "I think if we do that, then we'll probably have more fruitful conversations."[56]

Whether you agree or disagree with Holder's speech, the fact remains that the United States continues to have a serious problem with its criminal justice system. Not surprisingly, the population that has experienced and continues to experience the worst relationship with the criminal justice system is the African American population. History shows us, the current data show us, and now current policies show us that African Americans will continue to be affected disproportionately and negatively by the criminal justice system.

At one time in my early years of life, I was afraid of and felt threatened by police officers who patrolled our neighborhood. During those early years, police officers were a symbol that represented "the man" and "the system," both of which African Americans did not belong to.

Now that I am much older, I have come to greatly respect police officers and all those who try their best to protect all citizens in every neighborhood in America. Nonetheless, I do understand how some in my community, particularly young African American males, may see them as a threat and feel fearful of them. Yet it is up to us—African Americans—and all those who work in the criminal justice system to find new ways to come together in positive, constructive, culturally competent ways so that all Americans, particularly those who have been persecuted, imprisoned, incarcerated, and killed unjustly, can live and work in safe neighborhoods throughout all parts of America.

Maybe someday, there will be justice for all citizens of the United States.

Chapter 7

It's Time for Reparations

INTRODUCTION

Have you heard it? Can you feel it again? Have people been talkin' about it in the barbershops, hair salons, and churches across the country? Well, the rumblings are stirring up again in the black community about the issue of reparations.

As mentioned at the beginning of the book, reparations is a proposal made by some people in the United States that some type of compensation should be provided to the descendants of enslaved people. Reparations would be paid in consideration of the labor provided for free over several centuries, which has been a powerful and influential factor in the development of the country.[1] The issue of reparations has been a very touchy, sensitive, and polarizing topic in United States for years, simply because a majority of blacks and whites have opposing opinions about it. For the most part, blacks are in support of some type of reparations (financial or symbolic compensation) and whites are not. Although there are many exceptions to this broad generalization, just the word reparations can invoke an emotional response from an individual whether black or white.

A fascinating aspect of the issue of reparations is the fact that the federal government is bailing out U.S. banks, insurance companies, automobile industry, other financial firms, and states with billions and billions of dollars. On Tuesday, February 10, 2009, U.S. Treasury Secretary Timothy Geithner outlined the Obama administration's plan for an expanded taxpayer bailout of the banks. The plan will not only inject tens of billions of additional dollars into financial firms, but also use Treasury funds and Federal Reserve loans to offload worthless bank assets onto the public by means of a so-called Public-Private Investment Fund.[2]

With all this new-found money going from the U.S. taxpayers to the federal government and then to all the banks and auto industry, surveys were conducted to ask the general public what they thought about this massive bailout and how they felt about the fact that their money would be used to bail out these companies. In a *USA Today/Gallup* Poll conducted in March 2009 of 1,007 adults, 59 percent said they disapproved of even the federal loans already given General Motors and Chrysler last year to keep them out of bankruptcy court. Asked about their approval of five government policy actions in response to the recession, respondents disapproved most of the loans to automakers. The public's dislike of the auto loans may be one reason the administration moved to oust Chief Executive Officer (CEO) Rick Wagoner.

Senior auto industry analyst Stephen Spivey commented on this situation:

> The public is obviously very angry about all these bailouts the companies are getting. By showing Wagnoner the door, the administration can say, "Look, we're doing something here. We're not giving them money for no reason."[3]

The public's anger and discontent with the billions of bailout dollars going to these companies are particularly heartfelt in the African American community. One could hear the African American discontent through various media outlets, such as local talk radio stations and television programs across the country. Nationally, C-SPAN, public television, and radio stations captured the best and most vivid accounts of the general public's and African Americans' opinions about the bailouts.

This is exactly when the rumblings, the talk, and serious discussions among blacks returned to the issue of reparations. Speculation continued to grow in the black community as to how much more federal monies will go to these banks and automakers and not one red cent of the bailout monies will go to the black community for reparations. This lack of attention to the issue of reparations for slavery is particularly disheartening for African Americans because President Obama is African American. Of course, technically and professionally, it should not influence his decision regarding reparations, but it should at least be an issue that he considered to be culturally relevant, especially since the economic, social, and cultural issues related to reparations for slavery have not been resolved. From this African American perspective, that is the very least an African American president should do.

This was also the time during which I began to reflect on my childhood and teenage years in the 1960s and 1970s about the issue of reparations and to examine how African Americans in my familial and social network thought about this issue. The major reflections that I could recall was that blacks really felt empowered and much more proud of who we were, what we looked liked, and how we expressed ourselves. You could see and feel it every day whether it was at school or in the neighborhood. We had a sense of pride and accomplishment. Although we still were being denied basic civil rights across the country at this time, we knew that we had built this country, and it was built on our free, enslaved labor a century earlier.

In fact, during the year in which our country celebrated its bicentennial (1976), I graduated from high school. This year was special for the country and for my fellow high school graduates because we would be the one class from Xenia High School to graduate during our country's red, white, and blue bicentennial year. It was a special year for all citizens.

Yet in black communities across the country, it was a time of reflection. We were reflecting and self-evaluating our social, economic, and political status in this country simply because after some 200 years, blacks began to wonder why they should celebrate this bicentennial with the rest of America. The black experience was definitely different from other groups during the past 200 years. Yet because of this bicentennial year, African Americans came together as one once again.

Nonetheless, for some in the black community, this was asking too much. In fact, my favorite comedian of all time (even ahead of my second-most favorite comedian Eddie Murphy) and a favorite comedian of many younger African Americans at the time was Richard Pryor. Richard Pryor was a straight forward, witty, stylish, acting type of black comedian who made fun of everyday life. Pryor particularly contrasted African American culture and all of its humorous characters with ways that blacks had to adapt to white society.

Already a successful comedic-actor, Pryor continued to release his edgy comedy albums. During 1976, Pryor released his special bicentennial comedy album in which he specifically contrasted black society with white society. The major theme of Pryor's album, and particularly his comedic skit entitled "Bicentennial Prayer," was that he hoped that the United States finally would recognize the contributions of black Americans and that black America should recognize that blacks still are treated like second-class citizens even after 200 years.[4]

This is the very reason why 2009 feels so similar to the year 1976. As the country celebrates its first African American president, and with a renewed sense of togetherness shared among a vast majority of Americans, we are nonetheless reminded that a large percentage of African Americans are treated as second-class citizens in such areas as education, health care, housing, employment, criminal justice system, and poverty. So, it should not be shocking that African Americans have a renewed interest in the issue of reparations. If the current administration is able to allocate billions of dollars to companies that African Americans helped build and supported from the beginning, then African Americans, too, should receive their bailout. It may just be the only way for African Americans to get what is owed to them after 234 years.

A BRIEF HISTORY OF THE REPARATIONS ISSUE

To understand why the connection between sociocultural, economic, and political issues and the concept of reparations is so important to African Americans, we need to take a step backward to get a better sense of its significance to generations of African Americans and European Americans who helped settle and develop the United States. This is really the only way to recognize that this issue of reparations will not go away until it is truly resolved for all parties involved in the institution of slavery.

The first Africans arrived in the New World in 1502; by the time the slave trade ended in the 1860s, more than 100 million blacks had either been killed or transported from their homeland. Although statistics on the trade are imprecise, it appears that from 400,000 to 1 million of the 10 to 50 million Africans forcibly transported to the Americas came to North America between 1619 and 1808, when the legal slave trade ended. Hundreds of thousands more, captured in wars started by Europeans, were smuggled into the states illegally until 1860. Eventually, the raids of such groups as the Ashanti and Dahomey so disrupted and depopulated West African states that rulers began to protest against the trade. African rulers, unfortunately, were powerless to stop the trade.[5]

Legally, every African enslaved in the South and all of his or her descendants were bondsmen for life. Before 1800, however, it was relatively easy for planters to free slaves, and many of them did, especially among the Methodists in Maryland and the Quakers in North Carolina. Increasingly during the 19th century, however, Southern states erected hurdles to Emancipation, masters had to petition the legislature, post a bond (usually $500), and pay for transportation out of the state for any slave they liberated.[6]

There was no protection for the slave's family, because bondsmen were legally incapable of marriage, the family was nonexistent in the eyes of the law. The master could not only separate members of a slave's family at will, but also could avoid any punishment for committing adultery with his bondsman's "wife" or for the rape of the bondswoman. There was no enforceable minimum standard of labor, food, clothing, or housing for slaves.[7]

Whether an African-born slave or American-born slave, blacks pursued continuous rebellions, conspiracies, and attempts to escape from bondage. Slaves ran away and joined Native tribes, established small communities of runaways in southern swamps, murdered slaveholders, and resisted enslavement in countless ways. Although they were unarmed on most occasions, they waged war against slaveholders and risked retaliation from state militias and the U.S. Army. The most notable of these revolts occurred in 1831 when Nat Turner and his black army struck unsuccessfully for freedom in Southampton County, Virginia, and killed fifty whites in the attempt.[8]

In spite of the debates among economists, there is considerable evidence that slavery throughout the South was profitable for individual planters. In capitalistic America, no business enterprise could have lasted from 1619 to 1865 (almost 250 years) without being profitable. The planters and their slaves produced enough tobacco, rice, sugar, and cotton to form the foundation for American prosperity before the Civil War.[9]

From a historical perspective, the importance of the institution of slavery in the United States is evident in three areas. First, it was the major determinant of American race relations. The legacy of slavery led in the 19th century to the institution of Jim Crow laws—laws designed to separate blacks and whites—to segregated housing and schools, to discrimination in the dispensation of justice, to myths about interracial sex, and to economic and political oppression. Second, slaves played a crucial role in the transformation of African cultural elements and the creation of a unique black culture in the Americas.[10]

Third, although African slaves contributed much to American culture, they stood as America's accuser. As long as black people labored in chains, the Declaration of Independence and the Constitution symbolized America's ability to lie to itself. Having lived so long with this lie, European Americans found it increasingly difficult to resolve the dilemma between equality and discrimination once they had ended the conflict between slavery and freedom.[11]

Thus, reparations stem from a "breach of contract" between newly freed slaves and the U.S. federal government. The formal period of slavery ended as a result of the Emancipation Proclamation, signed in 1863 by President Lincoln. In January 1865, slaves were promised, among other things, "a plot of not more than (40) forty acres of tillable ground" in Special Field Order No. 15, issued by General William T. Sherman. But three months later, the order was rescinded by President Andrew Johnson, and the U.S. federal government seized the land it already had given to 40,000 blacks in Florida and South Carolina. In the end, approximately 4 million American-born slave men, women, and children across the nation were freed without one red cent.[12]

Although this initial act of reparations for blacks at the time of the Civil War and the Emancipation Proclamation was rescinded by President Andrew Johnson, it caught the attention of many other individuals and organizations thereafter. It was not until 1969 when James

Forman, a former executive secretary of the Student Nonviolent Coordinating Committee (SNCC) and organizer of the Black Economic Development Conference in Detroit, demanded at a church service in New York City that blacks receive a down payment of $500 million for unpaid servitude during slavery. Eventually, the controversy, debates, and events surrounding James Forman's incident, inspired liberal Yale law professor Boris Bittker to write "The Case for Black Reparations" in 1973.[13]

Bittker examined closely the idea of filing lawsuits over blacks' past mistreatment. For Bittker, it made sense to pursue reparations not through litigation but through legislation funded from government revenues. In the years that followed, the United States did just that by vastly increasing spending on social welfare, education, housing, and urban programs aimed at relieving black poverty.[14]

The movement reemerged in the late 1980s. This time, its advocates came mostly from law schools and embraced what Bittker had once ruled out: lawsuits against private parties.[15]

U.S. Rep. John Conyers, Jr.

In January 1989, U.S. Rep. John Conyers, Jr., representing Michigan's Fourteenth District, first introduced bill H.R. 40, the Commission to Study Reparation Proposals for African Americans Act. He has introduced H.R. 40 every Congress since 1989, and he will continue to do so until it is passed into law.

One of the biggest challenges in discussing the issue of reparations in a political context, is deciding how to have a national discussion without allowing the issue to polarize his party (Democrats) and the nation. Conyers has advocated for nearly two decades that the federal government should undertake an official study of the social, political, and economic impact of slavery on the nation.[16]

Conyers has requested the number of the bill, H.R. 40, as a symbol of the forty acres and a mule that the United States initially promised freed slaves. This unfulfilled promise and the serious devastation that slavery had on African American lives has never been recognized officially by the U.S. government.

Conyers legislation does four things:

1. Acknowledges the fundamental injustice and inhumanity of slavery
2. Establishes a commission to study slavery and its subsequent racial and economic discrimination against freed slaves
3. Studies the impact of those forces on today's living African Americans
4. Allows the commission to make recommendations to Congress on appropriate remedies to redress the harm inflicted on living African Americans.[17]

In fact according to this bill, the commission's recommendations should address, among other issues, the following questions:

- Whether the U.S. government should offer a formal apology on behalf of the people of the United States for the perpetration of gross human rights violations on African slaves and their descendants
- Whether African Americans still suffer from the lingering affects of slavery
- Whether, in consideration of the commission's findings, any form of monetary compensation of the descendants of African slaves is warranted
- Whether the commission finds that such compensation is warranted, what should be the amount of compensation, what form of compensation should be awarded, and who should be eligible for such compensation?[18]

Like the Dr. Martin Luther King Holiday bill, Mr. Conyers has seen the support for H.R. 40 increase each year. Currently, the bill has more than forty cosponsors, more than at any time in the past. What is also encouraging is the dramatic increase in the number of supporters for the bill among members of Congress who are not members of the Congressional Black Caucus (CBC). Support also extends outside of the Congress as various city councils and other local jurisdictions have supported his bill. The city councils in Detroit, Cleveland, Chicago, Dallas, Washington, D.C., and Atlanta have passed bills supporting H.R. 40.

Finally, Mr. Conyers said the following about reparations on his U.S. House of Representative Web site:

It is fact that slavery flourished in the United States and constituted an immoral and inhuman deprivation of African slaves' lives, liberty and cultural heritage. As a result, millions of African Americans continue to suffer great injustices. But reparations are a national and a global issue, which should be addressed in America and in the world. It is not limited to Black Americans in the U.S. but is an issue for the many countries and villages in Africa, which were pilfered, and the many countries, which participated in the institution of slavery. Our country can no longer afford to leave slavery in the past and the issue of reparations for African Americans must be resolved.[19]

The impact of this bill cannot be overlooked anymore because it says that the U.S. Congress is ready to address the issue politically, socially, economically, and most important, symbolically.

Randall Robinson

Randall Robinson is founder and past president of TransAfrica, the African American organization he established to promote enlightened, constructive U.S. policies toward Africa and the Caribbean. In 1984, Robinson established the Free South Africa Movement, which pushed successfully for the imposition of sanctions against Apartheid in South Africa, and in 1994, his public advocacy, including a twenty-seven-day hunger strike, led to the United Nations multinational operation that restored Haiti's first democratically elected government to power.

Robinson is probably best known for his book entitled "The Debt: What America Owes to Blacks" (2000). In this powerful and controversial book, Robinson made a persuasive case for the restoration of the rich history that slavery and segregation severed.[20] Drawing from research and personal experience, he showed that only by reclaiming their lost past and proud heritage can blacks lay the foundation for a viable future.

Throughout the book, Robinson described the national and local events of the days and how they conflicted or agreed with his personal philosophy on race relations. He challenges blacks and whites to truly reassess the issue of reparations and why it is so important to resolve:

> We would begin a healing of our psyches were the most public case made that whole peoples lost religions, languages, customs, histories, cultures, children, mothers, fathers. It would make us more forgiving of ourselves, more self-approving, more self-understanding to see, really see, that on three continents and a string of islands, survivors had little choice but to piece together whole new cultures from the rubble shards of what theirs had once been. And they were never made whole. And never compensated. Not one red cent.[21]

What readers and audiences brought away from his book and his lectures on the issues related to reparations was the clear fact that the United States has not provided any compensation, monetarily or symbolically, to African Americans since slavery ended in the 1860s. Simply put, African Americans deserve to be paid.

U.S. FEDERAL AND STATE GOVERNMENT INITIATIVES

Because of the increased interest among specific African American organizations regarding Conyers' proposed bill, an actual legislative resolution passed and was approved by U.S. House Representatives that apologized to black Americans for slavery. In late July 2008, Rep. Steve Cohen, a Jewish American, who represented a majority-black district in Memphis, sponsored the resolution. Interestingly, his measure was cosponsored by forty-two members of the CBC, including Rep. James E.

Clyburn (D-S.C.), the House majority whip; Rep. John Conyers, Jr. (D-Mich.), chairman of the Judiciary Committee; and Rep. Charles B. Rangel (D-N.Y.), chairman of the Ways and Means Committee. A total of 120 lawmakers, including two Republicans, cosponsored the resolution.[22]

After the resolution passed, Cohen said,

> I hope that this is part of the beginning of a dialogue that this country needs to engage in, concerning what the effects of slavery and Jim Crow have been. I think we started it and we're going to continue.[23]

Surprisingly, this U.S. House of Representatives' apology actually came after the apologies of six other states—Maryland, Alabama, North Carolina, Virginia, Florida, and New Jersey. In Florida, for example, the move was promoted by state senator Tony Hill, a black Jacksonville Democrat, who worked with ruling Republicans in the House and Senate to craft the resolution.

On Wednesday, March 26, 2008, the state of Florida passed a resolution apologizing for state slavery laws dating back to 1822—decades before Florida became a state. Legislators in both chambers sat in silence as historian John Phelps, a former House clerk, read a summary of state laws from the 19th century that denied even basic freedoms to slaves.

This former Florida state law stated:

> Slaves could be subject to 39 lashes of a whip, administered to a bare back, for raising a hand or addressing a white person with language deemed to be abusive or offensive. For crimes as common as robbery, slaves could have their ears nailed to wooden posts for an hour or even be sentenced to death.[24]

The Florida resolution punctuated the fact that although slave-era laws are gone, they should not be forgotten. The resolution calls for healing and reconciliation among all residents of the state.

Additionally two months earlier, the state of New Jersey, the first state north of the Mason-Dixon Line passed a resolution apologizing for slavery. New Jersey had 12,000 slaves, one of the largest populations in the Northern colonies. According to the state resolution number 270,

> The Legislature of the State of New Jersey expresses its profound regret for the State's role in slavery and apologizes for the wrongs inflicted by slavery and its after effects in the United States of America; expresses its deepest sympathies and solemn regrets to those who were enslaved and the descendants of those slaves, who were deprived of life, human dignity, and the constitutional protections accorded all citizens of the United States; and we encourage

all citizens to remember and teach their children about the history of slavery, Jim Crow laws, and modern day slavery, to ensure that these tragedies will neither be forgotten nor repeated.[25]

The growing support and resolutions from several states to apologize for slavery has caused many individuals to wonder about whether the U.S. federal government, particularly the Obama administration, will join in the movement not only to apologize for slavery but also to compensate blacks for the institution of slavery.

THE OBAMA ADMINISTRATION

Although President Obama and his administration have not spoken one word about reparations, and have not forwarded any federal initiatives to address the issue, an international event in April 2009 indicated the administration's stance. When the Obama administration announced it would boycott the United Nations Durban Review Conference on Racism in Geneva, Switzerland, designed as a follow-up to the 2001 World Conference Against Racism (WCAR) held in Durban, South Africa, mainstream American news media insisted the boycott had to do with Israel. But a decision that has followed the boycott seems to have indicated the second half of the Obama administration's demand—"that references to reparations be taken out of the document"—may have been just as, if not more, important.[26]

When Barack Obama was sworn in as president, many people believed that the U.S. position would change from the previous administration in that the United States would attend the conference and agree to the conferences' executive document on the issue of racism. But rather than simply deciding to participate, the Obama administration announced that it wanted to assess the negotiations on the outcome document. In February 2009, the announcement came that the United States would boycott the conference unless its outcome document changed to drop all references to Israel and the defamation of religion. A second U.S. demand (underplayed by the mainstream American media) was that the conference should not take up the issue of reparations for slavery. The Obama team announced that it would be prepared to reengage if the negotiations brought about a "shortened" text of the document that met the criteria.[27]

Apparently, the conference leaders and the United Nations High Commissioner for Human Rights made changes to the final document as requested by the Obama administration. The Durban review committee:

- Withdrew language related to reparations
- Removed the proposed paragraph related to the transatlantic slave trade being a crime against humanity

- Removed proposed paragraphs designed to strength the Working Group of Experts on People of African Descent
- Weakened overall efforts related to people of African Descent.

After these changes were implemented, the Obama administration still decided that the changes were not good enough and failed to attend the conference.

Reparations supporters and African American U.S. legislators such as CBC Chair Barbara Lee were disappointed in the Obama administration's boycott of the conference. Additionally, Vermillia Randall, law professor at University of Dayton, described the decision as devastating. In her March 2009 newsletter she stated,

> Unfortunately, the Durban Review Conference is being hijacked by governments and members of civil society, including the Obama administration, who may not have the elimination of racism and racial discrimination, especially for African and People of African Descent, as their highest priority.[28]

Actually, the Obama administration's decision to boycott this conference on racism and completely avoid talking about the reparations issue coincides with Obama's stance as a presidential candidate stance in which he completely opposed reparations for slavery. In August 2009 at a campaign rally, the Democratic presidential candidate said, "I have said in the past—and I'll repeat again—that the best reparations we can provide are good schools in the inner city and jobs for people who are unemployed."[29]

So why is President Barack Obama opposed to reparations? Obama said an apology would be appropriate but not particularly helpful in improving the lives of black Americans. Reparations could also be a distraction. When Obama was pressed for his position on apologizing to blacks or offering reparations, Obama said he was more interested in taking action to help people struggling to get by. Because many of them are minorities, he said, that would help the same people who would stand to benefit from reparations.[30]

Thus, I pose the question like I normally do in the college courses that I teach each semester: Dare to Speculate—Are there any other possible reasons why President Obama would be opposed to reparations to descendants of enslaved Africans?

Although at this time, I cannot find a clear reason as to why President Obama continues to oppose any form of reparations for descendants of enslaved Africans, I can speculate that it has to do with realistically being the president for all people of America not just being the president for blacks in America. By the end of his first or second term, this issue of reparations will have to be dealt with by

President Barack Obama and his entire administration, particularly as more African Americans begin to discover President Obama's core values. Are these values based in an American mainstream value system or are they based in an African American core value system? One would think that it really does not matter, but in the case on reparations, it seriously does matter for millions of Americans. Only time will tell.

THE COMMISSION TO STUDY REPARATION PROPOSAL FOR AFRICAN AMERICANS ACT

I agree with Rep. John Conyers Jr. of Michigan that the most effective political, social, and cultural approach in resolving this issue of reparations is to organize a commission to study reparations. On November 20, 1989, Conyers introduced H.R. 3745 and twenty years later (as of June 1, 2009), it still had not passed both the House of Representatives and the U.S. Senate.

This bill is designed to do the following:

- Acknowledge the fundamental injustice, cruelty, brutality, and inhumanity of slavery in the United States and the thirteen American colonies between 1619 and 1865
- Establish a commission to examine the institution of slavery, subsequent de jure and de facto racial and economic discrimination against African Americans, and the impact of these forces on living African Americans, to make recommendations to the Congress on appropriate remedies, and for other purposes.[31]

What is so fascinating about this Conyers' proposed bill is that this commission will not only attempt to thoroughly investigate how the federal and state governments supported the institution of slavery in constitutional and statutory provisions but also will examine the lingering negative effects of the institution of slavery on living African Americans and on society in the United States.

Another interesting aspect of Conyers' proposed bill is the selection of the commission. According to the bill, the commission shall be composed of seven members, who shall be appointed, within ninety days after the date of enactment of the Act and appointed as follows:

- Three members shall be appointed by the president.
- Three members shall be appointed by the speaker of the House of Representatives.
- One member shall be appointed by the president pro tempore of the Senate.

The most significant aspect in selecting the commission members is that all members of the commission shall be people who are especially qualified to serve on the commission by virtue of their education, training, or experience, particularly in the field of African American studies. In other words, commission members should be culturally competent regarding African American culture.

As a cultural anthropologist trained and experienced in African American culture, I highly support this requirement simply because it requires commission members who understand, appreciate, and respect the culture of African American people as well as its history. Therefore, a commission member can be of any racial, ethnic, gender, or political background just as long as they are committed to thoroughly investigation all the various factors related to the institution of slavery in the United States. This is a legislative proposal that I believe all Americans would be ready to support, particularly as we celebrate the election of the nation's first African American president.

CONCLUSION

As a young adult, I really did not give the issue of reparations much thought. I heard about the major issues related to reparations, yet did not think that it could be successful in any capacity. Just the ideal of repaying back an entire group of people (African Americans) for an event (slavery) that happened centuries ago did not seem plausible at the time. My opinion dramatically changed, however, as I learned more and more about the institution of slavery and its detrimental psychosociocultural affects on African Americans and European Americans.

Although I had learned about the institution of slavery as a young child from my parents, the local school system, public education programs, and television movies (for example, *Roots*), the issue did not resonate with me until I had to tell my children how we as African Americans were once enslaved in this country. To see their facial expression and witness their behavior when my wife and I explained to them that our African American ancestors were once enslaved in America, it made me feel empty inside as a human being. It was unimaginable to them that an entire group of people had no rights at all and that many of these people (enslaved Africans) in the past were related to us, which we discovered when we researched our genealogy.

As I reflected on my children's reaction to the news that our families were once enslaved, I naturally thought about my own childhood experience. I'm sure I asked my own parents the same questions. The questions that I often asked myself were as follows: How could this have happened? And what did our country do to make up for this terrible thing that they did to my people?

In time, I learned how my ancestors were forced to come to this country and were forced to live in a new world that instituted slavery for centuries. I also learned that even after the institution of slavery was ruled unlawful, the Jim Crow segregation system prevailed for decades, thereby keeping a vast majority of blacks in a permanent underclass situation.

I do not recall learning anything about how the nation apologized for this wrongdoing. Although the United States has come a long way with civil rights laws, mandates for equal opportunity and even the election of the first African American president, I cannot recall the country ever apologizing formally or paying monetarily for this unjust institution to descendants of enslaved Africans and African Americans.

As a proud African American who feels grateful to have been born and raised in the Midwestern part of our United States (also a proud Buckeye/Ohioan), I am still amazed how much we have become so much a part of American culture. Just imagine, in the same society that enslaved us for centuries, our people are now leaders (President Obama, Attorney General Eric Holder) of the major institutions that keep the United States functioning on a daily basis. That itself is re-markable.

I therefore think it would be possible for this country to honor and respect the people who significantly gave their hearts, souls, spirits, and lives. It would be the most honorable and symbolic thing to do. In the age in which we memorialize, commemorate, and ritualize practi-cally every group of people or specific cause in the United States, we need to find a respectful cultural way to resolve the issue of repara-tions for descendants of enslaved Africans and African Americans: It's time for reparations.

Chapter 8

Race Relations: Can We All Just Get Along?

INTRODUCTION

One of the most critical issues that has divided and brought together people of all ethnic and racial backgrounds in our United States is race relations. In our industrial society, race relations refers to the ability of two distinctively different populations to get along with each other whether it is living in the same or adjoining neighborhoods, sharing job situations, attending the same school systems, cohabitating or marrying, or even socializing in public venues. Throughout our melting pot history, Americans of all racial and ethnic backgrounds have had to endure varying types of race relations with each other. As we all know, some race relations went smoothly, whereas others have faced major confrontations physically, verbally, socially, politically, and culturally.

Historically, African Americans have had to constantly struggle to achieve positive race relations with whites in America. The one media project that truly captured this struggle between blacks and whites is the documentary and book entitled *Eyes on the Prize*.[1] The six-part PBS television series and book, which came out during the late 1980s, brought America's civil rights years to life with stories about the people and places of that time. The documentary and book featured the heroes and heroines, the brilliant strategies, the national politics and politicking, the violence, the people who defended segregation as a Southern "tradition," and the faces of the unheralded people, black and white, who were the soul of the movement. Overall, this *Eyes on the Prize* series chronicled these extraordinary times as a segregated America was forced, in a single decade, to take a giant step from a feudal state toward a free and open democracy.[2]

Seeing and reading how black and white race relations unfolded in the *Eyes on Prize* series reminded me again of my childhood experiences during the 1950s, 1960s, and 1970s. As I had mentioned earlier, my family moved from Springfield, Ohio, to Wilberforce, Ohio, in the early 1960s. Although these small rural towns were only a few miles apart, the impact that the move had on my socialization and exposure to mainstream white society was enormous.

Once we settled into the town of Wilberforce and the Valley neighborhood, my brother Dwight and I, along with all of my neighborhood African American friends, were bused to the predominant white elementary, junior high, and high schools of Xenia, Ohio. From second grade to my senior year in high school, I had to endure a thirty-five- to fifty-minute bus ride from Wilberforce (Route 42) to Xenia and a thirty-five- to fifty-minute ride back home when school was completed. Although the town of Wilberforce is only two miles outside of Xenia, it was the constant stopping and starting of picking up all the kids along the way that made our trip so long every day. What made it even longer was the fact that our stop in Wilberforce was usually the very first stop the bus driver made so therefore we had to be at the bus stop before the sun came up.

As a kid, you do not realize the importance of busing as much as an adult. It was just a means to get to a new school and experience new people. Yet busing during this time period was an attempt to get as many African American kids from Wilberforce and neighboring communities to integrate the primary and secondary schools of Xenia, Ohio, and to improve race relations between blacks and whites.

As a second grader, I was somewhat insulated from the tensions of black and white race relations. The experiences that my older brother had in sixth grade were dramatically different from my second-grade experiences.

For example, my best friend in second grade at Tecumseh Elementary was a Caucasian boy named John. We became best friends because we were in all the same classes together and we were both fairly shy. Both of us had a hard time "fitting in" with the rest of the kids so we tended to hang out together during lunch and recess. In fact, I even got to know his mom when she visited school, and his family invited me to their home on occasion. I do not know why, but they never made me feel different or out of place when I visited their home. That was one of my better race relations experiences at an early age.

Nonetheless, I had many other experiences that were quite the opposite. Some Caucasian children did not want to socialize with me or other African American children. Those kids stayed away from us, and we stayed away from them. Although we shared the same school building, classrooms, lunch areas, and teachers, most of us knew that certain people were simply not going to get along. Therefore, we stayed in our separate clichés or groups to avoid causing any more friction than need be, at least as it related to race relations.

In general, my race relations experiences in my primary and secondary school years in the Xenia public school system were positive. Indeed, there were times in which I heard and saw confrontations and fights between blacks and whites. There were times, in which I was called derogatory names by certain students, but I did not let it affect me and eventually I ignored them. Some days, you would think that race relations would never improve simply because so much dissention remained between blacks and whites, along with the social class issues between the haves and have-nots. Yet on other days, you felt that the school system was a shining example of how blacks and whites could get along based on the interracial social groupings, interracial academic groupings, interracial dating, and interracial sporting activities.

Another aspect that improved my race relations experiences with Caucasians at school was that I played sports. I was fortunate to have played and started on my junior high and high school football teams for six straight years. Although we still had our select racial and class groupings off the field, on the field, we played as one regardless of the racial issues in school. The friendships and bonds that I had with my fellow Caucasian teammates along with my African American teammates broke many of the racial barriers that existed in school.

Ironically, my race relations experiences with Caucasians during my primary and secondary school years in Xenia, Ohio, prepared me for the type of drastic race relations issues during my college years at Miami University (Ohio). From 1976 to 1983, I attended Miami University in Oxford, Ohio. At that time, approximately 1 to 2 percent of the student population at Miami University was black (and this is a mid-American public university).

As you can imagine, there were few blacks on and off campus. On most occasions, when I saw another black person walking in my same area or far away and we spotted each other, we would give each other a nod. This nod of the head was a reminder to help each keep that connection as African Americans regardless of the extremely low number of blacks on campus. It was our way of saying just keep doing what you are doing.

As for my relations with Caucasians at Miami University, it was similar to my primary and secondary school years. My best friends were Caucasians and we had the greatest times socially and academically from my freshman year to my senior year.

Yet there were also plenty of times and situations in which as a black person, I felt out of place, and the other students made you feel out of place. In those moments, I just ignored the racist looks and minded my own business. After awhile, I realized that these types of discriminatory experiences on campus not only made me stronger as a black person but also made me adapt in varying ways to overcome other people's prejudices.

Another aspect that improved my race relations experiences with Caucasians at Miami University was that I played on the football team. On several different occasions at social events on campus, I am sure that my football player status allowed me to overcome some of those discriminatory situations. As similar to my high school football team-mates, the friendships and bonds that I developed with my fellow Caucasian teammates along with my African American teammates broke many of the racial barriers that existed in college.

The major reason for highlighting my childhood and college experiences with race relations with whites was primarily to compare my experiences with documented scholarly reports on race relations. What I discovered in looking at my race relations with whites was that not only did I benefit socially and culturally from my early primary and secondary school years' exposure to a predominately white school system but also I benefited from being raised in a close-knit African American neighborhood in Wilberforce and the Valley.

There, I learned to know who I was ethnically. There, I learned to appreciate my history. There, I learned to connect with people who looked like me. There, I established my closest friends (Donnie, Karl, Leigh Anne, and Lucreatia). There, I learned that African Americans have the right to live like the rest of mainstream society. There, I learned to appreciate my skin color. Finally, there, I learned that I had a loving and hard-working family. All too often, we fail to recognize how our own experiences with race relations, even in small rural Mid-western towns such as Xenia and Wilberforce, Ohio, captured some of the similar issues that took place in large urban areas throughout history.

CONTEMPORARY RACE RELATIONS ISSUES

It is truly amazing to see how far race relations have improved between blacks and whites in our country since the civil rights movement years and my childhood years. Many of the issues that caused racial confrontations and tensions in the past, such as interracial friendships, interracial dating and marrying, primary and secondary school choice, college choice, job selections, voting, and even just sitting in the front portion of a bus are things of the past. So whether one is young, middle age, or elderly, a vast majority of Americans most likely would say that race relations have improved, right?

Interestingly, a Gallup Poll conducted during the summer of 2008, right before Barack Obama's nomination as Democratic presidential candidate, found that blacks and whites continue to have profoundly different perspectives on the prevalence of racism in America and a modest narrowing in some of those gaps along with a jump in optimism about the future. A record 58 percent of Americans said that race relations "eventually will be worked out," while 38 percent said there will "always be a problem." For the first time since the Gallup Poll began regularly asking that question in 1993, slightly more African Americans took the optimistic view over the pessimistic one.[3]

This latest Gallup Poll included 702 non-Hispanic whites, 608 non-Hispanic blacks, and 502 Hispanics and was conducted between June 5 and July 6, 2008. Sample comments from participants were as follows:

"I don't believe we've totally overcome everything that's necessary for equality, but I do believe things are getting better," said Ricardo Russell, a 30-year-old African American retail sales manager from Oak Park, Michigan.

"They're better than they used to be, that's for sure. It's the younger people who are doing this," said Susann Matarese, a 52-year-old medical receptionist from Port Charlotte, Florida who is Caucasian and who is not entirely comfortable with the interracial dating she increasingly sees.

"There was a time when people couldn't live in certain places, but now it seems as long as you have the money you can live anywhere. There are a lot more disadvantaged black people than there are white," said Angela Ross, a 44-year-old, African American stay-at-home mom from Houston, Texas.[4]

Additional major findings from the Gallup Poll were as follows:

- Blacks and whites continue to see different worlds when it comes to race. Two-thirds of non-Hispanic whites said they are satisfied with the way blacks are treated in the United States, and two-thirds of blacks say they are dissatisfied.

- Most blacks identified racial discrimination as a major factor in a list of problems the African American community faces, including shorter life expectancies than whites and a higher likelihood of going to prison. Most whites call racism a minor factor or not a factor in those situations.

- Blacks' views have improved a bit when it comes to equality in employment and housing, though a wide gap with whites' views remains. Now, 52 percent of African Americans said blacks have as good a chance as whites to get any housing they can afford, a jump of 8 percentage points from 2007. And 43 percent of African Americans said blacks have as good a chance to get any kind of job they are qualified for, up five points from 2007 and up ten points from 2005.

- The gap between blacks and whites in assessing race relations seems to be narrowing. In 2007, 75 percent of whites and 55 percent of blacks said black-white relations were good, a twenty-point gap. In 2008, that difference of opinion dropped to nine points.

- Most Americans said race relations are getting better. Eight in ten whites and seven in ten blacks say civil rights for blacks have improved in the past decade. Nearly as many say civil right will improve over the next decade.[5]

Four months after this Gallup Poll, Americans elected their first African American as president of the United States. Not surprisingly, another Gallup Poll was conducted immediately following the presidential election in November 2008. Apparently, Barack Obama's election inspired a wave of optimism about the future of race relations in the United States.

Confidence that the nation will resolve its racial problems rose to a historic level. Two-thirds of Americans predicted that relations between blacks and whites "will eventually be worked out" in the United States, by far the highest number since Gallup first asked the question in the midst of the civil rights struggle in 1963.[6]

In this poll of 1,036 adults, optimism jumped most among blacks. Five months earlier, half of African Americans predicted the nation eventually would solve its racial problems. Now, two-thirds see this as a possibility.[7]

Additional major findings from this postelection Gallup Poll were as follows:

- Those surveyed saw Obama's election as a seminal moment in African American history.

- One in three respondents called it the most important advance for blacks in the past 100 years.

- Thirty-eight percent of respondents described the election as one of the two or three most important advances in race relations.

- Ten percent of respondents described the election as not important on race relations.

- Twenty-eight percent said race relations in the country will get a lot better; and 42 percent said that race relations will get a little better.[8]

Perhaps one way to illustrate the significance of Barack Obama's election to African Americans as the first African American president of the United States comes from the commentary written by Robert Robinson, an African American deputy managing editor at *USA Today*.[9] In describing how he felt about the election, Robinson said the following:

> As I watched the election results on the big screen with my family Tuesday night and heard the announcement that the 44th president of the United States would be Barack Obama. I found myself fighting back tears as I thought of just how far we have come as a country.
>
> I thought about growing up in the Deep South and about my grandparents, who lived in a George Wallace governed Alabama.
>
> I thought about being born in 1955 and growing up in a city that was clearly black and white. I thought about how we'd go to the movies on Saturday, pay at the front box-office window and then have to go around to the side of the building and up the long iron steps to the balcony where the blacks had to sit. That was just the way it was.
>
> I thought about all the racial fights that interrupted my freshman year of high school because people still had not accepted integration. I can still see the rebel flags flying to this day.
>
> I thought about my single-parent mom working as a maid for most of her life, leaving her home to clean other people's homes and wash their clothes just to feed her six children.
>
> But Tuesday night, November 4th, 2008, showed me that if you persevere, anything is possible. Those things can change and will change if we would work together as one, believe in each other and look beyond our differences. Tuesday, November 4th, said that it is our differences that make us who we are and what we can be as a people and as a nation.
>
> I didn't think about the war, job layoffs, the sinking economy, the high cost of gas or the rising cost of food. None of that seemed to matter.
>
> Instead, I thought about what a great time it is to be alive and living in America.[10]

In general, that is how a vast majority of African Americans felt after the presidential election. Not only were we going to get our first African American president, but we also were able to release all of the pent-up frustration from past discriminatory and racist acts against us. Thus, the newly elected Barack Obama as president symbolized a change of status and a new day in race relations for all Americans, particularly African Americans.

THE OBAMA ADMINISTRATION

Let's face it; Barack Obama greatly benefited being an African American running for president of the United States during the 2008 presidential election. Not surprisingly, presidential candidate Barack Obama received a consistent high number of votes from blacks (95 percent) and other communities of color (Latino, Asian, Pacific Islanders, and Native Americans) throughout the primaries and general election. The fact that no other African American democratic candidate has been considered seriously to run for president since Jesse Jackson (1984 and 1988) and Shirley Chisholm (1972) tells us that our U.S. society still has an issue about race and politics.

As I had stated in my previous book *Black America, Body Beautiful: How the African American Image Is Changing Fashion, Fitness, and Other Industries,*[11] the current image of African Americans in mainstream American politics has changed significantly over the past few years. Gone are the days in which African American politicians touted their civil rights credentials and agendas as though they were special badges of honor and status that only African Americans achieved. The senior brigade includes Rep. Charles Rangel (D-N.Y.), Rep. John Lewis (D-Ga.), Rep. Bobby Rush (D-Ill.), Rep. Maxine Waters (D-Cailf.), Rev. Al Sharpton, and Rev. Jesse Jackson; these men and women, who regularly protested for civil rights, were considered street smart.

Ironically, African American politicians strive to assert more of their commonality with the mainstream populous and less with their African American base. An article titled "The New Black Brigade: Today's African American Politicians Have an Energy All Their Own" suggested that young African American politicians such as former U.S. senator Harold Ford, Jr., and former U.S. Senator and presidential candidate Barack Obama are part of a new guard of black leadership that is just waiting to burst forth.[12] Polished, suave, handsome, light-skin complexion, and highly educated, Barack Obama and Harold Ford targeted a wide range of ethnic groups and have downplayed racial identification and racial appeal. In fact, Obama was more successful than the older African American politicians in garnering crossover votes, while also recognizing a need to maintain the votes of his African American constituency.

For example, Barack Obama, the son of a Kenyan father and a white American mother and best-selling author of two books—*Dreams from My Father: A Story of Race and Inheritance*[13] and *The Audacity of Hope: Thoughts on Reclaiming the American* Dream,[14] differs markedly from the typical African American politician. When Obama delivered his inspirational keynote speech at the 2004 Democratic Convention, Americans witnessed a new image for an African American politician.

According to political reporter Benjamin Wallace-Wells, Americans encountered a new type of political character. He was black, but not quite. He spoke white, with the hand-gestures of a management consultant, but also with the oratorical flourishes of a black preacher.

Supporters and critics have likened Obama's popular image to a cultural Rorschach test, a neutral persona on whom people can project their personal histories and aspirations. Obama's own stories about his family's origins reinforce his "everyman" persona. In addition, Eugene Robinson, a *Washington Post* opinion columnist, characterized Obama's political image as "the personification of both-and, a messenger who rejects 'either-or' political choices, and [one who] could move the nation beyond the cultural wars of the 1960s."[15]

So regardless of all the political pundits in print and television media along with the president's press secretary, Robert Gibbs, President Obama's race and his style of downplaying his ethnicity not only helped him to capture the presidency but also is reflected in his popularity among the American public. This fact is not lost among the National Association for the Advancement of Colored People (NAACP) and even local school districts that have renamed their schools after President Obama.

For example, Ludlum Elementary School in Hempstead, New York, on Long Island, renamed their school after Obama just after the presidential elections in November.[16] Jean Bligen, principal of Barack Obama Elementary School on Long Island, said the idea for the name change came from fifth graders who held mock debates before the election and were excited about Obama's win. They therefore changed the name of school. How many times has this type of thing happen after a president is elected?

Another example of how President Obama's race plays a pivotal key role with his base constituency, African Americans, is reflected in the comments by Benjamin Todd Jealous, president and chief executive officer of the NAACP. During his second month as president of the United States, Jealous said that President Obama's election and presidency is even more heartfelt among African Americans during Black History Month.

"We celebrate whenever a glass ceiling is broken and the presidency may be the highest glass ceiling," said Benjamin Todd Jealous. While Obama's breaking of the color barrier in the White House may make the NAACP's job easier, Jealous said they will pressure Obama just as they have pressured past presidents. He specifically said, "We won't be post-racial until we are post-racism."[17]

So has the new Obama administration embraced the fact that his candidacy and now presidency are connected to how he handles race relations issues for the country? Some political pundits would say, yes, whereas others (such as me) say, no.

The Administration's Support for Race Relations Issues

There are two major visible areas in which the Obama administration has supported race relations issues in 2009: appointed cabinet positions and civil rights White House issues. The most visible sign in which President Obama wants to address race relations issues is through his nominations and confirmation of political appointees to his cabinet. Those who are selected and confirmed to a cabinet post with the administration not only help to support Obama's major political agenda but also help to symbolize a new beginning for the new administration. That is exactly what Obama attempted to do in his political appointments to his cabinet.

Overall, Obama picked five women, four blacks, three Hispanics, and two Asians as cabinet-level appointments. Although two of his nominations had to resign (Bill Richardson and Tom Daschle) because of their failure to pay taxes, Obama's cabinet is one of the most diverse in history. By comparison, President's Bush's first cabinet in 2001 had four women, two blacks, one Hispanic, and two Asians. Additionally, President Clinton's first Cabinet in 1993 had four women, four blacks, and two Hispanics.

President Obama's Cabinet is as follows:

- Hillary Rodham Clinton, Secretary of State (woman)
- Eric Holder, Attorney General and Justice (first African American)
- Gary Locke, Secretary of Commerce
- Tom Vilsack, Secretary of Agriculture
- Arne Duncan, Secretary of Education
- Robert Gates, Secretary of Defense
- Steven Chu, Secretary of Energy (first Asian American)
- Kathleen Sebelius, Secretary of Health and Human Services (woman)
- Jane Napolitano, Secretary of Homeland Security (Hispanic/ Latina)
- Shaun Donovan, Secretary of Housing and Urban Development
- Ken Salazar, Secretary of Interior (Hispanic/Latino)
- Hilda Solis, Secretary of Labor (Hispanic/Latina)
- Ray LaHood, Secretary of Transportation
- Timothy Geithner, Secretary of Treasury
- Eric Shinseki, Secretary of Veterans Affairs (Asian American)

Finally in one of President Obama's most controversial nominations, Sonia Sotomayor became the first Supreme Court Judge whose heritage is Puerto Rican. Ironically, her nomination and confirmation hearings provoked more debate about the issues of race than the administration anticipated. There was also lively discussion on how one's race or individual life experiences gives an individual a certain "empathy" to see and feel how other people live. Although this word "empathy" and some of her comments caused much controversy, by the end of the hearings this was a good thing for everyone—even Supreme Court Justices.

Ironically, one of the first interesting cases that Supreme Court Justice Sotomayor will have to rule is the "reverse discrimination" claim that arouse when a Connecticut city rejected results of a civil service test for firefighter promotions because whites scored disproportionately higher than blacks. In the firefighter's case, city officials in New Haven, Connecticut, offered a written civil service test to firefighters seeking promotions. Of the 118 applicants for promotion to captain or lieutenant, fifty were racial minorities. No blacks and only two Hispanic/ Latino applicants qualified for promotions based on their score.[18]

City officials said they feared that, if the results were certified, they would hurt black firefighters and the city would face bias lawsuits. Eighteen candidates (seventeen white and one Hispanic/Latino) sued under the Constitution's equality guarantee and Title VII of the Civil Rights Act. They said the results should not have been discarded. Lower courts rejected the case, saying there was no unlawful discrimination because the city threw out the results and no one received a promotion based on the test.[19] As for Supreme Court Justice Sotomayor, how she votes and decides on this case will definitely reflect the philosophy of the Obama administration on race relations.

The second most visible area in which the Obama administration addresses race relations issues is the civil rights area of the White House agenda. Although the word "race" is not included in any of the White House agenda issues, reexamining their two major programs for Civil Rights shows a connection.

For example, the two civil rights issues that the White House lists are the Anti-Discrimination Laws and the Criminal Justice Reform. Under the Anti-Discrimination Laws, President Obama signed the Lilly Ledbetter Fair Pay Restoration Act on January 29, 2009. The Lilly Ledbetter Fair Pay Restoration Act ensures that all Americans receive equal pay for equal work. The civil rights division of the Justice Department is to ensure that voting rights are protected and Americans do not suffer from increased discrimination during a time of economic distress. President Obama continues to support the Employment Non-Discrimination Act and believes that U.S. antidiscrimination employment laws should be expanded to include sexual orientation and gender identity. He supports full civil unions and federal rights for lesbian, gay, bisexual, and transgendered (LGBT) couples and opposes a constitutional ban on same-sex marriage.

As for criminal justice reform, the White House Web site states that the president will lead the fight to build a more fair and equitable criminal justice system. He will seek to strengthen federal hate crime legislation and will work to ensure that federal law enforcement agencies do not resort to racial profiling.[20]

Barack Obama's Race Relations Issues

First and foremost no one can possibly evaluate the trials and tribulations that Barack Obama has had to endure throughout his lifetime, particularly as it relates to his racial and ethnic identity. In his book *Dreams from My Father: A Story of Race and Inheritance,* Obama passionately traces his family's unique history and gives the reader a psychological and cultural insight into what it is like to be raised and to grow up as a biracial individual.[21] The description of his best-selling book is as follows:

> In this lyrical, unsentimental, and compelling memoir, the son of a black African father and a white American mother searches for a workable meaning to his life as a black American. It begins in New York, where Barack Obama learns that his father—a figure he knows more as a myth than as a man—has been killed in a car accident. This sudden death inspires an emotional odyssey—first to a small town in Kansas, from which he retraces the migration of his mother's family to Hawaii, and then to Kenya, where he meets the African side of his family, confronts the bitter truth of his father's life, and at last reconciles his divided inheritance.[22]

In fact, in the beginning of his book, Obama described the confusion many people often experienced when trying to figure out his racial and ethnic identity as a kid. He said:

> They know too much, we have all seen too much, take my parents' brief union—a black man and white woman, an African and an American—at face value. As a result, some people have a hard time taking me at face value. When people who don't know me well, black or white, discover my background (and it is usually a discovery, for I ceased to advertise my mother's race at the age of twelve or thirteen, when I began to suspect that by doing so I was ingratiating myself to whites), I see the split-second adjustments they have to make, the searching of my eyes for some telltale sign. They no longer know who I am.[23]

Even Barack admits that his personal history is not representative of the black American experience that most people think of when they think of the typical African American.

For all those who are still unfamiliar with his childhood history and roots, following is a brief history. Obama was born in Honolulu and lived with his mother and grandparents in a tenth-floor two-bedroom apartment. Obama's mother married an Indonesian and, in 1967, they moved to Jakarta. Obama's sister Maya was born there. They lived first in a humble home on Haji Ramli Tengah Street with chickens and ducks in the backyard, and later in a Dutch colonial-style house in one of the most prestigious neighborhoods in Jakarta. Obama first attended a Catholic school, Franciscus Assisi Elementary, and later a state-run secular school, Menteng 1 Elementary.

At age ten, Obama returned to Hawaii, where he lived with his grandparents until he was eighteen. He was a student at the Punahou School and played basketball on a team that won the state championship his senior year.

Obama's roots include his late mother who was born in Kansas and his maternal grandmother who grew up in Augusta, Kansas. His late father was from Kogelo, a village in western Kenyan. Obama's half-brother, step-grandmother, and other relatives still live there.[24]

Obama's unique family history and his historic rise to national political prominence caught the attention of mainstream American audiences when he delivered his speech at the 2004 Democratic National Convention. When Obama said, "There is not a black America and white America and Latino America and Asian America—there's the United States of America," it was exactly what Americans wanted to hear. In fact in his book *The Audacity of Hope* Obama said,

> For them, it seems to capture a vision of America finally freed from the past of Jim Crow and slavery, Japanese internment camps and Mexican braceros, workplace tensions and cultural conflict—an America that fulfills Dr. King's promise that we be judged not by the color of our skin but by the content of our character.[25]

Additionally, Obama stated that although many commentators and political pundits suggested that he meant that we have arrived at a "postracial politics" or that we already live in a color-blind society, he vehemently denied it. The fact that Obama recognized that his own upbringing hardly typified the African American experience and that his position as a U.S. senator at the time insulated him from most of the bumps and bruises that the average black man must endure; Barack specifically recalled how he was discriminated against because of being a person of color:

> I can recite the usual litany of petty slights that during my forty-five years have been directed my way: security guards tailing me as I shop in department stores, white couples who toss me their car keys as I stand outside a restaurant waiting for the valet, police cars pulling me over for no apparent reason. I know what it's like to have people tell me I can't do something because of my color, and I know the bitter swill of swallowed-back anger.[26]

Obama's public acknowledgment on the importance of race relations issues in his life as a private citizen, as a U.S. senator, and later as a presidential candidate came full circle when he had to make his now-famous race speech in Philadelphia. On March 18, 2008, presidential candidate Obama delivered a speech entitled "A More Perfect Union" and addressed the controversy surrounding the comments made by his former pastor Rev. Jeremiah Wright as well as several race relations issues associated with his presidential campaign. The massive media coverage over Obama's race speech not only elevated his presidential democratic candidacy but also enamored him with the mainstream media (including NBC, CBS, ABC, MSNBC, and CNN). The fact that mainstream media had a difficult time addressing the issues of race and race relations without coming off as "racist," particularly when talking about Obama as serious political candidate, gave candidate Obama the upper hand. He became the one and only political figure who could talk about race and racism. From that point forward, whatever presidential candidate Obama said became "gold" in the eyes of the mainstream media, mainstream America, and the African American community.

This speech that presidential candidate Obama delivered was exactly the type of race speech that the country needed to hear. In his speech, Obama even said the following about the legacy of slavery:

> But race is an issue that I believe this nation cannot afford to ignore right now. . . . We do not need to recite here the history of racial injustice in this country. But we do need to remind ourselves that so many of the disparities that exist in the African American community today can be directly traced to inequalities passed on from an earlier generation that suffered under the brutal legacy of slavery and Jim Crow.[27]

Whether or not President Obama feels the same about race and racism as he did when he was running for the Democratic presidential nomination, confronting race and race relations should be high priorities for the Obama administration. For some reason thus far in his presidency, they are not. Thus, I reaffirm what I said earlier in this chapter: The Obama administration has not confronted culturally the issues of race and race relations, particularly as they relate to the African American community. The time is now, not later, when it is politically correct or when the poll numbers say it is okay to talk about them.

THE RACE RELATIONS INITIATIVE

Most Americans recognize that we live in a global environment and that we must try to learn more about other people and other countries of the world. Most Americans also realize that we must try to find a better way to get along with as many cultures and varying political governments of the world as possible. This is a challenge for any country, and particularly so for the United States.

I say that the U.S. federal government will continue to struggle with the challenge of finding a better way to get along with other cultures and varying political governments of the world for two reasons. The first involves how the American ideologies of capitalism, democracy, and leadership tend to place the United States' policies and initiatives ahead or above other countries policies and initiatives.

For example, the Obama administration's boycott of the 2009 United Nations conference on racism illustrated how our federal government refused to take part in a worldwide conference that was attempting to examine all aspects of racism, including reparations. Although the U.S. representatives were successful in eliminating many of the sensitive racial topics that were to be discussed and documented at this significant conference, they were not successful in eliminating the frank discussion about racism and reparations around the world. Therefore, U.S. representatives from the Obama administration boycotted the event.

Interestingly, members of the Congressional Black Caucus felt that it was important for the Obama administration to attend, despite all the negative comments highlighted by the American mainstream media. In fact, Barbara Lee, the Congressional Black Caucus chair said,

This decision is inconsistent with the administration's policy of engaging with those we agree with and those we disagree with. By boycotting Durban, the U.S. is making it more difficult for it to play a leadership role on U.N. Human Rights Council as it states it plans to do. This is a missed opportunity, plain and simple.[28]

Since avoiding race relations issues appears to be the policy of the Obama administration, it is apparent that we need to start a race relations initiative not only to address global race relations issues but also—and primarily—to address domestic race relations issues that have been surely overlooked for decades in the United States.

If the Obama administration needs a model to follow or a framework for guidance on how to start a nationwide dialogue, discussion, and debate on race relations, it does not have to look far. In fact, former President Bill Clinton and his administration developed and implemented a Race Initiative during Clinton's second term.

On June 14, 1997, former president Bill Clinton announced "One America in the 21st Century: The President's Initiative on Race."[29] Although his Race Initiative did not fulfill its overall objectives and was highly criticized by political parties, ethnic groups, and scholars in various academic fields, Clinton nonetheless used his position as president of the United States and his own childhood experiences growing up in segregated Arkansas to engage the nation in a dialogue about race and race relations. The former president recognized that even as America rapidly became more of a multiracial democracy, race relations remained an issue that divided the nation.

Clinton's Race Initiative had five major goals:

1. To articulate the president's vision of racial reconciliation and a just, unified America
2. To help educate the nation about the facts surrounding the issue of race
3. To promote a constructive dialogue, to confront and work through the difficult and controversial issues surrounding race
4. To recruit and encourage leadership at all levels to help bridge racial divides
5. To find, develop, and implement solutions in critical areas such as education, economic opportunity, housing, health care, crime, and the administration of justice—for individuals, communities, corporations, and governments at all levels.[30]

The president convened an Advisory Board of seven distinguished Americans. Lead by respected African American scholar John Hope Franklin, the Advisory Board worked with the president to engage the many diverse groups, communities, regions, and various industries in the country. The Advisory Board consisted of Dr. John Hope Franklin, Angela E. Oh (lawyer), Linda Chavez-Thompson (American Federation of Labor–Congress of Industrial Organizations [AFL-CIO]), Gov. Thomas Kean (New Jersey), William Winter (former governor of Mississippi), Robert Thomas (businessman), and Rev. Suzan Johnson Cook (Bronx, New York). The Advisory Board was asked to join President Clinton in reaching out to local communities and to listen to Americans from all different races and backgrounds, so that the country could better understand the causes of racial tensions.

After the year-long community forums about race across the country, President Clinton presented his Race Initiative report to the American people and coordinated the efforts through a new White House Office headed by Ben Johnson.[31] A number of scholars and civil rights advocates said the board and the president squandered an opportunity to make a bold contribution to stimulating an informed discussion of race that moved beyond the familiar positions of liberals and conservatives. Critics claimed that the report offered only modest recommendations and a creation of a permanent presidential council on race.[32]

Overall, the report was filled with policy suggestions on education, affirmative action, health, the criminal justice system, and immigration. It underscored the following four recommendations as major:

- Creation of a permanent body, which would be known as the President's Council for One America, to promote harmony and dialogue among the nation's racial and ethnic groups.
- The government's development of an education program to keep the public informed about race in America.
- A presidential "call to arms" to leaders of government and the private sector to "make racial reconciliation a reality."
- Engagement of youth leaders in an effort to build bridges among the races.

In addition to their main recommendations, the report urged tighter enforcement of the nation's civil rights laws, an end to sentencing disparities for crimes involving crack on one hand and powder cocaine on the other, greater spending on teacher training and school construction in minority areas, and efforts to end income inequality. It reaffirmed the Clinton administration's support for race- and sex-based affirmative action, declaring that "for far too many minorities, a level playing field remains a mirage."[33]

Ironically, a decade later after President Clinton's Race Initiative and One America in the 21st Century, the country is still struggling with the issues of race and race relations. For some reason, no other administration (Bush and Obama) has followed up on Clinton's Race Initiative. This is particularly perplexing when we think about the fact that the Obama administration, with the most diverse cabinet in American history and led by the first African American president, does not have a race relations initiative. Think about that for a moment. Although there have been many reports over the past couple of years that President Obama does not really get along with former president Clinton, whether it is due to Hillary Clinton's presidential campaign, or the remarks that Bill Clinton made during her campaign, or the fact that former president Clinton is so well respected in the African American community (even Obama talks about Clinton's close relationship with the black community in his book, *The Audacity of Hope*), we have to give former president Clinton, a Caucasian male, credit and acknowledgment for forcing America to talk about the sensitive issues of race and race relations a decade ago. Surprisingly, the Obama administration and former president Bush steered cleared from this sensitive issue. Dare I ask this final simple question? Why have past and current administrations avoided the issues of race and race relations in America?

By now, you know the answer—politics.

CONCLUSION

It took only one simple press conference during President Barack Obama's early days in the White House to make him and the rest of the country realize that the country has a long way to go before we really are a "postracial society." The incident occurred at the end of President Obama's press conference on July 22, when he responded to the final question regarding the arrest of African American Harvard Professor Henry Louis Gates by a Caucasian Cambridge, Massachusetts, police officer. The key phrase that got President Obama in hot water and political trouble with the country was the "acted stupidly" remark about the Cambridge police.

Although the incident had started a national debate about racial profiling, the president's remarks heightened the race relations issue to a completely new level. Two days later, the Cambridge police officers defended their officer's arrest of Professor Gates in a press conference, and President Obama held his own press conference stating that he regretted saying those words to describe the incident. By the end of this race relations nightmare, President Obama invited both individuals—Professor Henry Louis Gates and Cambridge Police Sgt. James Crowly to the White House for beer. Unfortunately, this issue was never truly resolved, thereby causing blacks and whites to further hold onto their misperceptions of each another.

Interestingly some say that Barack Obama's election as president may be seen as an indicator of a colorblind society, but a new study suggests that derogatory racial stereotypes are so powerful that merely being unemployed makes people more likely to be viewed by others—and even themselves—as black. The fact that our westernized society has enculturated us to believe that certain occupations or status are more affiliated with certain racial and ethnic groups, such as being unemployed means that the individual is more likely to be black than white, does us all a disservice simply because we know those who are really unemployed encompass a wide array of racial and ethnic individuals. In a long-term survey of 12,686 people, changes in social circumstances such as falling below the poverty line or being sent to jail made people more likely to be perceived by interviewers as black and less likely to be seen as white.[34]

Andrew Penner, researcher, and Aliya Saperstein, a sociologist at the University of Oregon, examined data from the federal Bureau of Labor Statistics' National Longitudinal Survey of Youth. Though the ongoing survey is focused primarily on the work history of Americans born in the 1950s and 1960s, participants have provided interviewers with information on a variety of topics, including health, marital status, insurance coverage, and race.

On eighteen occasions between 1979 and 1998, interviewers wrote down whether the people they spoke with were "white," "black," or "other." The researchers found that people the interviewers initially perceived as white were roughly twice as likely to be seen as nonwhite in their next interview, if they had fallen into poverty, lost their job, or been sent to prison. People previously perceived as black were twice as likely to continue being seen as black if any one of those things occurred.[35]

For example, 10 percent of people previously described as white were reclassified as belonging to another race, if they became incarcerated. But if they stayed out of jail, 4 percent were reclassified as something other than white. The effect has staying power. People who were perceived as white and then became incarcerated were more likely to be perceived as black even after they were released from prison.[36]

What the study basically showed was that social status also affects the perception of race. Researchers have long recognized that a person's race affects his or her social status, but this study was the first to show that social status also affects perceptions of race. This is consistent with the view that race is not a fixed individual attribute, but rather a changeable marker of status.[37]

The major reason I highlighted this study at the end of this chapter is to shed light on what it is like to be an African American professor in mainstream academic institutions. During the past twenty-five years, I have been fortunate to have academic appointments as a teaching instructor and college professor at several universities. This is a profession that I spent years training to improve my skills as an instructor; this is a profession that I wanted to work extra hard at to ensure that I excelled as a professor; and most important, this is a profession that I loved from day one.

There is nothing like being a college professor. This is the one occupation that you get to share your knowledge with others, you get the freedom to express your views (some of the time), and you get to learn some thing new about life every day. Since I have always loved school as a child, it is a dream come true to be a college professor.

Yet I am somewhat disappointed, saddened, and still surprised to see the reaction from some of my students during the first day of class when the semester begins. When I walk into the classroom after all the students are seated and face the students to introduce myself, the reaction on their faces is always a "surprised look." There I am right in front of them—a short-stature (5'4"), dark-browned skinned, middle-age African American professor.

Students react in so many different ways. Some students simply stare, stare, and stare in amazement. Some students have a grin on their face. Some students have a frown on their face. Then some students simply get up and leave the classroom as soon as I begin to speak. Interestingly, these student reactions are not just from Caucasian students, but they come from all ethnicities (African American, Hispanic/Latino, and Asian). No student is exempt.

After trying to rationalize all types of reasons for the reaction from my students over the years, the major factor that surfaces is that I am an African American professor. In fact, many of my students have told me, after they had stayed in my class and felt comfortable with my lectures, that I was the first African American professor that they have had in college. Whether they were freshman, sophomores, juniors, seniors, or graduate students, they all were taken aback to see a black man teach a college course.

This is happening in our society today particularly as it relates to African Americans and black males. Our American society and culture is still trying to get used to African Americans being in occupations that are not considered to be typical of the so-called average African American. One would think that I should not have to prepare myself for this type of reaction from students in 2009 and 2010, but it is the reality.

The fact that the numbers of African Americans and persons of color as professors in higher education are still so low tells you that we have a long way to go in academia and in many other social status occupations. Sadly and quite honestly, the joke going around in the African American community today is that it is easier to become president of the United States than a college professor or a Division I college football coach. Dare I ask this final simple question? Why does American society still have this major disparity in certain occupations for African Americans particularly African American males?

By now, you know the answer.

Chapter 9

A New Cultural Rights Movement

INTRODUCTION

It should be apparent that American society is in need of a new movement right now. Not tomorrow, not in four years, not in eight years or not in ten years, but we need it right now. This movement that all of us are in desperate need of particularly African Americans is a cultural rights movement.

You can hear the concerns across America in each community and each neighborhood, whether you live in the urban enclaves of big cities or small rural towns, we are experiencing massive layoffs, massive unemployment, massive poverty, massive restructuring, massive bailouts, massive number of individuals who are uninsured, massive number of individuals who are undereducated, and massive number of individuals who are discriminated against just because of the color of their skin. You do not have to take my word for it. Just go to your neighborhood barbershop, or your neighborhood beauty salon, or local church, or neighborhood community center, and you will hear and get a sense of the underlying frustration and concern that keeps the government squandering opportunities after opportunities.

What you feel and hear, at least in the African American community, is this ironic twist of faith. On one hand, our wildest dreams came true, the country elected its first African American president in Barack Obama. On that day of the inauguration (January 20, 2009), millions of African Americans from the youngest of young to the oldest of old trekked across the country in all types of transportation to witness this historic event. To see this record number of people, particularly African Americans, at a presidential inauguration was quite unusual. Then the moment arrived. After all the ceremonial rituals were completed, Barack Obama took the oath of the presidency at 12:07 P.M. on the steps of the Capitol building in Washington. D.C.[1]

Just at that moment, a vast majority of the African Americans released a sigh of relief, which extended back in history to our African enslaved ancestors. A humorous comment about the election of Barack Obama was made by actress, comedian, and host of the television show the *View*, Whoopie Goldberg. She said, "I can finally put my bags down now." What she meant by that remark was that, as an African American, she never felt that American society had truly accepted her as an equal citizen. With the election of Barack Obama, maybe America had.

There we were by the millions witnessing this historic event in Washington, D.C., or viewing it from our homes across the country on flat-screened television sets. Without a doubt, this was a moment and day in which a substantial number of African Americans finally felt that they were accepted as Americans because the country had elected a black man to be commander-and-chief of the United States. This was also a moment and day in which all Americans, regardless of race, appeared to come together to share this historic event. Even the bitter partisanship between Democrats and Republicans appeared to disappear for the day.

Personally, I felt extremely proud to be an African American and overjoyed that Obama and his family were going to be our First Family. For the first time in the nation's history, not only were African American citizens going to have a black president but the country was going to have a black American family, including the president's mother-in-law, living in the White House for the next four to eight years.

Ironically, however, as blacks celebrate each day of Obama's presidency, we are placed in a perplexing position. Dare to speculate upon the following scenarios:

- What will we do as a people when the Obama policies and the administration's 2010 budget initiatives are implemented, and they fail to make a serious impact on the black community in the areas of health disparity (for example, increasing life span of black males and females; lowering heart disease, cancer, diabetes, homicide, and HIV/AIDS rates)?

- What will we do as a people when the Obama policies and the administration's 2010 budget initiatives are implemented, and they do not make a serious change in the poverty rate for black Americans in the inner cities and rural towns across America?

- What will we do as a people when the Obama policies and the administration's 2010 budget initiatives are implemented, and they do not make a serious impact on the high school graduation rates for African American adolescents?

- What will we do as a people when the Obama policies and the administration's 2010 budget initiatives are implemented, and they do not make a serious change in the black unemployment rate?

- What will we do as a people when the Obama policies and the administration's 2010 budget initiatives are implemented, and they do not make a serious change in the numbers of blacks who are incarcerated?

- What will we do as a people when the Obama policies and the administration's 2010 budget initiatives are implemented, and they do not address any of the related issues concerning reparations?

- What will we do as a people when the Obama policies and the administration's 2010 budget initiatives are implemented, and they do not improve race relations or eliminate blatant discriminatory practices in housing and the criminal justice system?

- What will we do as a people when the Obama policies and the administration's 2010 budget initiatives are implemented, and they do not uphold some of our basic civil rights as U.S. citizens?

Historically, the typical response from the black community has always preached patience, patience, and more patience. In the past, I would have even agreed that patience is a virtue, and we should give every "system" or in this case "administration" a chance to work.

The reality, however, is that we do not have any more time to wait and be patient. Thousand of African Americans are losing their lives each and every day needlessly because of the failed public health and medical systems that are not developing enough programs to eliminate or reduce health disparities. Even with the rush by the federal government and President Obama to reform the U.S. health care system with a universal health care program, key African American political leaders took a stand in demanding that the Obama administration do something serious about health disparities, particularly as they affect the African American community.

On June 7, 2009, the forty-one-member Congressional Black Caucus (CBC) sent a letter to President Obama stating that a health care reform bill should address disparities. Specifically, the letter said, "We . . . respectfully, but firmly urge you to ensure that efforts to reform the nation's health care system integrate aggressive solutions to the nation's current plight with health disparities."[2]

The letter was signed by CBC Chairwoman Barbara Lee (D-Calif.), Rep. Donna Christensen (D-V.I.), and Rep. Danny Davis (D-Ill.). The position of the CBC agreed with the Congressional Progressive Caucus, the Hispanic Caucus, and the Asian Pacific Islander Caucus stance on health care.

Interestingly, the very next day, the CBC joined with the Congressional Hispanic Caucus and the Congressional Asian Pacific Islander Caucus, otherwise known as the Tri-Caucus, in a news conference to promote their legislative bill entitled, "Health Equity and Accountability

Act." The Tri-Caucus announced that the bill pushed for (1) a public system that included mental health and dental benefits; (2) a strengthening of the Office of Minority Health within the Department of Health and Human Services; (3) progress on cultural and linguistic concerns, such as credentialing for medical translators; (4) the inclusion of racial and ethnic diversity in clinical trials to discover effects on a broad range of groups, and (5) establishing the National Center on Minority Health and Health Disparities at the National Institutes of Health as a true Institute instead of Center.[3]

This press conference was a clear case that more African American leaders and organizations as well as other persons of color organizations (Hispanic Caucus and Asian Pacific Islander Caucus) finally realized that the Obama administration most likely did not have any African American or ethnic health priority on their health care reform political agenda.

Another case that illustrated organizations' frustration with the Obama administration has to do with Washington, D.C., residents' voting rights. Although President Obama signed into law a number of new initiatives during the first four months of his presidency, thus far, he has not supported the D.C. residents' voting rights.

Rep. Eleanor Holmes Norton, a Democrat, released a statement on June 9, 2009. concerning President Obama's lack of support stating that she was "disappointed that they have received no help from the administration" regarding their voting rights bill. The bill would give the heavily Democratic D.C. a vote in Congress in exchange for an additional House seat for heavily Republican Utah, where the population has grown fast enough since the last census to qualify for another congressional district. The legislation appeared to be headed for passage until Sen. John Ensign (R-Nev.), attached an amendment that Norton said would effectively eliminate all of D.C.'s gun control laws, among the strictest in the nation. Norton expressed frustration with her party for not being willing to take on the gun lobby.[4]

What is so unfortunate about the D.C. voting rights issue is that D.C. residents have been waiting a long time for their vote. The history of Washington's struggle for voting rights dates to 1800, when Virginia and Maryland ceded the land that became the District of Columbia, and Congress took exclusive jurisdiction of the new capital. Congress stripped the 14,103 people who then lived in the city of the vote. More recently, Washingtonians have gradually regained a few footholds in the nation's democracy, winning the right to vote for president in 1964 and the right to elect their own mayor and city council ten years later. According to the latest U.S. Census, Washington, D.C., is now home to more than 588,000 people.[5]

Another aspect of this D.C. voting rights issue connected with a local radio station in the city. Radio talk-show host Mark Plotkin said he would announce every day on his radio show that Obama's presidential limo has gone without D.C. protest license plate "Taxation without Representation." At the time of his announcement, it was day 164. Apparently, Obama's car sports a more neutral license that bears the city's Web site address instead of the protest slogan. The only other president that placed the protest license plate on his car was President Bill Clinton. Clinton had placed the protest license plates on his limo as soon as they were issued.[6]

So the time is now, not later, to demand for not only these two issues (D.C. Voting Rights and the Health Equity and Accountability Act) but also for all the issues described in this book—including the War on Poverty, education reform, medical and health care reform, criminal justice reform, a new race relations initiatives, and reparations (whether symbolic or monetarily) for slavery. If the Obama administration does not address these issues significantly, then it is time to start an African American cultural rights movement.

CULTURAL RIGHTS MOVEMENT

A cultural rights movement is defined as a system of shared beliefs, values, and traditions associated with a group of people who share a common background that are passed down from generation to generation through learning for the purpose of asserting one's rights as a human being. Being able to assert one's human rights *culturally* is important not only for the individual and the group but also for all citizens. Asserting one's human rights *culturally* gives that individual or the group the right to define who they are to others, the right to express themselves the way that they want, and the right to fight for their equal status in their own society and the world.

With all the change that is occurring in America and the world, it is time for all citizens, especially African Americans, to start a cultural rights movement. Starting a cultural rights movement will serve three major objectives:

1. To embrace, value, and respect the diversity of African American culture and how it should be integrated into the totality of American culture.

2. To embrace, value, and respect every group's diverse cultural traditions, values, and history.

3. To start a door-to-door, neighborhood, community, county, regional, national, and global movement among all cultures of the world that want to assert their rights as human beings and to change any national government policies that do not include cultural rights.

The Cultural Framework

The cultural rights movement is based within a cultural framework. One of the best methods that I use to get individuals and groups to learn more about themselves and others is to incorporate a cultural framework into the issue. In this case, examining each one of the nation's major issues (poverty, education reform, medical and health care reform, criminal justice reform, a new race relations initiatives, and reparations for slavery) and reevaluating them culturally. So how does this work?

The major components of the cultural framework that helps us to better understand the deeper cultural issues connected to a significant issue include the following attributes:

- Learned
- Symbolism
- Meaning to Reality
- Integrated
- Differently Shared
- Adaptive

By breaking down or reexamining each significant group issue through these six cultural attributes, we will be able to truly see how important these issues relate to African American communities throughout the United States.

For example, let's look at two issues—poverty and health care—and see how using a cultural framework helps us to better understand these issues from an African American perspective.

Poverty

As mentioned in chapter 3, we need to restart a War on Poverty program that is similar to the War on Poverty initiatives of the 1960s. Although both programs will share similar general issues, the specific details will be quite different, because of different issues affecting the African American population in the early 21st century.

For example, we learned that poverty in 2009 affects more ethnic and disparity groups than ever before. Although the face of poverty has changed dramatically since the 1960s, African Americans are nonetheless still experiencing higher rates of poverty than other groups. The fact that blacks continue to have the highest percentage of children in poverty of any group (33.4 percent) tells us that this is an issue that has been, and continues to be, neglected for more than forty years by federal and state agencies and individuals who can do something about it.[7]

Unfortunately, those who live in poverty experience a wide array of verbal and nonverbal stigmatization. Whether it comes from society, friends, or even extended family members, those who live in poverty are always reminded of their impoverished status. Although U.S. society touts that it is designed to help the underprivileged to get up on their feet and maintain a lifestyle without the help of the government, the practical and informative steps to improve one's status is not shared with those who need this information the most. Therefore, those who are born into poverty have a difficult time getting out of poverty, particularly African Americans.

For those who are impoverished, the reality is that many of the opportunities afforded to those who are labeled middle class and upper class simply are not offered to the lower class. Thus, education, employment, and housing opportunities are not readily available to obtain, primarily because of the persistent barriers that exist. Whether this lack of availability is due to the lack of transportation, income, the criminal justice system, or other tangible barriers, U.S. society makes it difficult for those who are impoverished to see their reality as anything else. That is one of the real unfortunate aspects about being born into and living in poverty in America.

For those who are impoverished, they also are affected by how their lives, like the rest of society, are integrated into the total fabric of society. Their lives are connected to the social, economic, political, and health care fabric of society. If the U.S. economy experiences a recession, then those who are impoverished are suffering at least three times as much as the so-called middle-income U.S. citizen. Thus, their health status, their income, and their education are at least three times worse than the average U.S. citizen. As Ruby Payne stated in her book entitled *A Framework for Understanding Poverty* (1996), individuals who are trying to get out of poverty recognize that it is more than just overcoming financial resources; it involves emotional resources, mental resources, spiritual resources, physical resources, and a support system.[8] That is another very real and unfortunate aspect about being born into and living in poverty in America.

For those who are impoverished, their lives vary from one person and one family to another. All too often, U.S. society paints a picture or promotes an image of a person or a group of people that represent "the poor" in America. In the past and even today, most people's images of the poor are primarily black people. Yet as we have described in this book, the impoverished includes all types of people, not just African Americans. Thus, Caucasians, Hispanic/Latinos, Asian and Pacific Islanders, Native Americans, and all other populations have thousands of individuals and families who are living in poverty now. Yet, for some reason in America, we still want to *perceive* that those who are in poverty are only black people. That image must change because it does all Americans a disservice, particularly when so many people of all walks of life need help to get out of poverty.

For those who are impoverished, they have to be adaptive in their living conditions, their social status, their education level, the type of medical care that they receive, and their aspirations to succeed in America. Most American citizens cannot imagine how those who are impoverished must adapt individually and collectively to survive each and every day. Yet, they continue to adapt and survive without most Americans knowing or even wanting to know. That is yet another very real and unfortunate aspect about being born into and living in poverty in America.

Health Care

The fact that African Americans' life expectancy (sixty-nine years for men and seventy-four years for women) and major causes of death and disability (heart disease, cancer, and stroke) represent the worst health outcomes and have the highest disparity rates than all other populations illustrates the reality that the African American population is experiencing a health care crisis unlike any other group in the United States. Some people question the seriousness of African American health status today, because more African Americans are living a better quality of life in their older ages. When viewing their health status through the cultural framework (learn, symbolize, meaning to reality, integrated, differently shared, and adaptive), however, we can begin to better appreciate their health and medical plight.

For example, African Americans still adhere to the health beliefs and practices that they learned from their immediate or extended familial network as opposed to their health care provider. When a health care crisis occurs, African Americans tend to seek and trust health care information from their immediate or extended familial network or a lay health professional first, and then opt for professional care.

Health care is transmitted by symbols verbally and nonverbally. African Americans are acutely aware of nonverbal body language that indicates whether a health care provider is comfortable or not treating an African American person. If the African American patient perceives the nonverbal language as positive, he or she most likely will return for care. If, however, the African American patient perceives the nonverbal body language as negative, he or she most likely will not return for care and not adhere to the prescribed regimen.[9]

Health care adds meaning to reality. African Americans respect and honor those who train, graduate, and serve in the health professional fields. Often, African American health care professionals feel a commitment to serve their community. Yet African Americans also realize that all major health and medical fields are still experiencing low numbers of African Americans. The low numbers of African Americans in the health profession suggest to many African Americans that these fields are not as receptive in training and recruiting new African Americans to the discipline. Thus, the reality is that the health care field is still a new field of expertise for many African Americans.

Health care is integrated. Like all Americans, African Americans are connected to the social, economic, political, and current health care reform debate issues. Whatever the outcome of the current health care reform for the citizens of United States, a large percentage of African Americans know that they still will have to fight for good quality health care services. For some reason in U.S. society, this has always been the situation for a vast majority of African Americans.

Health care is shared differently. African Americans perceive health and the health care system in different ways. The fact that African American men perceive and use the health system differently and less often than African American women indicates a problem. This problem is reflected in the lower life expectancy for black men and the belief among many African Americans and non–African Americans that the black male is an endangered species.

Health care is adaptive. Traditionally, African Americans have always had to adapt to social, economic, political, and health care barriers to mainstream society. Whether the barriers are actual or perceived, African Americans learn alternative patterns of obtaining care (use of alternative medical medicine, herbal remedies, or practitioners). Once the U.S. public health system implements health care reform, it will be quite interesting to see how African Americans adapt to a universal health care system.

HOW DO WE BEGIN A CULTURAL RIGHTS MOVEMENT?

Now that we have a cultural understanding of the particular issues such as poverty and health care as they relate to the African American population or any other ethnic or cultural group, we can engage our local population by holding small meetings in and around community settings or use the Internet to hold virtual meetings. In the fields of cultural anthropology and public health, we often refer to these meetings as "focus groups" and in the field of art they are referred to as "creative conversations."[10]

Focus groups are a qualitative research method that provides rich data on dynamic attitudes of individuals interacting in a group about a designated topic. Focus group methodology uses a standardized series of questions to elicit individual responses within the context of a group. This method benefits from both group interaction and group dynamics. In this environment, participant responses include the interplay of group members, which allows for greater depth of response, social context, and emotion. In addition, focus groups allow the researcher to hear directly from participants, using their own vocabulary, language, and communication patterns—essential components when engaging a group of individuals with like interest.[11]

Over the years, I have held a number of focus group sessions for all types of health care research studies (for example, prenatal care, diabetes, hypertension, HIV/AIDS, and community health screening programs). Yet now I use this focus group method to start a cultural rights movement on issues that are of great concern to me as well as many African Americans.

For example, as a college professor for more than twenty years, I have been concerned and disappointed about the continual low numbers of African American professors at mainstream universities. At each university that I have worked, there always has been a much smaller percentage of African American professors than white professors. In fact, a recent study examining the racial gaps in faculty job satisfaction found that African American professors had lower levels of job satisfaction and perceived more unfair treatment at their jobs than white faculty.[12]

To find out whether this perception held true at the university where I worked, I collaborated with a Caucasian professor and held focus groups called "Faculty Talks." These faculty talk sessions started a groundswell of interest and discussion on faculty diversity issues within the college. The result of these faculty talks sessions are still being evaluated, yet it has empowered the African American professors on campus to speak more about faculty diversity issues and got the administration to pay attention to our special concerns, which were once ignored.

Focus groups also can be conducted online through the various virtual meeting software applications. After establishing Internet outlets (Web site, blog, Facebook page, and Twitter page), moderators can hold virtual chat sessions to discuss and debate issues described in this book or topics that are more specific to each group's priorities. Despite being miles apart, these virtual chat sessions are a cost-effective method to get groups of like-minded people together to discuss an important and culturally, sensitive topic.

For example, to continue the dialogue, discussion, debate, and development of all the major issues described in this book (poverty, health care, criminal justice system, education, reparations, and race relations), I incorporated the use of the Internet to start a new Web site, blog, Facebook page, and Twitter site focused specifically on the cultural rights movement. Our new movement begins at www.culturalrights-movment.org.

Website: CulturalRightsMovement.Org

As an applied academician who extends his research and teaching activities to the real world, I have developed this new cultural rights movement Web site for the sole purpose of bringing folks of all ethnicities and all walks life together on the Internet so that we can assert and fight for our cultural human rights. The three major objectives of this Web site are as follows:

1. To embrace, value, and respect the diversity of African American culture and how it should be integrated into the totality of American culture.
2. To embrace, value, and respect every group's diverse cultural traditions, values, and history.
3. To start a door-to-door, neighborhood, community, county, regional, national, and global movement among all cultures of the world that want to not only assert their rights as human beings but also want to change any national government policies that do not include cultural rights.

This new Web site will provide detailed culturally competent data on as many groups as possible who are struggling to find a way to assert their cultural human rights. We will feature a brief cultural historical profile on each group along with their major sociocultural political issue. This feature is designed to inform, educate, and activate the world about real-life cultural issues that we all should know about in our global environment.

Blog: CulturalRightsMovement.Org

Along with the Web site, our blog, http://culturalrightsmovement. blogspot.com, provides an update of current activities and programs in which we are involved each and every month. The blog is designed for visitors to share their own cultural rights movement activities, whether a local neighborhood, town, county, state, nationwide or global event. The more visitors become involved in the process of sharing their cultural rights issues in a professional manner on the blog, the more we can embrace, value, and respect all groups of the world.

Facebook: CulturalRightsMovement.Org

In collaboration with the Web site and the blog, we have created a Facebook page. Our Facebook page provides an additional opportunity for us to visually see and interact with one another on a daily basis. This page will have an exclusive membership that will feature specific organizations fighting for their cultural human rights.

Twitter: CulturalRightsMovement.Org

In collaboration with the Web site, blog, and Facebook page, we will also feature a Twitter site. Our Twitter site will give followers a

minute-by-minute update of our activities and our thoughts. We look
forward to interacting with individuals and groups who want to follow
our activities and we look forward to the opportunity to follow all the
other cultural rights advocate Twitters in the world.

Connect with Key Decision Makers

For our cultural rights movement to be recognized, grow, and
expand, we need to connect with as many local, county, state, national,
and international key decision makers as possible. We emphasize decision makers primarily because those who are in leadership positions
and appointments are not necessarily good decision makers. Many
elected or appointed leaders today are representatives of a certain populous of constituents who have lobbied for their person to represent
them. Unfortunately, many of these elected or appointed leaders must
adhere to the obligations (that is, new legislation, laws, funding, policies) driven by their main supporters. In other words, they are compro-
mised, and many times they have their own agenda once in office.

We are looking to connect with people who are respected in their
communities, towns, cities, states, and nations, who are committed to
their cultural human rights cause, and who most likely are not a populous representative of their cause. They are considered the "activist,"
"advocate," or "foot-soldier" to their cause. These are the people who
are more than likely to be the best decision makers for their cause.

Congresswoman Barbara Lee

If there is one person on a national level who represents the mission,
vision, and objectives of the cultural rights movement and who is an
outstanding decision maker, it is Rep. Barbara Lee—Democratic Representative of the Ninth District of California. As mentioned earlier in
this book, Lee has always proudly been a civil rights advocate and a
person who has walked the walk and now talks the talk. As chair of
the CBC, she consistently challenges the establishment and the administration on issues that need to be challenged.

As stated on the book jacket of her recent autobiography, *Renegade
for Peace and Justice: Congresswoman Barbara Lee Speaks for Me* (2008),

> Congresswoman Barbara Lee's willingness to stand on principle
> earned her unsolicited international attention when she was the
> only member of Congress to vote against a resolution giving
> President George W. Bush virtually unlimited authority to wage
> war against unspecified organizations, and unspecified individuals
> for an unspecified period of time in the wake of the horrific events
> of September 11. Some praised her vote opposing this "blank check"
> to use force as heroic and inspirational; others called for her death.

But this was not her only profile in courage. In addition to being one of Congress's most vocal opponents to the war in Iraq, Lee has been a leader in promoting policies that foster international peace, security, and human rights and she has been an advocate for communities of color and for the poor. Her principled stands include disavowing the doctrine of preemptive war, offering legislation to address the HIV/AIDS pandemic, and helping to lead the bipartisan effort in Congress to end the ongoing genocide in the Darfur region of the Sudan of Africa.[13]

Finally, in her book, Lee shares with readers a reason why I feel that she will continue to be a key decision maker in Congress for years to come. She says,

> Although I consider myself a proud African American woman, that scar has been a constant reminder of where I came from and that no matter how much black people have accomplished, it was still less than forty years ago when we couldn't even share a bathroom, drinking fountain, or classroom with whites. Less than a century ago, black people were treated with little more regard than farm animals. This history keeps me grounded and is part of why I work so hard for my constituents and our great country. It is why I try to fight injustice wherever I see it, no matter how uncomfortable it may be for me.[14]

Tavis Smiley: Television Journalist, Host, and Author

Another person who really deserves to be mentioned as an outstanding decision maker who is not a politician but rather a television journalist, host of a PBS talk shows and radio shows, and best-selling author is Tavis Smiley.[15] One of America's most celebrated and respected media personalities, Tavis Smiley hosts a half-hour nightly talk show on PBS, *Tavis Smiley*, that reaches 92 percent of America's households and is seen in 187 countries through the American Forces Network. *The Tavis Smiley Show* from Public Radio International (PRI) reaches 800,000 listeners each weekend. His annual symposium, State of the Black Union, featuring America's premiere thought leaders, engages thousands of attendees and more than 100 million viewers worldwide. Published under Smiley Books, his most recent book *The Covenant in Action* hit the *New York Times* Best-Seller List's top ten in 2007.

One of the major reasons why Tavis Smiley is recognized as my other national outstanding decision makers is that he was the only television journalist and host to ask the once presidential candidate Barack Obama tough questions during the democratic presidential primaries. At that time in 2008, a strong and committed contingent of folks was still supporting Sen. Hillary Rodham Clinton for the Democratic presidential nominee. Despite the overwhelming support and endorsement of the African American community for presidential candidate Barack Obama, Tavis Smiley held true to his profession and asked the tough questions.

Unfortunately, what was surprising after the debates was that a large percentage of the African American community criticized Tavis Smiley for questioning Barack Obama on his political campaign proposals and for his support of Hillary Rodham Clinton. It was truly sad to read and hear the type of nasty criticism directed at Tavis Smiley, a professional, community-based, spiritually based African American man, and to see him get ostracized from his own people. Interestingly, after the months passed and Barack Obama became our forty-fourth president, the black community finally realized that Tavis Smiley did the right thing and stood up for what he believed in.

I often asked myself after this event where it says in the *black credo* that all blacks must think, act, and vote in the same way. If any population should have the most diverse views, perspectives, orientations, and lifestyles, it should be black people in America. Yet for some reason, we (African Americans) still hold ourselves back in many ways (educationally, economically, socially, politically, and culturally) because we do not want to ask the serious questions, or challenge a long-standing cultural tradition, or take a stand against the establishment. During the civil rights years, we always asked the serious questions, challenged our own traditions, and even took a stand against the establishment. I for one will not hold myself back, and I will take a stand against the establishment if it does not respect the rights of all people. I will also take a stand against the establishment even when the establishment looks like me.

TAKE A STAND FOR CULTURAL RIGHTS

Throughout the fifty years of my life, I realized that I tend to admire and respect those women and men who have taken a stand for their beliefs and individual rights particularly when few people supported them. I guess that is the reason why I have admired individuals in the entertainment, sporting, and political worlds—individuals such as Muhammad Ali, Jim Brown, Martin Luther King Jr., Malcolm X, Jesse Jackson, Barbara Jordan, Mrs. Johnnie Carr, Adam Clayton Powell, Jr., Randall Robinson, John Conyers, John Hope Franklin, Julius Erving, Kareem Abdul Jabaar, Jack Tatum, Walter Payton, Tiger Woods, Oprah Winfrey, Tavis Smiley, Spike Lee, Denzel Washington, Sidney Poitier, Richard Pryor, Eddie Murphy, Michael Jackson, Lena Horne, Vanessa Williams, Tyra Banks, Barbara Lee, Shirley Chisholm, and former president Bill Clinton.

I also have realized after fifty years of living that our American democracy and our U.S. Constitution support our individual beliefs, thoughts, and actions as American citizens. I am proud to be an American citizen. That is why it was so refreshing when I heard Joseph Wilson—former special assistant to President Bill Clinton, senior director for African Affairs on the United States National Security Council, and most notably, writer of an op-ed piece on the Bush administration's intelligence reports to exaggerate the Iraqi threat—speak at a university event in 2009.

Wilson spoke about the entire controversy surrounding the build up to the Iraqi war and the disclosure of his wife, Valerie Plame as a Central Intelligence Agency agent. From his talk and book entitled *The Politics of Truth: Inside the Lies that Led to War and Betrayed My Wife's CIA Identity: A Diplomat's Memoir,* Wilson reminded the audience that it is our right and responsibility as American citizens to "speak truth to power."[16] We are supposed to hold governments (local and national) accountable for their actions and if the government policies are wrong and unfair, we are supposed to *speak truth to power*. He was, and still is, right on all points.

This is one of the major reasons why our cultural rights movement is needed and necessary now more than ever. It is our time to take a stand for cultural rights and follow through on the rights given to all of us simply because we are human and not because we are of a particular ethnicity, skin color, social class, professional class, education level, gender, age, political party, or special interest group.

Most important, this new cultural rights movement is not about us collectively, but it is about you. It is about you because you deserve to be embraced, valued, and respected as a human being. You deserve to be integrated into the total fabric of society. You deserve to be educated equally just like everyone else in society. You deserve to be treated fairly in the court system. You deserve to receive quality health care. Finally, you deserve to be properly compensated for the atrocities committed against your ancestors.

So let's no longer chant the catchy political phrase, "Yes, We Can! Yes, We Can!" because that gives the power and decision making to someone else. It is time to take a stand and chant the new phrase, "Yes, I Can! Yes, I Can!" That is right. You have the right and the power to live your life the way that you want to. This is what the cultural rights movement is all about: "Yes, I Can! Yes, I Can!"

CONCLUSION

When I began my journey to write this book, I knew it was going to be one of the most difficult journeys that I have ever had to do. This book tested my psychic, my internal soul, my ethnicity, my history, my professionalism, my self-esteem, my heart, and my love for this country. In the end, I know that I have come out as a better person because

I not only have empowered myself, but I believe that I will empower you as well—the reader.

My parents always taught my brothers and I when we were growing up that each and every one of us were special and that we could be anything that we wanted to be in this world. Being born and raised in the rural Midwestern towns of Springfield and Wilberforce, Ohio, during the 1950s, 1960s, and 1970s, I felt just like any other kid in America. Yet I really was not. By society's definition and categorization, I was black and a minority.

Although my parents tried their best to insulate us from the subtle and blatant discriminatory practices, all of us experienced varying degrees of the discriminatory and racist actions of the time. Being the youngest, I was really fortunate because I did not have to endure the same type of discriminatory practices that my older brothers experienced. Yet if it was not for our parents perseverance and commitment to improve our lives, we would have remained in a social class and neighborhood setting relegated to the "have-nots."

From the very moment in which our lifestyle changed to more of a working middle-class neighborhood, my outlook on life and the possibility to be anything that I wanted to be became clearer. Even with all the societal changes happening throughout the nation and in the small rural towns of Xenia and Wilberforce, Ohio, at the time (such as integration of schools, busing, race riots, protests), I remained focus on what our parents told us: "you can be whatever you want to be in this society."

Although I did not know what I wanted to be at that time in my life, I felt that my love for school and education could open up doors of opportunity for me, so that is why I stuck with my education even when it was not cool. In fact, many of my closest African American friends thought I was wasting my time—getting degree after degree. Eventually, as the years passed, I completed my doctoral degree in anthropology and got a job as an assistant professor.

Now that I have been a professor for the past twenty years, I feel even more committed to follow and share with my students what my parents told me when I was a kid: "you can be whatever you want to be." The fact that our United States has elected its first black president in Barack Obama is testament to my parent's advice. Yet is this possibility really true for most African Americans in the 21st century?

Of course, the politically correct answer is yes. You can be whatever you want to be in U.S. society. However, the sad reality is that fewer and fewer African Americans, and particularly African American males, are not making it through the U.S. education system. They are getting sidetracked and misdirected by a whole host of social ills.

Over the past twenty years of teaching college courses, I have seen fewer numbers of African American males on mainstream college campuses particularly in my introductory and upper-level courses. Quite naturally, I am empathetic to this issue because I am a proud black male. I want others like myself to do well and get a college education.

So I wonder more and more each year, what is happening to the black male? I also wonder why there are fewer African American male professors. Is our society giving up on the black male? Why can't we provide special recruitment and retention programs to retain black males in college?

Obviously, the answer to the first question is, yes, we are giving up on black males. Our society does not want to keep black males in the education system. Our society actually prefers to keep black males in the prison system as opposed to the education system. What makes this trend even worse is that no one is doing anything about it. Everyone knows what is going on, but no one wants or thinks that they can do anything about it.

Well, I am ready to do something about it. I am ready to stand up and say enough is enough. I am ready to say, "Yes, I Can." I am ready to not only talk the talk but also walk the walk. In fact, I have already talked about this issue to the powerbase at the University of North Carolina college system and still nothing has been done to address this issue.

Because our country has a black male president, we should be able to do something for other black males in our society. Why can't we extend a helping hand to other young black males in society, just as our president received a helping hand when he was younger and struggling through college as well? It only makes common sense to help those who need help. Besides, if our U.S. Senate can finally pass a resolution apologizing to African Americans for the institution of slavery in America (June 18, 2009), then President Obama surely can use his executive power to save the black males in the United States.

Ironically, whether President Obama or his administration moves forward on any of these civil rights issues for African Americans does not really matter. What really matters is whether you and I move forward to address these civil rights issues that are not just for African Americans but for all citizens. This is exactly what the new cultural rights movement is all about: "Yes, I Can!"

Notes

CHAPTER 1

1. Ricky Hill, "The Study of Black Politics: Notes on Rethinking the Paradigm," in *Black Politics and Black Political Behavior: A Linkage Analysis*, ed. By Hanes Walton, Jr. (Westport, CT: Praeger Publishers, 1994), 11–17.

2. Ibid.

3. Barack Obama, *Dreams from My Father: A Story of Race and Inheritance* (New York: Three Rivers Press, 2004).

4. Barack Obama, *The Audacity of Hope: Thoughts on Reclaiming the American Dream* (New York: Three Rivers Press, 2006).

5. Benjamin Wallace-Wells, "The Great Black Hope: What's Riding on Barack Obama?" *Washington Monthly*, November 2004.

6. Eugene Robinson, "The Moment for This Messenger?" *Washington Post*, March 13, 2007.

7. Thomas Sowell, *Civil Rights: Rhetoric or Reality?* (New York: William Morrow, 1984).

8. Ibid., 15.

9. Ibid., 16.

10. Ibid.

11. Amaad Rivera, Brenda Cotto-Escalera, Anisha Desai, Jeannette Huezo, and Dedrick Muhammad, "Foreclosed State of the Dream 2008" (Boston: United for Fair Economy, 2008).

12. Department of Housing and Urban Development (HUD), *Housing Discrimination Study 2000* (Washington, DC, 2008).

13. Ibid.

14. Robert Blendon, Tami Buhr, Elaine Cassidy, Debra Perez, Tara Sussman, John Benson, and Melissa Herrman, "Disparities in Physician Care: Experiences and Perceptions of a Multi-Ethnic America," *Health Affairs* 27, no. 2 (2008): 507.

15. L. A. Bell, "More Good News, So Why the Blues?" *Academe* 86, no. 2 (2000): 11–95.

16. National Center for Education Statistics, *Gender and Racial/Ethnic Differences in Salary and Other Characteristics of Postsecondary Faculty: Fall 1998,* NCES 2002-170 (Washington, DC: U.S. Department of Education, 2002).

17. Ibid., 25.

18. NCES, *Gender and Racial/Ethnic Differences,* 2002; Caroline Sotello Viemes Turner, *Diversifying the Faculty: A Guidebook for Search Committees* (Washington, DC: Association of American Colleges and Universities, 2002).

19. American Council on Education. *Minorities in Higher Education 2008 Twenty-Third Status Report* (Washington, DC: ACE, 2008).

20. Ibid.

21. Marc Mauer and Ryan King. *Uneven Justice: States Rates of Incarceration By Race and Ethnicity* (Washington, DC: Sentencing Project, 2007).

22. The Sentencing Project, *Reducing Racial Disparity in the Criminal Justice: A Manual for Practitioners and Policymakers* (Washington, DC: The Sentencing Project, 2008).

23. Ibid.

24. Ibid.

25. "Reparations for Slavery," Wikipedia. http://en.wikipedia.org/wiki/Reparations_for_slavery (accessed October 3, 2009).

26. Ibid.

27. National Urban League Policy Institute, *2006 Census Poverty and Income Data* (Washington, DC: National Urban League Policy Institute, 2007).

28. Ibid.

29. Ibid.

30. Ibid.

31. Carmen DeNavas-Walt, Bernadette D. Proctor, and Jessica C. Smith, "Income, Poverty, and Health Insurance Coverage in the United States: 2007." U.S. Census Bureau, Current Population Reports, P60-235, (Washington, DC: U.S. Government Printing Office, 2008).

32. Randall Robinson, *The Debt: What America Owes to Blacks* (New York: Plume Books, 2001); John Conyers, "Reparations," www.johnconyers.com/issues/reparations, 2008; Charles Ogletree, "Stanford Alumnus Seeks Reparations for Survivors of Deadly 1921 Tulsa Race Riot," http://news-service.standford.edu/news/2005/february16/tulsa-021605.html, 2005.

33. Darryl Fears, "House Issues an Apology for Slavery." *Washington Post.* July 30, 2008.

34. Ibid.

35. Christopher Wills, "Obama Opposes Reparations for Slavery," Associated Press, August 2, 2008.

36. Ibid.

CHAPTER 2

1. "Civil and Political Rights," Wikipedia, http://en.wikipedia.org/wiki/Civil_rights_and_liberties (accessed October 3, 2009).

2. Juan Williams, *Eyes on the Prize: America's Civil Rights Years, 1954-1965* (New York. Penguin Books, 1987), xi.

3. John Hope Franklin and Alfred Moss, Jr., *From Slavery to Freedom: A History of Negro Americans*, 14th ed. (New York. Alfred A. Knopf, 1988).

4. Ibid., 444.

5. Ibid., 445.

6. Ibid., 447.

7. Ibid., 448.

8. Mary Frances Berry and John W. Blassingame, *Long Memory: The Black Experience in America* (New York: Oxford, 1982).

9. Gloria Bailey, "Analyzing Present and Future Affects of Civil Rights Legislation and Diversity in Human Resource Planning and Management" (paper printed in the Proceedings of Humanities, 2008).

10. Williams 1987; Lawson 2003; Mary Frances Berry and John Blassingame, *Long Memory: The Black Experience in America* (New York: Oxford, 1982).

11. Desiree Hunter, "Johnnie Carr, 97: A Civil Rights 'Spark Plug," *Washington Post*, February 25, 2008.

12. Ibid.

13. Jill Nolin and Alvin Benn, "Civil Rights Leader Carr Dies at 97," *Montgomery Advertiser*, February 24, 2008.

14. National Public Radio, "In the Presence of a Giant: Johnnie Carr," February 24, 2008.

15. PBS Tavis Smiley Interview, "Johnnie Carr," December 1, 2005.

16. Ibid.

17. Sandra Parham, "Barbara C. Jordan: Selected Speeches" (Washington, DC: Howard University Press, 1999).

18. Megan Scarborough, *A Voice That Could Not Be Stilled* (Austin: University of Texas Archives, 2003).

19. Ibid.

20. Ibid.

21. Ibid., 63–69.

22. Nichola Gutgold, *Paving the Way for Madam President* (New York: Rowman & Littlefield, 2006), 51–52.

23. Ibid., 52.

24. Ibid., 64.

25. Jo Freeman, "Shirley Chisholm's 1972 Presidential Campaign," Shirley Chisholm Web site, www.uic.edu/orgs/cwluherstory/jofreeman/polhistory/chisholm.htm (accessed January 9, 2009).

26. Ibid.

27. Shirley Chisholm, "Chisholm '72—Unbought and Unbossed," www.chisholm72.net/campaign.html (accessed October 3, 2009).

28. Camille Cosby, and Renee Poussaint, *A Wealth of Wisdom: Legendary African American Elders Speak* (New York: Atria Books, 2004), 70.

29. Ibid.

CHAPTER 3

1. National Poverty Center, "Poverty Facts," www.npc.umich.edu/poverty (accessed October 3, 2009).

2. U.S. Bureau of the Census, *2007 U.S. Poverty Threshold* (Washington, DC, 2007).

3. National Center for Children in Poverty, www.nccp.org (accessed October 3, 2009).

4. John Herbers, "Black Poverty Spreads in 50 Biggest U.S. Cities," *New York Times*, January 26, 1987.

5. National Urban League, "2006 Census Poverty and Income Data" (Washington, DC, 2007), 1.

6. Ibid.

7. National Center for Children in Poverty, www.nccp.org (access October 3, 2009).

8. Douglas Glasglow, *The Black Underclass: Poverty, Unemployment, and Development of Ghetto Youth* (San Francisco: Jossey-Bass Publishers, 1980), 5.

9. Ibid., 6.

10. Wikipedia.org, "War on Poverty," http://en.wikipedia.org/wiki/War_on_Poverty (accessed October 3, 2009).

11. Wikipedia.org, "Adam Clayton Powell, Jr.," http://en.wikipedia.org/wiki/Adam_Clayton_Powell_Jr. (accessed October 3, 2009.

12. Economic Opportunity Act of 1964. "Hearings Before the Subcommittee on the War on Poverty Program of the Committee on Education and Labor House of Representatives: Eighty-Eighth Congress, Second Session on H.R. 10440" (Washington, DC. U.S. Government Printing Office, 1964), 1–2.

13. Ibid., 2.

14. Ibid., 3 [emphasis added].

15. Absolute Astronomy.com, "Head Start," http://www.absoluteastronomy.com/topics/Head_Start#encyclopedia (accessed October 3, 2009).

16. Ibid.

17. White House Web site, "Poverty," http://www.whitehouse.gov/agenda/poverty (accessed October 3, 2009).

18. Sam Stein, "Barack Obama's Innovative War on Poverty," Huffingtonpost.com, October 13, 2008.

19. Nichola Gutgold, "Shirley Chisholm: Ms. Chis," in *Paving the Way for Madam President,* 50–77 (New York: Rowman & Littlefield, 2006), 61.

20. C-SPAN TV Interview, "Barbara Lee," February 22, 2009.

21. Barbara Lee Web site, www.lee.house.gov, 2009.

22. Katrina Vanden Heuvel, "Barbara Lee's War on Poverty," *The Nation,* http://www.thenation.com/blogs/edcut/301907/print, 2009.

23. Ibid.

24. War on Poverty Florida, Inc., http://waronpoverty.org (accessed October 3, 2009).

25. Ibid.

26. New York City Center for Economic Opportunity, "News and Events," http://www.nyc.gov/html/ceo/html/events/past_events.shtml (accessed October 3, 2009).

27. New York City Commission for Economic Opportunity Report (New York: NYC CEO, 2006), 8–9.

28. Ibid., 40–41.

29. Martha Moore, "With Cities' Programs for Poor, It Pays to Save," *USA Today*, February 19, 2009.

CHAPTER 4

1. American Council on Education, "Generational Gains in Postsecondary Education Appear to Have Stalled, New ACE Report Finds" (Washington, DC: ACE, October 9, 2008).

2. Ibid.

3. Ibid.

4. Ibid., 2.

5. American Council on Education, "Generational Gains in Postsecondary Education"; and Bryan Cook and Diana Corova, *Minorities in Higher Education: Twenty-Second Annual Status Report: 2007 Supplement* (Washington, DC: American Council on Education, 2007).

6. "Black Faculty in Higher Education: Still Only a Drop in the Bucket," *The Journal of Blacks in Higher Education,* http://www.jbhe.com/features/55_blackfaculty.html, 2009; "Blacks Making Solid Progress in Graduate School Enrollments: Women Are in the Lead," *The Journal of Blacks in Higher Education,* http://www.jbhe.com/news_views/61_gradschoolenrolls.html, 2009; "African Americans in Higher Education: Now for the Good News," *The Journal of Blacks in Higher Education,* http://www.jbhe.com/news_views/48_blacks_higher education.html, 2009.

7. American Council on Education, "Generational Gains in Postsecondary Education."

8. "Black Faculty in Higher Education."

9. Dione Danns, *Something Better For Our Children: Black Organizing in Chicago Public Schools, 1963-1971* (New York: Routledge, 2003).

10. Ibid.

11. Ibid.

12. Ibid., 14.

13. Ibid., 27.

14. Ibid., 118.

15. Ibid., 27.

16. Ibid.

17. Ibid., 118.

18. Ibid., 2.

19. Ibid., 3.

20. Michael Rebell and Jessica Wolff, *Moving Every Child Ahead: From NCLB Hype to Meaningful Educational Opportunity* (New York: Teachers College Press, 2008).

21. Ibid., 2.

22. Ibid., 3.

23. Ibid., 7.

24. *Measuring Up 2008. The 2008 National Report Card: Modest Improvements Persistent Disparities, Eroding Global Competitiveness,* http://measuringup2008.highereducation.org/commentary/callan.php, 2008.

25. Ibid.

26. Ibid.

27. Ibid.

28. White House Web site, "Education," http://www.whitehouse.gov/agenda/education, (accessed October 3, 2009).

29. Gloria Boutee, *Multicultural Education: Raising Consciousness* (Belmont, CA: Wadsworth Publishing Company, 1999); Jean Madsen and Reitumetse Obakeng Mabokela. *Culturally Relevant Schools: Creating Positive Workplace Relationships and Preventing Intergroup Differences* (New York: Routledge, 2005); Mary Beth Klotz, "Culturally Competent Schools: Guidelines for Secondary School Principals" National Association of School Psychologists, http://www.nasponline.org/resources/principals/Culturally%20Competent%20Schools%20NASSP.pdf, March 2008.

30. Klotz, "Culturally Competent Schools."

31. Boutee, *Multicultural Education*; Madsen and Mabokela, *Culturally Relevant Schools*.

32. Klotz, "Culturally Competent Schools," 13.

33. David Hefner, "Where the Boys Aren't: The Decline of Black Males in Colleges and Universities Has Sociologists and Educators Concerned about the Future of the African American Community" (Washington, DC: American Council on Education, 2006).

34. Ibid.

35. Black Male Initiative, City University of New York, www.mec.cuny.edu, 2009; Inside Higher Education, "The Missing Black Men," http://insidehighered.com/news/2005/12/05/blackmale, 2009.

36. Black Male Initiative.

37. Ibid.

38. Ibid.

CHAPTER 5

1. Medline Plus, http://www.nlm.nih.gov/medlineplus, 2009.

2. Ibid.

3. Eric Bailey, *Medical Anthropology and African American Health* (Westport, CT: Bergin & Garvey, 2002).

4. Office of Minority Health, U.S. Department of Health and Human Services, www.omhrc.gov, 2008.

5. Ibid.

6. Ibid.

7. Ibid.

8. Ibid.

9. Ibid.

10. Ibid.

11. Ibid.

12. Centers for Disease Control and Prevention, *National Center for Health Statistics. Health Behaviors of Adults: United States, 1999- 2001*, Vital and Health Statistics, Series 10, no. 219 (Washington, DC: U.S. Department of Health and Human Services, 2004).

13. S. Daniels, S., D. Arnett, R. Eckel, S. Gidding, L. Hayman, S. Kumanyika, T. Robinson, B. Scott, S. Jeor, and C. Williams, "Overweight in Children and Adolescents: Pathophysiology, Consequences, Prevention, and Treatment," *Circulation* 111 (2005): 1999–2012; P. Gordon-Larsen, L. Adair, and B. Popkin, "The Relationship of Ethnicity, Socioeconomic Factors, and Overweight in U.S.

Adolescents," *Obesity Research* 11, no 1. (2003): 121–129; National Center for Health Statistics, *Health United States 1996-97 and Injury Chartbook* (Hyattsville, MD: DHHS Publication PHS 97-1232, 1997).

14. K. Flegal, M. Carrol, C. Ognen, and C. Johnson, "Prevalence and Trends in Obesity Among U.S. Adults, 19990-2000," *Journal of the American Medical Association* 288 (2002): 1723–1727.

15. Robert Staples, "Towards a Sociology of the Black Family: A Theoretical and Methodological Assessment," *Journal of Marriage and Family* 33 (1971): 19–138.

16. Bailey, *Medical Anthropology and African American Health.*

17. John Hope Franklin and Alfred Moss, *From Slavery to Freedom: A History of Negro Americans* (New York: Alfred A. Knopf, 1988).

18. Bailey, *Medical Anthropology and African American Health.*

19. White House Web site, www.whitehouse.gov/health_care/, 2009.

20. Obama-Biden Health Plan, http://barackobama.com/pdf/issues/Health-CareFullPlan.pdf.

21. The Office of Management and Budget, *The 2009 President's Budget,* http://www.whitehouse.gov/omb/budget/fy2009.

22. "What Is an Hispanic?" *Latin American Wave,* Indianapolis, October 1997, 6.

23. Andrew Vazquez and Aurora Ramirez-Krodel, *America's Hispanic Heritage: An Overview of Hispanics in the United States* (Ann Arbor: University of Michigan Press, 1989).

24. Office of Minority Health, U.S. Department of Health and Human Services, www.omhrc.gov, 2008.

25. U.S. Department of Commerce, *We the American Asians* (Economics and Statistics Administration, Bureau of Census, 1993); *We the First Americans* (Economics and Statistics Administration, Bureau of Census, 1993); *We the American Hispanics* (Economics and Statistics Administration, Bureau of Census, 1993).

26. Office of Minority Health, U.S. Department of Health and Human Services, www.omhrc.gov, 2008.

27. Alan Harwood, "The Hot-Cold Theory of Disease," *Journal of the American Medical Association* 216: 1153–1158; Rachel Spector, "Health and Illness in the American Indian Community," in *Cultural Diversity and Health Care,* ed. R. Spector, 235–257 (New York: Appleton-Century Crofts, 1985); Edward Spicer, *Ethnic Medicine in the Southwest* (Tucson: University of Arizona Press, 1979).

28. L. Saunders, *Cultural Differences in Medical Care* (New York: Russell Sage, 1954).

29. Harwood, "The Hot-Cold Theory of Disease."

30. G. Lucero, "Health and Illness in the Chicano Community" (lecture given at Boston College School of Nursing, March 1975).

31. Harwood, "The Hot-Cold Theory of Disease"; Spector, "Health and Illness in the American Indian Community."

32. R. Beals, and L. Cheran, "A Sierra Tarascan Village," *Publications of the Institute of Social Anthropology,* Smithsonian Institution 2 (1946): 1–225; M. Clark, *Health in the Mexican American Culture* (Berkeley: University of California Press, 1959); Richard Currier, "The Hot-Cold Syndrome and Symbolic Balance in Mexican and Spanish American Folk Medicine," *Ethnology* 5 (1966): 251–263; Arthur Rubel, "Concepts of Disease in Mexican American Culture," *American*

Anthropologist 62 (1960): 795–815; F. McFeeley, "Some Aspects of Folk Curing in the American Southwest" (master's thesis, University of California, 1949); George Foster, "Relationship between Spanish and Spanish American Folk Medicine," *Journal of American Folklore* 66 (1953): 202–218.

33. Currier, "The Hot-Cold Syndrome."

34. Beals and Cheran, "A Sierra Tarascan Village"; Clark, *Health in the Mexican American Culture* Currier, "The Hot-Cold Syndrome"; Rubel, "Concepts of Disease in Mexican American Culture"; McFeeley, "Some Aspects of Folk Curing in the American Southwest"; Foster, "Relationship between Spanish and Spanish American Folk Medicine."

35. Rubel, "Concepts of Disease in Mexican American Culture."

36. Beals and Cheran, "A Sierra Tarascan Village"; Clark, *Health in the Mexican American Culture* Currier, "The Hot-Cold Syndrome"; Rubel, "Concepts of Disease in Mexican American Culture"; McFeeley, "Some Aspects of Folk Curing in the American Southwest"; Foster, "Relationship between Spanish and Spanish American Folk Medicine."

37. William Madsen, *Mexican Americans of South Texas* (New York: Holt, Rinehart, and Winston, 1964).

38. I. F. Abril, "Mexican American Folk Beliefs: How They Affect Health Care," *The American Journal of Maternal Child Nursing* (May/June 1977): 168–173; Margarita Kay, "Health and Illness in a Mexican American Barrio," in *Ethnic Medicine in the Southwest*, ed. E. Spicer, 99–160 (Tucson: University of Arizona Press, 1979).

39. Madsen, *Mexican Americans of South Texas*.

40. Rubel, "Concepts of Disease in Mexican American Culture."

41. Harwood, "The Hot-Cold Theory of Disease"; Spector, "Health and Illness in the American Indian Community"; Rubel, "Concepts of Disease in Mexican American Culture."

42. Rubel, "Concepts of Disease in Mexican American Culture."

43. Harwood, "The Hot-Cold Theory of Disease."

44. Kay, "Health and Illness in a Mexican American Barrio."

45. Beals and Cheran, "A Sierra Tarascan Village"; Clark, *Health in the Mexican American Culture* Currier, "The Hot-Cold Syndrome"; Rubel, "Concepts of Disease in Mexican American Culture"; McFeeley, "Some Aspects of Folk Curing in the American Southwest"; Foster, "Relationship between Spanish and Spanish American Folk Medicine."

46. Louis Sullivan, "Keynote Address at the Surgeon General's National Workshop on Hispanic/Latino Health," Washington, DC, September 1992.

47. U.S. Department of Health and Human Services, *Black and Minority Health: The Secretary's Task Force on Minority Health* (Washington, DC: U.S. Government Printing Office, 1985).

48. K. Gould-Martin and C. Ngin, "Chinese Americans." In *Ethnicity and Medical Care*, ed. A. Harwood, 130–171 (Cambridge, MA: Harvard University Press, 1981).

49. Ibid.

50. Ibid.

51. Harwood, "The Hot-Cold Theory of Disease."

52. Gould-Martin and Ngin, "Chinese Americans."

53. Ibid.

54. George Ulett, Jishen Han, and Songpin Han, "Traditional and Evidence-Based Acupuncture: History, Mechanisms, and Present Status," *Southern Medical Journal* 91 (1998): 1115–1120.

55. Salvador Ceniceros and George Brown, "Acupuncture: A Review of Its History, Theories, and Indications," *Southern Medical Journal* 91 (1998): 1121–1125; Kathryn Braun and Colette Brown, "Perceptions of Dementia, Caregiving, and Help Seeking among Asian and Pacific Islander Americans," *Health and Social Work* 23 (1998): 262–274.

56. Harwood, "The Hot-Cold Theory of Disease."

57. Ibid.

58. Office of Minority Health, U.S. Department of Health and Human Services, www.omhrc.gov, 2008; U.S. Department of Commerce, *We the American Asians, We the First Americans, We the American Hispanics.*

59. Office of Minority Health, U.S. Department of Health and Human Services, www.omhrc.gov, 2008.

60. Office of Minority Health, U.S. Department of Health and Human Services, www.omhrc.gov, 2008; U.S. Department of Commerce, *We the American Asians, We the First Americans, We the American Hispanics.*

61. Harwood, "The Hot-Cold Theory of Disease."

62. Ibid.

63. Ibid.

64. Stephen Kunitz and J. Levy, "Navajos," in *Ethnicity and Medical Care*, ed. A. Harood, 337–396 (Cambridge, MA: Harvard University of Press, 1981); Virgil Vogel, *American Indian Medicine* (Norman: University of Oklahoma Press, 1981).

65. Kunitz and Levy, "Navajos."

66. Ibid.

67. Vogel, *American Indian Medicine.*

68. Harwood, "The Hot-Cold Theory of Disease."

69. Ibid.

70. Spector, "Health and Illness in the American Indian Community."

71. Harwood, "The Hot-Cold Theory of Disease."

72. Office of Minority Health, U.S. Department of Health and Human Services, www.omhrc.gov, 2008.

73. Jesse Washington, "Obama's True Colors: Black, White ... or Neither," *Washington Post*, December 14, 2008.

74. Ibid.

75. Health Care Forum, http://cgi.cnn.com/2009/POLITICS/03/05/health.care.cummit, 2009.

76. Thomas LaVeist, *Minority Populations and Health: An Introduction to Health Disparities in the United States* (San Francisco: Jossey-Bass, 2005).

77. Ibid.

CHAPTER 6

1. Ashley Nellis, Judy Greene, and Marc Mauer, *Reducing Racial Disparity in the Criminal Justice System: A Manual for Practitioners and Policymakers* (The Sentencing Project.org, 2008).

2. Mary Frances Berry and John Blassingame, *Long Memory: The Black Experience in America* (New York: Oxford University Press, 1982).

3. Ibid.

4. Rich Phillips, "Snipes Gets the Max—3 years—in Tax Case," CNN, www.cnn.com, May 13, 2009.

5. Ibid.

6. Wikipedia.org, "Timothy Geithner," http://en.wikipedia.org/wiki/Timothy_Geithner (accessed October 3, 2009).

7. Ibid.

8. Ibid.

9. Ibid., 234.

10. Ibid., 235.

11. Ibid.

12. Ibid., 236.

13. Ibid., 241.

14. Ibid.

15. Ibid.

16. Marc Mauer and Ryan King, *Uneven Justice: State Rates of Incarceration by Race and Ethnicity* (The Sentencing Project, July 2007).

17. Ibid., 5.

18. Ibid., 7.

19. Ibid., 10.

20. Ibid.

21. Ibid.

22. Nellis, Greene, and Mauer, *Reducing Racial Disparity.*

23. Eileen Poe-Yamagata and Michael Jones, *And Justice for Some: Differential Treatment of Minority Youth in the Justice System* (Building Blocks for Youth, April 2000).

24. Vernetta Young, Rebecca Reviere, and Yaw Ackah, "Behind Bars: An Examination of Race and Health Disparities in Prison," in *Praeger Handbook of Black American Health,* ed. Ivor Livingston, 638–652 (Westport, CT: Praeger, 2004).

25. Ibid.

26. S. Whitman, N. Benbow, and G. Good, "The Epidemiology of Homicide in Chicago," *Journal of the National Medical Association* 88 (1996): 781–787.

27. Ibid.

28. Ibid., 785.

29. U.S. Bureau of Justice Statistics, http://www.ojp.usdoj.gov/bjs (accessed October 3, 2009).

30. "Study: Murders among Black Youths on the Rise," *USA Today,* November 29, 2008.

31. Ibid.

32. Jeff Carlton, "Freed Prisoner Reflects on His Ordeal," AOL. News, January 4, 2008.

33. Ibid.

34. Ibid.

35. The Innocence Project, www.innocenceproject.org (accessed October 3, 2009).

36. Ibid.

37. "Fla. Mulls Payments for Wrongful Imprisonments," *USA Today,* January 19, 2008.

38. Nellis, Greene, and Mauer, *Reducing Racial Disparity*, 9.

39. Ibid.

40. White House Web site, "Civil Rights," www.whitehouse.gov/issues/civil_rights (accessed October 3, 2009).

41. Ibid., 82.

42. The Justice Center, Council of State Governments, "Second Chance Act," http://reentrypolicy.org/government_affairs/second_chance_act (accessed October 14, 2009).

43. Gary Fields, "Senate Clears Prisoner Bill," *Wall Street Journal*, March 12, 2008.

44. Ibid.

45. Nellis, Greene, and Mauer, *Reducing Racial Disparity*.

46. Ibid.

47. Ibid., 30.

48. Ibid., 31.

49. S. Orchowsky and K. Taylor, "The Insiders Juvenile Crime Prevention Program: An Assessment of a Juvenile Assessment Program" (Research and Reporting Unit, Division of Program Development and Evaluation, Virginia Department of Corrections, 1981).

50. Jarrett Bell, "Reaching Out, Lifting Up: Prison Ministry Now Dungy's Priority," *USA Today*, April 21, 2009.

51. Ibid.

52. Ibid.

53. Dayo Olopade, "Visible Man," The Root, http://www.theroot.com/print/5858?page=0%2c1 (accessed October 3, 2009).

54. Ibid.

55. "Obama Gently Departs from Holder's Race Comment," *USA Today*, March 8, 2009.

56. Ibid.

CHAPTER 7

1. John Conyers, "Reparations," http://www.johnconyers.com/issues/reparations, 1989; Randall Robinson, *The Debt: What America Owes to Black* (New York: A Plume Book, 2001); Charles Ogletree, Jr., "The Case for Reparations," *USA Today Weekend*. August 18, 2002; Wikipedia.org., "Reparations for Slavery," http://en.wikipedia.org/wiki/Reparations_for_slavery (accessed October 3, 2009).

2. World Socialist Web site, http://www.wsws.org, 2009.

3. Sharon Silke Carty, "GM's Future at Stake as Obama Team Steps In." *USA Today*, May 15, 2009.

4. Richard Pryor, "Bicentennial Prayer," (Warner Brothers, 1976).

5. Mary Frances Berry and John Blassingame, *Long Memory: The Black Experience in America* (New York: Oxford University Press, 1982).

6. Ibid.

7. Ibid., 8.

8. Ibid., 11.

9. Ibid., 13.

10. Ibid., 15.

11. Ibid., 15.

12. Ogletree, "The Case for Reparations."

13. Walter Olsen, "Slavery Reparations: What Happened?" *Los Angeles Times*, October 31, 2008.

14. Ibid.

15. Ibid.

16. Conyers, "Reparations."

17. Ibid.

18. Ibid.

19. Ibid.

20. Robinson, *The Debt.*

21. Ibid., 208.

22. Darryl Fears, "House Issues an Apology for Slavery," *Washington Post*, July 30, 2008.

23. Ibid.

24. Josh Hafenbrack and John Kennedy, "Florida Legislature Makes Formal Apology for Slavery," Common Dreams.org, March 27, 2008.

25. State of New Jersey, Assembly Concurrent Resolution No. 270, November 8, 2007.

26. Ida Hakim, http://reparations.wordpress.com, April 12, 2009.

27. Ibid.

28. Ibid.

29. *USA Today*, "Obama Opposes Slavery Reparations," August 2, 2008.

30. Ibid.

31. Conyers, "Reparations."

CHAPTER 8

1. Juan Williams, *Eyes on the Prize: America's Civil Rights Years, 1954-1965* (New York: Penguin Books, 1988).

2. Ibid.

3. Susan Page and William Risser, "Poll: Racial Divide Narrowing But Persists," *USA Today*, July 23, 2008.

4. Ibid.

5. Ibid.

6. Susan Page, "Poll: Hopes Are High for Race Relations," *USA Today*, November 7, 2008.

7. Ibid.

8. Ibid.

9. Robert Robinson, "How Far We Have Come," *USA Today*, November 7, 2008.

10. Ibid.

11. Eric Bailey, *Black America, Body Beautiful: How the African American Image Is Changing Fashion, Fitness, and Other Industries* (Westport, CT: Praeger, 2008).

12. Sindya Bhanoo, "The New Black Brigade: Today's African American Politicians Have an Energy All Their Own," *Berkeley Journalism*, November 3, 2006, http://journalism.berkeley.edu/projects/election2006/11/the_new_black_brigade_today.

13. Barack Obama, *Dreams from My Father: A Story of Race and Inheritance* (New York: Three Rivers Press, 2004).

14. Barack Obama, *The Audacity of Hope: Thoughts on Reclaiming The American Dream* (New York: Three Rivers Press, 2006).

15. Eugene Robinson, "The Moment for This Messenger?" *Washington Post*, March 13, 2007, http://washingtonpost.com/wp-kyn/content/article/2007/03/12/AR2007031200983.html.

16. Marisol Bello, "Renamed Schools, Streets Mark Early Tributes to Obama," *USA Today*, January 26, 2009.

17. Rebecca Kern. "Black History Month Has Added Meaning in 2009," *USA Today*, February 2, 2009.

18. Joan Biskupic, "Civil Rights in Court Spotlight," *USA Today*, February 18, 2009.

19. Ibid.

20. White House Web site, http://www.whitehouse.gov (accessed October 3, 2009).

21. Obama, *Dreams from My Father*.

22. Ibid.

23. Ibid., xv.

24. Obama, *Dreams from My Father*; Beth Harpaz, "Trace Obama's Roots from Kenya to Chicago," *USA Today*, November 25, 2008.

25. Obama, *The Audacity of Hope*, 26.

26. Ibid., 233.

27. "Obama Race Speech," The Huffington Post, http://wwww.huffingtonpost.com/2008/03/18/obama-race-speech-read-th_n_92077.html (accessed October 3, 2009).

28. "U.S. to Boycott U.N. Racism Meeting," *USA Today*, April 18, 2009.

29. Bill Clinton, "One America in the 21st Century: The President's Initiative on Race," http://clinton4.nara.gov/Initiatives/OneAmerica/about.html (accessed October 3, 2009).

30. Ibid.

31. Bill Clinton, *My Life* (New York: Alfred A. Knopf, 2004), 758.

32. Steven Holmes, "Clinton Panel on Race Urges Variety of Modest Measures," *New York Times*, September 18, 1998.

33. Ibid.

34. Andrew Penner and Aliya Saperstein, "How Social Status Shapes Race," *PNAS* 105, no. 50 (2008): 19628–19630.

35. Ibid.

36. Ibid.

37. Ibid.

CHAPTER 9

1. Eric Bailey, personal observation notes of the Forty-Fourth Presidential Inauguration, January 20, 2009.

2. TriCaucus Congressional Group, *Health Equity and Accountability Act*, conference held on June 12, 2009.

3. Mike Soraghan, "CBC Backs Public Medicare-Like Program," *The Hill.com*, June 7, 2009.

4. Kathy Kiely, "Obama Wimping Out?" *Washington Times*, June 12, 2009.

5. Ibid.

6. Ibid.

7. Ruby Payne, *A Framework for Understanding Poverty*, 3rd rev. ed. (Texas: aha Process, Inc., 2003).

8. Ibid.

9. Eric Bailey, *Medical Anthropology and African American Health* (Westport, CT: Bergin & Garvey, 2002).

10. America for the Arts, "Creative Conversations," www.artsusa.org, 2008.

11. Bailey, *Medical Anthropology and African American Health.*

12. "Racial Gaps in Faculty Job Satisfaction," *Chronicles of Higher Education*, http://www.insidehighered.com/news/2008/12/05/coache#, 2009.

13. Barbara Lee, *Renegade for Peace and Justice: Congresswoman Barbara Lee Speaks for Me* (Lanham, MD: Rowman & Littlefield, 2008).

14. Ibid., 4.

15. Tavis Smiley, www.tavistalks.com (accessed October 3, 2009).

16. Joseph Wilson, *The Politics of Truth: Inside the Lies That Led to War and Betrayed My Wife's CIA Identity* (New York: Carrol & Graf, 2004).

Index

About the Author

ERIC J. BAILEY, PhD, MPH, is a professor of anthropology and public health and director of the Online Certificate Program in Ethnic and Rural Health Disparities at East Carolina University. He served as health scientist administrator at the National Institutes of Health, the National Center on Minority Health and Health Disparities, and the National Cancer Institute. He completed a postdoctoral fellowship at the Centers for Disease Control and Prevention and Emory University's Rollins School of Public Health. In earlier roles, he served as program director for the Master's of Public Health Program in Urban Public Health at the Charles R. Drew University of Medicine and Science and as assistant and associate Professor at the University of Arkansas for Medical Sciences, Indiana University at Indianapolis, and the University of Houston.